# Praise for *It's Not You*

"A compassionate road map and survival guide for people in narcissistic relationships that helps them understand how to heal and thrive during and after these challenging relationships."
—Jay Shetty, *New York Times* bestselling author of *Think Like a Monk* and host of the *On Purpose with Jay Shetty* podcast

"A must read. Dr. Ramani will teach you how to heal from any toxic relationship. With her expert advice based on decades of research and clinical experience, she makes the impossible seem possible."
—Mel Robbins, *New York Times* bestselling author of *The High 5 Habit* and host of *The Mel Robbins Podcast*

"In writing *It's Not You*, Dr. Ramani directly addresses victims of narcissistic abuse with targeted advice developed through years of clinical experience and research. I would highly recommend this book to anyone struggling in a relationship with a narcissist. Once you realize it's not you who is the problem, you can become the solution."
—W. Keith Campbell, PhD, professor of psychology at the University of Georgia and author of *The Narcissism Epidemic*

"*It's Not You* tackles a subject matter so wildly misunderstood and offers a path forward for those who have been or currently are in narcissistic relationships. With deep compassion, Dr. Ramani masterfully helps the reader shift from self-blame to seeing the picture clearly. What a profound gift it is to those who will see their experience written about in this book and feel a little less alone." —Vienna Pharaon, bestselling author of *The Origins of You* and host of the *This Keeps Happening* podcast

"Whether you are looking to avoid damaging relationships, leave one, or finally move on from one, Dr. Ramani has produced a work that is utterly essential for understanding the patterns we were never built to see coming. *It's Not You* is not just lifesaving, but life restoring. More than a way out, it's a way back—to yourself."
—Matthew Hussey, host of the *Love Life with Matthew Hussey* podcast

"Emotionally abusive relationships take away our voice and our power, and Dr. Ramani gives us the tools and teaches all of us how to take ourselves back and feel whole again."

—Debra Newell, author of *Surviving Dirty John*

"Dr. Ramani is one of the most respected experts on healing and narcissism. In this important book, I'm grateful she includes the often unseen world of grief and narcissism."

—David Kessler, author of *Finding Meaning*

"What sets Dr. Ramani apart is her valuable emphasis on healing from the damaging effects of a narcissist's destructive behavior. With a direct and compassionate approach, she reminds us that it *is* possible to heal. As always, Dr. Ramani gives comfort and validation to the 'lions.' *It's Not You* is a gift."

—Jenifer Faison, host of the *Betrayal* podcast

"*It's Not You* is, simply put, brilliant. In straightforward, clear language, Dr. Ramani has created a framework for deeply understanding the complexities of, and healing from, this most insidious form of abuse. She challenges misconceptions and glaring gaps in knowledge of current paradigms in traditional psychology and with compassion and refreshing candor, guides us through hell—and back to our true selves."

—Mark Vicente, NXIVM whistleblower and director of *Empathy Not Included*

# It's Not You

*Identifying and Healing
from Narcissistic People*

## Ramani Durvasula, PhD

THE OPEN FIELD | PENGUIN LIFE

VIKING
An imprint of Penguin Random House LLC
penguinrandomhouse.com

The Open Field/A Penguin Life Book

THE OPEN FIELD is a registered trademark of MOS Enterprises, Inc.

LIBRARY OF CONGRESS CATALOGING-IN-PUBLICATION DATA
Names: Durvasula, Ramani, author.
Title: It's not you: identifying and healing from narcissistic people /
Ramani Durvasula, PhD. Other titles: It is not you
Description: [New York] : The Open Field/Penguin Life, [2024] |
Includes bibliographical references and index. |
Identifiers: LCCN 2023040075 (print) | LCCN 2023040076 (ebook) |
ISBN 9780593492628 (hardcover) | ISBN 9780593492635 (ebook)
Subjects: LCSH: Narcissism. | Autonomy.
Classification: LCC BF575.N35 D877 2024 (print) |
LCC BF575.N35 (ebook) |
DDC 155.2/32—dc23/eng/20231109
LC record available at https://lccn.loc.gov/2023040075
LC ebook record available at https://lccn.loc.gov/2023040076

Printed in the United States of America
4th Printing

*Designed by Alexis Farabaugh*

All names and identifying characteristics have been changed
to protect the privacy of the individuals involved.

THE OPEN FIELD

Dear Reader,

Years ago, these words attributed to Rumi found a place in my heart:

*Out beyond ideas of*
*wrongdoing and rightdoing,*
*there is a field. I'll meet you there.*

Ever since, I've cultivated an image of what I call the "Open Field"—a place out beyond fear and shame, beyond judgment, loneliness, and expectation. A place that hosts the reunion of all creation. It's the hope of my soul to find my way there—and whenever I hear an insight or a practice that helps me on the path, I love nothing more than to share it with others.

That's why I've created the Open Field. My hope is to publish books that honor the most unifying truth in human life: We are all seeking the same things. We're all seeking dignity. We're all seeking joy. We're all seeking love and acceptance, seeking to be seen, to be safe. And there is no competition for these things we seek—because they are not material goods; they are spiritual gifts!

We can all give each other these gifts if we share what we know—what has lifted us up and moved us forward. That is our duty to one another—to help each other toward acceptance, toward peace, toward happiness—and my promise to you is that the books published under this imprint will be maps to the Open Field, written by guides who know the path and want to share it.

Each title will offer insights, inspiration, and guidance for moving beyond the fears, the judgments, and the masks we all wear. And when we take off the masks, guess what? We will see that we are the opposite of what we thought—we are each other.

We are all on our way to the Open Field. We are all helping one another along the path. I'll meet you there.

Love,
Maria Shriver

*To my mother, Sai Kumari Durvasula—*
*and the story still to come.*

*In memory of my great-grandmother Gunupudi Venkamma*
*and the grandmothers who came before her.*

*To all survivors of emotionally abusive relationships.*

Within tears, find hidden laughter.

Seek treasures amid ruins, sincere one.

RUMI

Every betrayal contains a perfect moment, a coin
stamped heads or tails with salvation on the other side.

BARBARA KINGSOLVER

# CONTENTS

# Preface

Once upon a time, an eight-year-old girl sat on the floor of a stuffy cafeteria in an elementary school in New England and watched as a troupe of circus performers from New York City gave a show at her school. It was the 1970s, an era before any kind of multicultural awareness, and the little girl with her foreign name, brown skin, and two tight braids in her hair had taught herself to be invisible. The circus chose their volunteers from the gaggle of children, one boy to be an elephant, a girl to be a juggler's assistant, the luckiest boy was the ringmaster.

Finally, the circus folks held up a costume; it was satin, a deep shade of purple, festooned with fringe and sequins. All of the girls swooned, including the little girl with the braids. Every girl's hand shot up except hers. "Pick me, please, *please* pick me," they shrieked. *How did they have the courage*, thought the girl with the braids. *Why weren't they afraid?* The head of the troupe ignored the children with their hands up and chose the little girl with the braids. She trembled and put her head down, tears welling up, and quietly said, "No thank you, sir." He looked at her and gently asked, "Are you sure?" And she quietly nodded. The girl sitting next to her grabbed at the opportunity and wore the costume with pride. He asked the girl with the braids what part she wanted, and she said she would be content as part of the horse's costume where she would be hidden. She would spend years thinking about what it would have felt like to wear that purple-sequined wonder of a dress, but that day she was so frightened of the taunts of her classmates . . . and simply of being seen.

From the very beginning of her life, she had internalized the message that her wants, dreams, and needs weren't worthy of being seen, and that she wasn't enough. Her kind and compassionate mother's dreams had been thwarted and silenced, and the little girl felt she didn't have the right to them, either.

Until she did.

While I still may not own a fabulous purple-sequined dress, I recognize that we can pull ourselves out of the stories of the narcissistic people who defined us, silenced us, clipped our wings, taught us our dreams were grandiose, filled us with shame, and for a time, stole our joy. That we can have love stories, success stories, and happiness, yet comprehend that there will still be dark nights of the soul, and that the shadow of self-doubt remains a fellow traveler. And we can pay it forward, and let folks know that what happened was real and that they are enough. I did, and every day I see more and more people who do. We can begin to break intergenerational cycles of devaluation and invalidation and psychological self-harm. These stories must be told.

I still don't know if I would have the courage to grab hold of that spangled dress today, but I'd like to think that the little girl with the braids and the big brown eyes, and the name no one could pronounce, would have rocked it.

And from my little girl heart to all of you . . . I know you can, too.

# Introduction:
## How Did We Get Here?

Neutrality helps the oppressor, never the victim.
Silence encourages the tormentor, never the tormented.

ELIE WIESEL

## 9:00 a.m.

Carolina has two children and was betrayed and cheated on by her husband several times during their twenty-year marriage, including with friends and neighbors. After he denied it repeatedly, and then after enduring his rage for her "paranoid accusations," she was told the affairs were her fault for making him feel like he wasn't important. She would minimize her career so he felt "safe." She struggles with missing what she believed was the beautiful life and family they created, with feeling not enough, believing that maybe she was misunderstanding him and the situation, knowing it was breaking her heart every time he criticized her and betrayed her trust. Carolina didn't understand it; she has parents who had been happily married for forty-five years until her father died. She believed in family and now with the impending divorce, she felt she had failed. She was also experiencing regular panic attacks and debilitating anxiety, and sometimes ruminated about a reconciliation.

## 10:30 a.m.

Nataliya has been married for fifty years to a man who told her that she was being "ridiculous" for expecting so much of him when she had cancer. He said it was "disruptive" and throwing him off because now he was supposed to feel sad for her and up-end his busy schedule to pick her up from chemotherapy appointments. She found it difficult to walk after developing neuropathy following years of cancer treatment, and he would shame her and call her "the empress" for asking to be dropped off in front of a restaurant instead of walking five blocks on a cold night. However, they have adult children and grandchildren, and a life filled with travel and family time. Nataliya doesn't want to be the one responsible for messing up a lifestyle that everyone is enjoying, and she acknowledges that on more than a few days, she enjoys her husband's company—they still have a decent sex life and a shared history. Despite her having both medical and law degrees, he treats her like a personal assistant. She has struggled with ongoing health conditions, self-blame, and shame, and has become socially isolated from everyone except her close family.

## 1:00 p.m.

Rafael's father has compared him unfavorably to his brother since childhood, and he works constantly with the fantasy that once he makes enough money, he will get noticed. His father often perceived him as weak, would take some glee in telling him about his brother's latest successes (Rafael had long since distanced from his brother), and had been emotionally abusive toward his wife, Rafael's mother. This resulted in a tremendous psychological toll on her, which Rafael believed resulted in her premature death. Rafael knows that his grandfather did the same thing to his father—it was just how it was for them culturally—and he also wanted to make allowances for the racial biases and limitations his father and grandfather faced throughout their lives. Rafael has not been able to sustain successful intimate relationships and keeps telling himself, "If I can just show Dad my success, then I will be okay and ready to start the rest of my life." Rafael works around the clock, relies on a mix of drugs and remedies to sleep and to get going, rarely socializes, and craves social contact, but says it feels "indulgent" to go on vacation or hang out with people when there is so much work to do.

LET'S CALL THIS a hypothetical day in my office. Over the years, having listened to enough of these stories, it became clear that in just about every case like Rafael's, the parent would remain invalidating, and with folks like Carolina and Nataliya, their partners would continue to blame them. But it wouldn't have been helpful for me to tell Rafael, Carolina, and Nataliya up front that the people in their lives would likely continue their harmful behavior. Instead, our work became about teaching them what constitutes acceptable and unacceptable behavior and what healthy relationships are about, while creating a safe space for them to explore their feelings, these relationships, and their true selves. We had to make sense of the confusion and explore why they were blaming themselves for something they didn't do or feeling guilty when they were doing nothing wrong. As a therapist, I would have found it easier to just focus treatment only on the anxiety, health issues, depression, confusion, dissatisfaction, frustration, helplessness, social isolation, and obsessive work tendencies and not include the context. That's what we are taught to do: focus on the maladaptive patterns of the person in the office instead of what's going on around them.

But there was something else happening. Week after week, my clients' panic and sadness ebbed and flowed alongside the patterns and behavior within their relationships. It became clear that the relationships were the horse and the anxiety that got them into therapy was the cart. I was struck by the similarities in so many clients' stories, yet these clients were very different people with different histories. But where they didn't vary was that all of them felt they were to blame for their situations—they doubted themselves, ruminated, felt ashamed, were psychologically isolated, confused, and helpless. Increasingly, they censored themselves in these relationships and became progressively more numb and restrained to avoid the criticism, contempt, or anger from these challenging people in their lives. They were trying to change themselves with the hope that this would change this person and relationship.

There was another significant similarity: the behaviors that were happening in their relationships. Regardless of whether it was a spouse, partner, parent, other family member, adult child, friend, colleague, boss—my clients consistently shared stories of being invalidated or shamed for having a need or for expressing or being themselves. Their experiences, perceptions, and reality itself were regularly challenged. They were blamed for the problematic behavior of these people in their lives. They felt lost and isolated.

Yet at the same time, all of them shared that it wasn't bad all the time. There was sometimes laughter, good sex, enjoyable experiences, dinners, shared interests and histories, even love. In fact, just when things seemed as though they were becoming untenable, there would be a decent day, just enough to reseed the self-doubt. I gave my clients what had helped me in my own healing—validation and education. Focusing on their anxiety without educating them about the patterns within these relationships was like fixing engine problems by putting air in the tires. And those engine problems always seemed to track back to the same place: narcissistic relationships.

There is a proverb that says *Until the story of the hunt is told by the lion, the tale of the hunt will always glorify the hunter.* The person who holds the narrative holds the power. Until now, we have only told the story of the hunter. Books about narcissism tend to talk about narcissists. We are deeply curious about these charming people who seem to get away with so much bad and hurtful behavior with so few consequences. We are compelled to understand why they are ostensibly so successful and why they do what they do. As much as we may not like narcissism, we glorify people with these personality styles—they are our leaders, heroes, entertainers, and celebrities. Unfortunately, they are also our parents, partners, friends, siblings, children, bosses, and neighbors.

But what about the lion? What about the person whom the hunter goes after or harms?

Much of what's written about narcissism tends to forget the more important part of the story: *What happens to the people who are in the wake of the narcissist?* How are people affected by folks with narcissistic personalities and the behaviors? When people are hurt, there is a preoccupation with understanding the "why"— as if this could somehow ease their pain (it doesn't). We become so curious about the hunter in an almost obsessive zeal to understand why they do what they do. Why would someone lack empathy or gaslight or manipulate or lie so skillfully or rage so suddenly? But in focusing on why people with narcissistic personalities do what they do, we lose sight of what happens to the people who fall in love with, have children with, are raised by, are related to, work for, work with, get divorced from, share apartments with, become friends with, and raise narcissists. What happens to them?

The short answer: it's not good.

This is an uncomfortable conversation. You don't want to cast aspersions on the people you love, admire, respect, and care about. It's easier to take responsibility for your difficult relationships yourself, or write it off to the ebbs and flows of life, rather than accept that you are facing predictable, unchangeable, and harmful patterns from someone you love or respect. As a psychologist who has worked with hundreds of survivors of narcissistic abuse, who maintains a program for thousands of more survivors, and who has written books and created thousands of hours of content on this topic, I grapple with whether it is even a worthwhile conversation to focus on narcissism, because the issue is really the harm the narcissistic person's behavior causes you.

Can we separate the personality from the behavior if the personality is not likely to change? Does it matter if their harmful behavior is intentional or not? Can you heal without understanding narcissism? And most importantly, can you heal from these relationships? This book will explore those complex questions.

There is pushback from people who ask me, "How do you know the partner/parent/boss/friend is narcissistic?" Fair question. When I am working with a client in therapy, I have typically not met the other people in their lives, but I am getting a detailed history, often reading emails and text messages that have been sent to them by the antagonistic person and witnessing the impact on my client. I use the term *antagonistic relational stress* to describe what happens to survivors of these relationships, and I prefer to characterize the behavior of the psychologically harmful person in my clients' lives as antagonistic, which is a broader and less stigmatized term than narcissistic. This is the term I use when teaching other professionals about these patterns, because it captures the breadth of antagonistic behaviors and tactics that we observe in narcissism—manipulation, attention-seeking, exploitativeness, hostility, arrogance—but also in other antagonistic personality styles, such as psychopathy, and positions it as a unique stress that antagonistic relationships evoke. But the narcissistic cat is out of the bag, and the term *narcissistic abuse* is familiar to most of you, though I will also use the term *antagonistic* throughout this book to capture the full breadth of these patterns.

YOU DON'T GET into this work unless it is personal, and yes, for me, it's personal. I have encountered narcissism-induced invalidation, rage, betrayal, dismissiveness, manipulation, and gaslighting in my family relationships, intimate relationships, workplace relationships, and friendships. It hit me in the gut as I listened to the pain being shared by the clients I was working with, then going into my own therapy and sharing my own pain, and slowly realizing it was my story, too. Narcissistic abuse has changed the course of my career and my life. I was so gaslighted, I thought up was down, that I was to blame, that my expectations for people were not realistic, and that I was not worthy of being seen, heard, or noticed. It was foundational for me, and that fear of grasping the purple dress morphed into feeling unworthy of success, love, or happiness as an adult. There was no penny-drop moment, no singular defining relationship. Narcissistic abuse happened in many different relationships and ways in my life, so I believed this must be me, it can't be all of these other situations in my life. I never learned about narcissistic abuse in graduate school; I didn't think that this confusing and abusive behavior was a thing until I finally saw it clearly. I spent years grieving and then wishing I could get back the years I wasted in rumination and regret. I felt guilty and disloyal for viewing family members and people I loved as narcissistic. I slowly set boundaries, radically accepted that none of this behavior would change, stopped trying to change the antagonistic people in my life, and disengaged from them and their behavior. I lost relationships that once mattered to me and faced criticism for violating ancient cultural norms about family loyalty and current norms about needing to figure out a way to get along with people who have sharp elbows. I now realize that if you spend enough time with sharp elbows, you will end up bleeding to death.

A little over twenty years ago, I was supervising research assistants who were reporting back about certain patients in outpatient clinics wreaking havoc on nurses, physicians, and everyone else who worked there through their entitled, dysregulated, contemptuous, and arrogant behavior. That observation led me to start a research program looking at personality, particularly narcissism and antagonism, and how it affects health.

Simultaneously, I have had the privilege of hearing the stories of thousands of people who have endured these relationships. Unfortunately, I kept hearing that many times the partners, family members, friends, colleagues, and even therapists were blaming the person experiencing the abusive behavior for being too sensitive, not trying harder, being too anxious, not being more forgiving, staying, leaving, being judged as harsh for using the term *narcissist*, and not communicating more clearly. I have read descriptions of therapist-training programs that pushed back on clients who believed their families or relationships were toxic, or believed clients who came into therapy to talk about manipulative relationships were simply whining. There were countless books and articles written about narcissistic personalities and how to do therapy with narcissistic people. There were virtually none that addressed what happened to people in these relationships or how to do therapy with people who were in relationships with narcissistic folks, even though everyone in the field of mental health knew that these were unhealthy relationships. Once I unclenched my fists, I turned my anger into a focus on education, not only for clients and survivors of narcissistic abuse but also for clinical professionals.

The clients I have worked with have gone through divorces that spanned years; been doubted by the leadership in their company when they made documented claims of harassment and abuse and watched the workplace perpetrator be moved to a new post in a different location; been cut off by their families when they set a boundary; had grandchildren withheld as punishment; watched elderly parents be financially abused by narcissistic siblings; survived invalidating childhoods just to have to survive invalidating adulthoods; had narcissistic friends start online smear campaigns when they didn't get their way; and had narcissistic parents manipulate them from their deathbeds. I have worked in organizations where gaslighting was the preferred mode of communication, and I witnessed the most toxic people be enabled by the systems they worked in, to the detriment of the best and brightest in those places. Personally, there are roads and neighborhoods in Los Angeles I still avoid because I don't have the bandwidth to deal with the memories. I have experienced threats to my safety and felt compelled to leave jobs, and I have watched family be more concerned with protecting a family member's reputation than in offering solace to someone who is suffering. It takes me a long time to build trust with new people.

The only thing you need to understand about narcissism is that in almost all cases this personality pattern was there *before you came into the narcissistic person's life* and it will be there after you leave. These relationships change you, but out of that shift comes growth, a new perspective, and greater interpersonal discernment. Recognizing and coming out of these relationships can be a wake-up call to excavate your authentic self, dust it off, and take it into the world. The traditional therapeutic goal of teaching clients to understand their role and responsibilities in a relationship and to learn to think differently about situations that aren't working doesn't consider that the deck is stacked when it comes to managing these situations with a narcissistic person. Short of deluding yourself about the relationship, how differently can you think about someone who is manipulating you and negating your existence as a person? Instead of learning to think differently about the person, it's time we started learning about what constitutes unacceptable and toxic behavior.

I hope that this book shines a light on a simple premise that narcissistic patterns and behaviors really don't change and you are not to blame for another person's invalidating behavior. I want you to land on a simple yet profound truth:

It's not you.

I have heard from people around the world that simply receiving a framework for narcissism and what these relationships do to them marked the first time they felt normal in years. This isn't about calling out narcissistic people but rather about identifying unhealthy relationship behavior and patterns. To be given permission to disengage. To learn that multiple things (good and bad) can be true in a relationship. To learn that understanding narcissism doesn't mean you have to leave or end contact with people you have complicated relationships with, but instead that you can interact with them differently. To understand that it is a basic human right to be seen and to have your own and separate identity, needs, wants, and aspirations expressed and recognized. To become aware that instead of thinking differently about yourself, it's time to start thinking differently about the behavior of someone whom you love or respect but who is also harming you. To finally be told, clearly and definitively, that you were never going to be able to change another person's behavior. All of this was like turning the house lights on and the gaslights off.

This is a book for you, the survivors of invalidating relationships with narcissistic people. This is not a book about how they tick but rather how you heal. There will be a brief overview about narcissism to ensure we are all on the same page, but the rest of it is *for* and *about* you. The story of the hunt told by the lion, as it were. It will review the effect of narcissistic people's behavior on you and how you can move forward, recover, and heal from a place of grace, wisdom, compassion, and strength. This is a book written from both my head and my heart.

Often when you get out of a narcissistic relationship or disengage from one, you think of it is as an end, but in fact the healing and all that follows is where everything begins. This is the beginning of your story, of stepping out of the invalidating shadow and finally allowing yourself to be you.

# It's
# Not You

# PART I

# The Narcissistic Relationship

# Clarifying Narcissism

The personality susceptible to the dream of limitless
freedom is a personality also prone, should the dream
ever sour, to misanthropy and rage.

JONATHAN FRANZEN

Carlos is the guy who will help everyone in the neighborhood. He is devoted to his ailing mother, is very involved with his son from a brief relationship with his ex, and would even describe himself as an "overgrown child" who loves his toys and football. Everyone, including his longtime girlfriend, will say he is empathic and cares about their lives. He may do things like forget birthdays, but he remembers the day of your job interview and sends you a "good luck!" text. One weekend, he went to a music festival with a group of friends, drank too much, and kissed another woman. Filled with shame and sadness, he came home and confessed to his girlfriend because he didn't want to lie to her. She then wrote numerous social media posts about Carlos's "narcissism."

Joanna has been married to Adam for about five years. He works hard but his career has stumbled, and Joanna has encouraged him to pursue what he really wants to do while she acts as the primary provider. Initially, Joanna was drawn to Adam's discipline, loyalty, and work ethic. But he has often made light of her career, has called her sadness after a miscarriage "drama," and has reactive tantrums if she asks him to help around the house, then criticizes her for wasting money when she hires a cleaner. He will often be quite dismissive of her desire to spend time with friends and family, calling her friends "parasites" and her family a "swamp of domestic boredom," which deeply hurts her, and he is very selfish with his time. But he remembers birthdays and anniversaries and celebrates with great fanfare, even if he can't afford it. Joanna feels guilty because Adam's dreams never took off, so she attributes his spotty empathy to his belief that his life didn't work out the way he wanted it to. When things turn around he will be nicer, she thinks, and so what if he doesn't empty the dishwasher? He puts so much effort into her birthday every year—though she would rather he emptied the dishwasher and was nicer to her friends.

Who do you think is more likely to be narcissistic? Careless Carlos or Angry Adam?

*Narcissism* is the word of our time, and yet it's deeply misunderstood. It would be easier if narcissistic people were simply mirror-gazing, self-involved poseurs, but they are much more than that. They are an emotionally abusive romantic partner who belittles you but with whom you sometimes have fun. A toxic boss who berates you in front of your colleagues but whose work you greatly admire. A parent who is jealous of your success but who showed up to all your soccer games when you were a child. A friend who is forever a victim and drones on endlessly about what's going on in their life with little interest in yours but who has been in your life since you were thirteen. Even these snapshots fail to capture the complexity that is narcissism. You yourself have likely had one or more relationships with a narcissistic person—and may not have even known it.

But how do you identify what narcissism is, what it isn't, and whether being able to understand it really matters? This chapter explores why narcissism is misunderstood and debunks many of the myths surrounding it. You will also discover why being clear on narcissism may actually muddy your own waters.

## What Is Narcissism?

Narcissism is an interpersonally maladaptive personality style that encompasses a wide spectrum of traits and behavioral patterns that present in different ways, from mild to severe, vulnerable to malignant. What separates a narcissistic person from someone who is self-centered or vain or entitled is the consistency and sheer number of these traits in one person. Just being superficial doesn't mean someone is narcissistic.

It is also looking at the function of these traits—which is to protect the narcissistic person. Narcissism is about a deep insecurity and fragility offset by maneuvers like domination, manipulation, and gaslighting, which allow the narcissistic person to stay in control. The variable empathy and lack of self-awareness mean that they do not stop to consider the harm their behavior is creating for other people. The traits aren't really the issue, but rather how these traits translate into consistently harmful behaviors.

Because traits, especially those in a rigid and unaware personality style such as narcissism, really do not change, the behavior is also unlikely to change. And because there is such a wide spectrum of narcissism, from mild to severe, we may be having very different experiences of this personality style in our relationships. The middle of this spectrum—with enough bad days to take a toll and enough good days to keep you hooked—is where many people are stuck, and that "moderate narcissism" is where we will focus.

Let's take a closer look at some of these traits.

## A Need for Narcissistic Supply

Narcissistic people need validation and admiration, and this need motivates much of their behavior. They seek out status, compliments, excessive recognition, and attention, and this may happen through ostentatious wealth, physical appearance, friends who fawn over them, or social media likes and follows. This validation from other people or the world at large, whatever form it takes, is called *narcissistic supply*. Their moods can turn rather dark, and they can become irritable, resentful, sullen, and aggrieved when they do not get the validation or supply they feel entitled to. Anyone around them must bring supply or face their wrath.

## *Egocentricity*

Narcissistic people are egocentric, but this goes beyond mere selfishness. It is selfishness with a devaluation chaser. For example, a selfish person will choose the restaurant they want, but a narcissistic person will choose the restaurant they want *and* tell you they had to do that because you are too dumb about food to choose one. In short, a narcissistic person's needs will always come first in any relationship.

## *Consistent Inconsistency*

Narcissism is consistent. However, there is a consistency to it that can make it feel inconsistent. When the narcissistic person is well regulated, feels they are in control, and has sufficient narcissistic supply—for instance, work is going well, they are getting compliments, they are in a fun new relationship, or they just got a new car—they may be less antagonistic and more pleasant. Unfortunately, the narcissistic supply gets stale for them quickly, so they always need more, new, better. I recall working with a narcissistic person who said one afternoon, "I am having the best day ever, I scored a big new deal, I am the man, I slay it every time, right?" That evening, he left a message saying that he was angry and that his life isn't fair. I came to find out that this change in his emotional state was because the new person he was dating had to reschedule dinner.

It can turn that quickly.

## Restlessness

There is a restless quality to the narcissistic personality, a pursuit of novelty and excitement, which is why we may observe infidelity or frequently shifting romantic partners, overspending and shopping, or frenetic activity. Narcissistic people often seem perpetually bored, disenchanted, or contemptuous if things are not interesting and engaging enough for them.

## Delusional Grandiosity

A defining characteristic of narcissism is grandiosity, which shows up as exaggerated beliefs about the person's importance in the world, fantastical beliefs about ideal love stories and their current or future success, a sense of superiority over other people and of a uniqueness and specialness about themselves not observed in others. Grandiosity also means that the person believes they are better than others. It is "delusional" because for most narcissistic people, there is little to no evidence supporting any of these beliefs, and they hold on to them despite the discomfort or harm this stance is causing to other people.

## Shifting Masks

The confusion comes from the narcissistic person going between charming, fun, and charismatic, or at least normal and regulated, to abusive, sullen, and enraged. Their self-appraisal is high when things are going their way, and when things are not, they blame the world and shift to viewing themselves as a victim. As a result, you can't always anticipate which version of the narcissist you will be dealing with—the grandiose and cheerful one or the dejected, victimized, and angry one. Makes for a bit of a wild and uncomfortable ride.

## Entitlement

Entitlement is a core pattern of narcissism, and one of the most problematic. Theories of narcissism suggest that entitlement may be the core pillar of this personality style and that all other dynamics tie back to it.[1] Narcissistic people believe that they are special, must be given special treatment, can only be truly understood by other special people, and that the rules should not apply to them. If rules *are* applied to them or they are held accountable, narcissistic folks become quite angry and push back because *those rules are for ordinary people!* If they have to follow the rules, then they aren't so special. They feel entitled to doing and saying what they want, whenever they want. Their entitlement serves as a way for them to create a reality in which they can exert their specialness, and it drives their anger when they don't feel they are being regarded as a VIP.

Most of us can probably recall a time when a narcissistic person's entitlement left us feeling uncomfortable. One woman shared with me the mortification she would feel when her husband would raise his voice and bark at restaurant servers when he didn't get his way. She said that she got good at keeping her head down in shame in those situations so that she never had to make eye contact with the people left in her husband's wake. Sadly, she felt complicit in their mistreatment because she didn't stop him, yet stopping him meant enduring his tantrums or silent treatment for days.

## Overcompensating for Insecurity

This takes us to the bedrock of narcissism, which is insecurity. Narcissism is *not* about high self-esteem or low self-esteem as much as it is about inaccurate, inflated, and variable self-appraisal. The narcissistic person always harbors a lurking sense of inadequacy that is close to the bone, since they are unable to reflect on what they sound like or how their behavior impacts others. This can be confusing—how could someone who seems so sure of themselves be so fragile? All of this narcissistic stuff—the grandiosity, entitlement, arrogance, charisma—is a defensive suit of armor designed to protect the narcissistic person, a sort of adult superhero cape they can tie around their fragile psyche.

## Being Thin-skinned

Narcissistic folks can dish it out but they cannot take it. When you give them even the mildest critique or feedback, you must be prepared for rapid, rageful, and disproportionate reactions, and it can be doubly confusing because they will frequently retaliate by criticizing you in far harsher terms. This is often juxtaposed against their chronic need for reassurance: they will not ask for it, but despite their arrogant exteriors, it's clear they need to be soothed and told that everything is going to be okay.

Offering reassurance is a treacherous dance, however, because if your soothing is too transparent, they will lash out at you for reminding them of their weakness. I worked with a woman who was obsessed with appearances. For her birthday party, she decorated her home with impeccable care but took little consideration of other people's financial or time limitations. When her family was busy with work responsibilities, small children, illness, or life, she experienced this as a direct attack and complained that nobody appreciated her. Her son tried to reassure her: "Don't worry, Mom, we will make sure we are right on time for your birthday, and we're going to get you that cake you love, and ice cream, and have lots of presents and a big dinner. It's going to be the best birthday ever." She lashed back, "Don't treat me like I am a six-year-old, you make it seem like I am crazy." The dance between the narcissistic reactive sensitivity to feedback, their need for reassurance and chronic sense that they are a victim, and their shame and subsequent rage at having these vulnerabilities reminds us of the essence of narcissistic relationships: *you can't win*.

## Inability to Self-regulate

Narcissistic people cannot manage their emotions. They don't know how to express them because that would be too shameful and vulnerable, and so they cannot regulate them. The narcissistic person isn't saying, "Hey, I am going to cover my insecurity with some grandstanding," nor are they rubbing their hands together wondering, "How can I hurt you?" Their lashing out is unprocessed stuff, which is why even a mild critique or crisis can set off shame about their vulnerability or imperfection being on full display. These ego injuries then set off their rage and blame shifting, which allow them to reduce tension, maintain their grandiose facade, and feel safe. The lack of empathy and impulsivity mean that they can't stop to catch themselves and consider how their lashing out may hurt you. Instead, they will issue a hollow apology and get frustrated if you try to hold them accountable.

## *Need for Dominance*

Narcissistic folks are motivated by dominance, status, control, power, and the desire to be special. Affiliation, intimacy, and closeness are not motivating for them. Thus they are always going to need to have the upper hand in any relationship. This means if *your* relationship motivation is deep emotional connection or intimacy, the two of you are dancing very different steps. Relationships exist largely for the narcissistic person's benefit and pleasure. They aren't interested in the give-and-take that a healthy relationship requires, or in the needs of others.

## *Lack of Empathy*

It's not accurate to say narcissistic people are devoid of empathy. Their empathy is hollow and variable. Narcissistic people have *cognitive empathy*—they may understand what empathy is and why someone feels a certain way, and they may use it to get what they want. Once they get what they want, or they can't be bothered, the empathy fades. Narcissistic empathy can also be performative—to look good to other people, to win someone over—and it can also be transactional, mustering it to get what they need from someone else. This can feel really galling because it shows you that they know that empathy is valued but they may only deploy it as a tactic.

Narcissistic people tend to be more "empathic" when they feel safe and supplied. For example, on a day when things went well for them, they may come home and hear about a bad day you had at work and reassure you everything is going to be okay. A week later, you may think, *Well, they were so supportive last week when I raised this with them, let me talk it out with them again.* But this time they may not have had that same kind of validating day, so you are met with, "When are you going to stop complaining about work? I'm tired of hearing your whining."

## *Contempt for Others*

Narcissistic people need people, and they resent that they need people. Needing people means other people have power, and they cannot tolerate thinking of themselves as dependent on anyone. This can drive the contempt that is often observed in narcissism—contempt for other people and their feelings, vulnerabilities, and needs. Other people's vulnerabilities become an unwitting mirror for the narcissistic person's own insecurities, and instead of embracing others, they have contempt for any reminders of their own fragilities. The contempt can come out directly, but quite often it surfaces as passive-aggressive digs and jabs.

## *Projection of Shame*

Projection is also a common pattern in narcissism. It is a defense—which means it operates unconsciously to protect the ego—and manifests as a person projecting unacceptable aspects of themselves onto another person. For example, a person who is lying accuses another person of lying, then the "projector" gets to continue to view themselves as honest after psychologically flinging their bad behavior onto someone else. Narcissistic people project the shameful parts of their personalities and behavior onto others to maintain their grandiose ideal of themselves and to shelter themselves from the discomfort of shame. It can be confusing because the narcissist may accuse you of the hurtful things they themselves are doing (e.g., you are out together at a coffee shop and they accuse you, out of the blue, of flirting with the barista, but in reality the narcissistic person is the one cheating on you).

## *Being Incredibly Charming*

If narcissistic people are entitled, rageful, manipulative, and invalidating, why don't we see these behaviors early and get the hell away? Because narcissistic people have great game. They are charming, charismatic, confident, curious, and often very well put together and intelligent. While you may not consider arrogance to be desirable, there is often the assumption that behind that arrogance and confidence, a person has the goods to back it up. You may also be willing to excuse a lot of bad behavior if you

believe someone is smart or successful. Narcissism is often con-
flated with success, and instead of being viewed as a toxic and
unhealthy pattern, it is viewed as swagger and unbridled ambition. Narcissistic people are skilled shape-shifters and chame-
leons. They have an uncanny ability to camouflage themselves,
get close, and then behave badly.

## The Continuum of Narcissism

Most of us think of narcissism as a binary: either you are or you're
not. We can get caught up in the zeal and idea that if it is an
either-or, then there is a way to identify narcissism clearly and
steer away from people with these traits. But nothing in the world
of psychology or mental health is that simple.

The reality is that narcissism is on a continuum. On the milder
end you have your superficial social-media narcissists, locked
into a perpetual and emotionally stunted adolescence, which may
be annoying but not necessarily harmful. At the severe end, you
observe callousness, exploitation, cruelty, vindictiveness, dominance, and even physical, sexual, psychological, or verbal violence,
which may be terrifying and traumatic. Moderate narcissism is
the form of narcissism that most of us are dealing with and that
this book will address.

Marcus has been married to Melissa, a kind, self-deprecating
people pleaser who will exhaust herself to be there for others, for
twenty-five years. Together they have two children. People see
Marcus as a hard worker and pillar of the community, but at

home he wants what he wants when he wants it, and the household runs around his schedule. Melissa has a busy well-paying job, but he still expects her to drop what she is doing to meet his needs, even if it causes her tension at work. And yet, the relationship is peppered with good days and moments. When Marcus feels content and satisfied with where things are in his life, he encourages family hikes, camping trips, and dinners out. Just when Melissa was about to consider seeing an attorney because she was tired of living in the "Marcus Show," he suggested they go on a beach vacation and reconnect. She blamed herself for misreading the situation and not recognizing how lucky she is. Until they got home, when it all began again.

Moderate narcissism is not the immature, cotton-candy froth of the low-grade superficial narcissist nor the coercive terror of the malignant, violent, or more severe narcissist. The moderate narcissist offers enough good days to keep you invested and enough bad days that hurt you and leave you utterly confused. Moderate narcissistic people have cognitive empathy, so they sometimes seem to "get it." They are entitled and seek validation and have a cocky, but not menacing, arrogance. They are hypocritical and believe that there is one set of rules for them and another for everyone else. They often feel that they are the victim in situations that do not go their way. They do not take responsibility for their behavior and will shift blame onto others for anything that makes them look bad. They are deeply selfish and will choose what works for them to the detriment of you or anyone else.

Moderate narcissists have just enough insight to know that their behavior is not okay—but not enough regulation, mindfulness, or empathy to stop themselves. Because they are aware enough to know that their behavior is inappropriate, they do it out of sight of others, which can leave you with no support. As a result, they are often a devil at home and an angel in the street. They might compliment you in a meeting in front of colleagues then verbally eviscerate you behind closed doors in their office. This two-faced mask-on-mask-off behavior is a trademark of the moderate narcissist. People will see a relatively composed and charming person in public, which is a complete disconnect from what you are experiencing in private.

## The Different Types of Narcissism

There are several types of narcissism. The core traits remain the same, but the way it manifests and how it affects us varies. Because so much of the content on narcissism focuses on the grandiose narcissist, it can be frustrating if you are dealing with a type of narcissistic person whose behavior doesn't fully align with what is commonly seen as narcissism. Usually one type predominates, although a narcissistic person can be a hybrid of these types. Within each of these types there is a continuum of severity—for example, a mild communal narcissist may be a preachy, exercise- and health-obsessed person who proclaims positivity but is very judgmental of her friends and family, while a severe communal narcissist may be a cult leader.

## Grandiose

> I'm going to be a billionaire by the time I'm thirty, and the world will see me as the genius I am. I will create a legacy bigger than you can even imagine. Nothing will ever stop me. I can't be bothered with the petty lives of the folks out there who aren't dreamers—they just bring me down, and I deserve to have people lift me up all the time.

Grandiose narcissism is the classical depiction of the narcissistic personality style. These are the charismatic, charming, attention-seeking, arrogant, "shiny" narcissists we associate with success, glamour, and celebrity. They look good when things are going well but when disappointment arises, the cracks appear, and they become rageful and project blame onto you. It can be exhausting to try to live in real life while they live in their fantasy worlds. The grandiosity is this narcissistic person's suit of armor against deep-seated inadequacy and insecurity. They believe their hype to a seemingly delusional, albeit convincing, level, which can make it easy to get sucked in. These relationships, with the ups and downs, good days and bad, can leave you excited, exhausted, and riddled with confusion.

## Vulnerable

> I am every bit as smart as all these start-up types, but I didn't have the connections or Daddy's money to get ahead. I'm not wasting my time in college or working

*some BS job for an incompetent; I would rather do nothing than work for Ivy League A-holes. I blame my parents for not giving me more money and setting me up better, because then I would have totally been the best in the business.*

Vulnerable narcissists are the victimized, anxious, socially awkward, sullen, broodingly angry, irritable, sad, and resentful narcissists. This type is sometimes termed *the covert narcissist*. The *covert/overt* distinction actually refers to the patterns we can and cannot see: overt behaviors, like yelling or manipulating, versus covert behaviors, meaning the narcissist's thoughts and feelings. Some people also use the term *covert narcissist* to refer to the narcissistic person's ability to pass as a nice person when there are people to impress—in essence they are hiding their narcissism from plain view (but behaving badly when there is no audience). In a vulnerable narcissistic person, instead of the grandiosity presenting as charismatic and pretentious prattling about their next big thing, it translates as a victimized grandiosity ("I never get a fair chance, because the world is too stupid to recognize my genius") and a victimized entitlement ("Why should I have to work when other people have trust funds?"). People with vulnerable narcissistic styles will attribute your success to good luck and their own lack of success to life being unfair to only them. They are also chronically malcontented. Vulnerable narcissists can be oppositional and argumentative, and asking them to do anything can feel like trying to compel a teenager to fold the laundry. They also struggle with abandonment and rejection sensitivity and may burn you out through their constantly victimized anger. Vulnerable narcissists can be awkward in social situations and compensate for that anxiety and the insecurity it evokes by criticizing you or devaluing and mocking you when you are enjoying other people or experiences or you are succeeding at something. Because vulnerable narcissists don't have the charismatic and charming exterior, most people, including therapists, will believe that they are struggling with self-esteem, anxiety, depression, or just bad luck. But even if these other issues are addressed, the sense of victimization lingers.

## *Communal*

> *I'm saving the world. I am a humanitarian who understands real people and real issues, and frankly, I get tired of people complaining about their lives when there are so many struggles out there, and they could be saving the world, too. I need people to see all the good I'm doing, and I know that people who don't notice it are just jealous that in their small lives they don't do any good for anyone.*

Typically, narcissistic people get their validation and other narcissistic needs by focusing on themselves ("I'm so rich/attractive/ a great person/smart"). But the communal narcissistic folks get those same narcissistic needs met in a collective way, resulting in a grandiose identity based on what they do for others ("I'm so giving, I always put others first"). They participate in activities that seem generous, like raising money, volunteering, organizing fundraising galas, going on humanitarian trips, helping a neighbor, or even just proclaiming positivity on social media, but the behavior is designed to allow them to maintain a grandiose sense of themselves as a saintly person and to receive validation for that.[2] Their "do-gooding" can range from small-ticket actions, such as going to a beach cleanup (and making sure they post to Instagram when they do it), to much bigger ones, like creating large nonprofit foundations (but treating the staff horribly). Regardless of how they do their humanitarian deeds, they make sure the world knows how much good they are doing, drink up the praise and recognition they receive, and get indignant if it doesn't come.

Communal narcissists also occupy spiritual and cult-y spaces where they can pontificate about self-improvement and positivity, such as religious, new age, or yoga communities where abuse and shame are used to control anyone who opposes the narrative or goes against the charismatic communal leader. Growing up with a communal narcissistic parent meant hearing that your parent was a pillar of the community while enduring their disinterest and anger behind closed doors.

## *Self-righteous*

> *There is a right way and a wrong way, and I'm disgusted by the people who do not understand that. I work hard, I save my money, I maintain tradition, and I don't have time or patience for people who cannot live in a responsible way. When I see people out there who*

*say they are struggling, I know it's because of their bad
choices. It's not my responsibility to help them out. If
you can't do it my way, then don't waste my time with
your problems. Figure it out.*

Self-righteous narcissists are hypermoralistic, judgmental, coldly
loyal, extremely rigid, and almost black-and-white in their worldview and belief systems. Their grandiosity is related to their almost delusional belief that they know better than everyone, and
they truly believe that their opinions, work, and lifestyle are su-
perior to others'. They imperiously stand above people and have
contempt for them. They mock everything from their food
choices to lifestyle habits to partner choices to careers. They expect an almost robotic obedience to their beliefs and devalue
emotion, human frailty, mistakes, and joy.

The self-righteous narcissist expects you to fall into line with
how they do things, and any variance from that is not tolerated.
They often live precisely engineered lives: waking up early, having a strict morning routine, eating similar meals every day, following an exact schedule, and keeping their items in an orderly
manner (and expecting everyone in their environment to do the
same). They make little time for joy, laughter, silliness, or other
people. They may have an obsessive work ethic, and they will
sneer at anyone who makes time for the "wrong" kind of leisure
or who they think is not working hard enough. They may also be
obsessive about their leisure activities—it has to be the right golf
game at the right place or spinning at the right class.

## Neglectful

> *If I need you, you will know. Otherwise, I'm doing my*
> *own thing and really can't be bothered with you.*

Neglectful narcissists are completely detached. Their lack of empathy manifests in their utter disregard for others, and their arrogance manifests in their belief that they are above having to deal with human relationships. Their validation seeking may happen in public spaces such as work, but almost never within the confines of a close relationship. They barely respond when you talk to them, and they have little to no interest in you. If you are in any kind of relationship with them, you may feel like a ghost in your own home, as if you cease to exist around them. They may not be argumentative or engaged with you in any way; at least if they were fighting, they would be talking to you.

## Malignant

> *The reason I'm always in control is because people fear*
> *me, and I'm good with that. If anyone messes with me,*
> *I will make them and anyone around them regret it for*
> *the rest of their lives. If anyone gets in my way, or*
> *doesn't give me what I want, I will make sure I get it.*

Malignant narcissism represents the dark tetrad, which is the crossroads of narcissism, psychopathy, sadism, and Machiavellianism or the willingness to use and exploit other people.[3] The malignant narcissist is only differentiated from the psychopath in that the malignant narcissist still has that nagging insecurity and sense of inadequacy, which they compensate for through domination, while the psychopath doesn't experience the anxiety we observe in narcissism. When they feel threatened or frustrated, the malignant narcissists' vindictive rage can escalate and become noisy and bombastic, while the psychopathic person is able to remain calm and composed even when they are angry.

There is an almost sadistic glee malignant narcissistic people derive from exacting revenge. They malign people publicly, or harm their reputations. They are highly manipulative, transactional, and judge everyone based on how useful they are—whether for power, profit, pleasure, or validation. In the simplest framing, the malignant narcissist is a bully: mean, menacing, unrelenting, and overpowering. This is the most dangerous form of narcissism—a sort of last stop on the personality train before it veers into psychopathy station. They have a willful disregard for your needs and safety and exploit and manipulate just about everyone. Their aggressiveness can be manifested physically through violence and abusive displays of anger, insults, and interpersonal cruelty. They have a heightened sense of suspiciousness bordering on paranoia, frequently believing that other people are "out to get them," which also fuels their aggression.

# The Battle over Narcissism vs. Narcissistic Personality Disorder

There has been backlash about using the term *narcissist* to describe people. People are using this word to describe jerks, politicians, celebrities, toxic family members, and ex-partners. Narcissism is a lot more complicated than someone being a jerk. Many therapists, media pundits, judges, lawyers, and others feel the term is too diagnostic, too label-y, too defeatist, or just kind of mean, especially when it is used without distinguishing between trait and behavior. I understand the fear of labeling: it reduces the complexity of a person to a single word. We regularly use personality terms to describe people—*introverted, humble, neurotic*—and yet the term *narcissism* is met with stronger reactions.

There is, however, a danger in overusing the term *narcissism*, not only because it might erroneously label someone, but because it loses its descriptive potency. Too many people use it to describe someone who is boastful, attention-seeking, superficial, or unfaithful but not actually narcissistic. This creates multiple risks: First, that people may minimize the plight of those who are in actual narcissistic relationships, which may mean that you do not get the support or empathy you need. Second, that you don't receive an accurate understanding of what narcissism really is, subsequently miss the opportunity to protect yourself, and therefore become more likely to blame yourself for the narcissistic person's behavior. And third, it simplifies the nuanced dynamics of the narcissistic person's experience in the world, which can foster even more misunderstanding. For this reason, it's important that we use this term correctly, sparingly, and judiciously, but it's also important that we do call these traits, patterns, and behaviors by their proper name.

Calling something by its proper name means that we know how to interact with it, maintain realistic expectations, and enter a situation with our eyes wide open. If someone is usually empathic and compassionate but on the day he loses his job is a bit snappier than usual, yet ultimately apologizes, is accountable, and returns to his respectful, kind self, he is not narcissistic, he just had a bad day. When a person is usually superficially charming but unempathetic, entitled, and disrespectful, then on a bad day is really nasty, doesn't apologize, and blames you, that is more likely to be narcissism. Understanding that narcissism encompasses a series of traits that translate into a series of interpersonally harmful behaviors, and is not just someone's bad day, is crucial to ensuring that we do not waste lifetimes trying to fix these relationships or stay in impossible situations.

There is also the pervasive yet misleading idea that narcissism is a diagnosis or an illness. Many online communities and therapists believe you cannot diagnose people without proper training and evaluation (and there is truth to that). They inadvertently shame survivors of actual narcissistic and antagonistic relationships by saying that if a person has a "disorder," it is wrong to characterize their behavior as abusive because they are not in control of it—even though we know narcissistic people can be quite tactical about how they show their different faces. This has pushed some survivors into believing that perhaps they have no right to view the patterns in the relationship as toxic or abusive, and that maybe they themselves are the issue.

However, this is problematic in several ways. First, narcissism is a personality style, not a disorder. A personality style is the collection of traits that together represent a given individual's personality, and is associated with how they would behave, cope, approach, and respond to life. Yes, there is a diagnosis called *narcissistic personality disorder* (NPD), which is characterized by all the patterns we observe in a narcissistic person. But to receive the diagnosis, the patterns must be observed by a trained clinician as being pervasive, stable, and consistent *and* the patterns must result in significant impairments in social and occupational functioning, or distress, for the person. We cannot diagnose a patient on the basis of what other people are experiencing, even if those other people are experiencing distress and harm. NPD is a paradoxical illness that may harm the people the narcissistic person interacts with more than it harms the narcissistic individuals themselves. People who have narcissistic personality styles won't typically show up to therapy for evaluation, and it can take several weeks or months to definitively determine NPD. If narcissistic people do show up to therapy, it may be because they are experiencing their own negative mood states (e.g., anxiety or depression) or co-occurring issues such as substance use, are being forced to go for good optics, or their lives have taken a turn they don't like (e.g., their relationship ends), but they don't necessarily show up because they are experiencing guilt for hurting others (in fact, most narcissistic people are more likely to think the other person is the one with the issue, not them).

I personally believe the diagnosis should be disbanded altogether, because there is little substantial evidence for accessible treatment, and because there is little reliability across clinicians in assigning this diagnosis. It is beyond the scope of this book to address the nuanced issues around this diagnosis, but this term *narcissistic personality disorder* has muddied the waters of the conversation on narcissism. We all have a personality; some are just easier to get along with than others.

For purposes of this book, we are not concerning ourselves with whether someone has been "diagnosed." The descriptor *narcissism* will reflect a personality style and not a clinical diagnosis. Too many survivors are minimizing their experience on the premise that "Well, my parent/partner/friend/colleague/boss/child hasn't been diagnosed with anything, so maybe I am just overreacting, and it is just me." Some of you reading this may be healing from a relationship with someone who actually has been diagnosed with NPD, some of you may be healing from a relationship with someone who was sufficiently narcissistic for it to be a problem, and some of you may be healing from a relationship with someone who would have been diagnosed with NPD but never saw a clinician. The effects are the same all around.

## Myths about Narcissism

We miss something important when we try to simplify narcissism or boil it down to one trait. Narcissistic patterns and behaviors, such as delusional grandiosity or the framing of cruel discourse as "straight talk," are becoming more normalized in the world at large, so more people are being harmed by them, which makes getting clarity even more essential. We'll explore and debunk a few of the most popular myths to help you avoid falling into narcissistic traps.

## Narcissistic People Are Always Men

Not quite, and enough of you have narcissistic mothers to know that this is not true. While the research does show that grandiose narcissism is more common among men, narcissism can be found in all genders.[4] The prototype of the grandiose alpha male may perpetuate this myth, but it is a misleading stereotype that leads us to miss or doubt toxic patterns.

## It's Just Bragging and Arrogance

Arrogance is pretentious superiority. The person who looks through you when you talk to them because they decide that you aren't worth their time, or who shows little interest in anyone unless they believe that they are "at their level" or are useful to them at that moment. All narcissistic people are arrogant, but the narcissistic person isn't content to just believe they are better than everyone else—they generally also have to leave the other person feeling "less than" through contemptuous dismissal and criticism or snobbery and confused through manipulation and gaslighting.

Arrogance is tripping the person; narcissism is laughing at them when they fall. An arrogant person may simply be privileged or entitled, while the narcissistic person has a more complex psychology that includes insecurity and fragility. Arrogance is interpersonally uncomfortable and off-putting; narcissism is unhealthy.

## They Can't Control Their Behavior

Have you ever been to a party with a narcissistic person you are close to? In front of others, they were charming and charismatic, and you were surprised they didn't react when a person tossed a playful jab at them. You may have thought, "Oh, maybe I was wrong about them, everybody really likes them, and they managed themselves well." Then you get into the car at the end of the evening and they lay into you, just expel their rage all over you. You recognize that, in fact, they were bothered by what was said but were able to make the choice to not react so as to not look bad in front of others, just as they also made the choice to let loose on you when there were no witnesses.

Narcissistic people *can* manage their behavior. They may lose it in front of others they're close to (e.g., family members), but generally not in front of "high-status" people or new people whose validation they desire. A woman once told me her narcissistic sister would sometimes call when she was in the car and ask in a sweet voice if she was alone, knowing she was on speaker. If she answered yes, the sister would let it rip and go off on her. That's a choice. She didn't like the idea that people would hear her rageful behavior, so she knew rage was not a good look. Unlike people who have personality styles that are more uniformly dysregulated and will yell at you in front of your friends, clients, and strangers alike, narcissistic people tend to be much more tactical and less disorganized. Narcissistic people know what looks good and bad, and how to choose their audience to maintain a public image while privately using those closest to them as punching bags and pacifiers.

## Narcissists Can Significantly Change

Take a minute and reflect on your own personality. Are you introverted? If you are, could you morph into wanting to go out four nights a week and spend lots of time in big groups? Or are you agreeable? Agreeableness, a personality style characterized by empathy, altruism, humility, trust, and a willingness to adhere to the rules, happens to be associated with better mental health and better emotional regulation.[5] Let's say that you are agreeable. Do you want to change that? Do you feel you *could* change that? Do you think that tomorrow you could go from being empathic, humble, and ethical to entitled, manipulative, attention-seeking, and egocentric? Not likely, and you may even ask, "Why would I want to do that? It wouldn't feel good, and it would hurt people around me."

It's not easy to change a personality. Personality is generally viewed as stable and relatively unchanging. Some researchers believe that a significant experience like trauma could result in personality change, as can physical trauma such as a head injury or a stroke.[6] However, to even nudge personality, a person must be committed to change and believe it will yield a desirable outcome. Even then, under conditions of stress, our baseline personality will pop through. Narcissism is termed a *maladaptive* personality style because it often puts a person at odds with other people. However, the more maladaptive the personality, *the more resistant it is to change*. People with this personality have little desire to change, especially since many narcissistic people are thriving financially and professionally, and because they have little self-awareness or self-reflective capacity, they don't take notice of other people's experience and their contribution to it. Instead, they blame everyone else when something goes wrong and are firm in their self-righteous resolve that they are good. If a narcissistic person does not believe there is a reason to change—and in fact, they may believe it would hurt them or take away their "edge"—they will be no more likely or able to make that switch to agreeableness or to become self-aware than you would be able to switch over from agreeableness to disagreeableness. Personality change may be possible, but the changes require tremendous buy-in from the person making the change. For example, a person who really wants to be more conscientious because they think it would make them a better student may be willing to do the work to make the change, but it would still be very difficult.

Everyone loves a redemption story. The myth is that all people can change, and if all people can change, so can a narcissistic person. If you love them enough or soothe their insecurity or figure out how best to talk to them, or if *you* are enough, the relationship will work out. But the reality is, this is extraordinarily unlikely, and anyone citing the case of a narcissistic person who made a complete turnaround from tyrant to sweetheart is talking about a unicorn. There is minimal research supporting the outcome of sustained clinically significant narcissistic behavioral change, so let's keep it simple and recognize the likelihood that the narcissistic people in your life are probably not going to be the exception to the rule.

## Mental Health Issues That Overlap with Narcissism

People who have moderately narcissistic people in their lives may struggle with differentiating the personality style from other mental health issues. This is because narcissism can magnify or look similar to other mental health patterns. Unfortunately, the presence of narcissism makes treatment for other mental health issues that much more complicated.

We most often observe overlaps and association between narcissism and the following: attention deficit hyperactivity disorder (ADHD),[7] addiction,[8] anxiety, depression,[9] bipolar disorder,[10] impulse control disorders,[11] and PTSD. These overlaps may be more pronounced with certain subtypes of narcissism, for example, how social anxiety is commonly observed in vulnerable narcissism.[12] The grandiosity and variable, irritable, and reactive moods we observe in narcissism can sometimes result in the narcissistic person's patterns being attributed to bipolar disorder or to hypomania (a lower-level mania where a person is able to work and function). Bipolar disorder is completely distinct from narcissism; however, it is not unusual for a person to have co-occurring bipolar disorder and narcissism,[13] a combination that can result in the grandiosity persisting long after the manic episode has passed. Irritable mood is often a presenting characteristic of depression, and irritability is a quality observed in many narcissistic people. While we know that narcissism and depression are associated,[14] it is not uncommon for the depression observed in vulnerable narcissism to be so pronounced that the therapist misses the narcissistic patterns, so even as the depression improves, the narcissistic patterns mean ongoing victimhood, irritability, and apathy.

People who are narcissistic often have co-occurring attention deficit hyperactivity disorder (ADHD), or evidence of problems with attention.[15] This is challenging because the ADHD can be deployed as an excuse for why the narcissistic person is impulsive or can't pay attention when you are talking (but is able to stay on point when the conversation is about them or they are focused on something that matters to them)—and ADHD in and of itself is not associated with manipulation, entitlement, or lack of empathy.

Narcissism can complicate substance-use treatment, increasing the likelihood of relapse, and the grandiosity means that a narcissistic person may think they don't need therapy and drop out of treatment, or not get it at all.[16] Addiction may muddy the waters for you in the relationship, as you may believe that their bad behavior will subside once they are sober, or you may worry that ending the relationship may lead to a relapse.

It's not unusual for people who develop narcissistic personalities to have had childhood experiences of trauma, neglect, or chaos, and researchers such as Tracie Afifi and colleagues have suggested that narcissism, especially the impulsivity and anger, is related to adverse childhood experiences.[17] However, a large proportion of people with narcissistic personalities have not experienced significant trauma, and most people who experience trauma do not go on to develop narcissistic personalities. That said, if you are aware that the narcissistic person in your life has a history of trauma, you may have struggled with guilt and even the belief that it isn't fair to hold that person accountable if their behavior is posttraumatic in nature.

These overlaps can get very confusing, and you may find yourself justifying their behavior ("Maybe they are just anxious . . ." but most anxious people aren't abusive). The key to remember is that personality is consistent, a sort of backbeat that constantly plays behind the vocals. Other mental health patterns may only flare up at times or be manageable with medication and intervention. Many narcissistic people commandeer mental health explanations for their chronically invalidating behavior as a more excusable explanation, and then will still not enter treatment to address their behavior. You may also find it more difficult to set boundaries or walk away from the relationship when you subsume their narcissistic patterns under other mental health issues. Ironically, it's almost always the people who are in the relationships with the narcissistic people who are getting into therapy, while the narcissists rarely show up for treatment themselves.

Narcissism still represents a murky and frustrating backwater of the mental health world. The mental health establishment may have abdicated responsibility for understanding and accounting for narcissism, perhaps because of the sense of futility these personalities raise for clinicians, but that's not an excuse. It's a rare conundrum in the world of mental health: understanding a personality style in one set of people to protect others.

SO, WHAT ABOUT Carlos and Adam? After reading this chapter, it is probably more clear that Adam has the chronic, hurtful, invalidating, and unyielding patterns consistent with narcissism, even though to the world he may look like a stand-up guy. Carlos's careless and selfish behavior caused pain, yet there was also awareness, contrition, and other long-standing empathic and healthier behaviors. One behavior does not a narcissist make.

Narcissism is a series of traits that hang together as a personality style, and lies on a continuum from mild to severe. The traits in and of themselves aren't the issue; it's the tactics and behaviors that follow from these traits that are so harmful. The behaviors the narcissistic people engage in to dominate and protect their fragility are where the harm begins. You may feel guilty when you believe someone close to you is narcissistic, and you may avoid identifying the behavior as harmful because it all feels uncomfortable. This guilt and discomfort with using the word *narcissism* has kept many of you in the shadows, and if that is the case, don't get lost in naming the personality, but instead allow yourself to clearly observe the behavior.

Most of us aren't dealing with the villainous version of narcissism but rather with the folks somewhere in the middle. The question is, how does narcissistic behavior play out in your relationship? You know what it is, you know the types; now it's time to unpack these relationships and the associated behaviors. Once you understand the cycle of narcissistic abuse, you will be in a better place to stop blaming yourself—and to start healing.

# Death by a Thousand Cuts: The Narcissistic Relationship

Imagine how much easier it would be for us to learn
how to love if we began with a shared definition.

bell hooks

Jordan was disgusted that he still wanted to please his father; he felt like a forty-five-year-old boy who was trying to get his father to throw a baseball with him. Childhood for him had been a roller coaster. The good times felt like a surprise warm day in the middle of winter, and he would cherish them and wish they wouldn't end, because he knew it would be an eternity before another one came along.

Jordan saw his father as a big fish in the medium-sized city they lived in. He would drive around in vintage cars and hold court at local establishments as people lavished praise on him. But he would also fly into rages when he didn't get his way. Merely going to a restaurant was a harrowing experience. His father would scream at anyone who didn't treat him with deference, and actually said things like "Don't you know who I am? I could shut this place down if I wanted to." The entire family was organized around his father's interests. Weekends would have to be turned around to accommodate his golf schedule and the family was expected to come and cheer him on at every tournament. His parents had been married for fifty years, and his mother had become a shell of her former self—she often seemed sad, anxious, and skittish, and it was almost impossible for Jordan to conceive that she had once had a thriving career. It was painful to watch how callous his father was to his mother, and Jordan spent many nights hearing his mother's crying.

Jordan noticed his father gave more attention to his friends' children than to him and his sister. So he learned to avoid his father while also craving his attention. He wondered, *What is it about me? Why am I not enough for him?* Jordan was an excellent student, a top violin player in the school orchestra, and a kind person. Yet his father mocked his musicianship ("What are you going to do, become a professional fiddle player?"), ridiculed his emotions, and never attempted to really get to know him. His mother was so lost in her unhappiness and exhaustion at trying to please an unpleasable man that she barely registered Jordan's needs. Jordan even tried to learn to play golf so he could connect with his father but found himself hating the game. The one time Jordan played with him, he insulted Jordan's abilities the entire time.

As Jordan grew into adulthood, he kept finding himself underemployed, selling himself short, and entering relationships with people he wanted to "fix." Jordan's first marriage to a difficult woman ended in divorce, and he had been trying to find his footing ever since. He didn't feel he could fully pull away from his family. He still felt compelled to protect his mother—though he also felt angry that she put up with his dad's behavior—and was inexplicably drawn to winning over his father. He blamed himself for his lackluster career, for his failed marriage, for not being able to "figure out" his father.

Jordan's story illustrates what narcissism does to other people. His father's personality translated into behavior that harmed his family. His father's rage, entitled behavior, unrealistic expectations that his family simply be an audience for his validation-seeking behavior, the ridicule and the contempt—all harmed not only Jordan but his mother as well. This behavior is called *narcissistic abuse.*

Oftentimes, the patterns and traits of narcissism can translate into relationship behaviors that are unhealthy and harmful, such as invalidation, manipulation, hostility, arrogance, and entitlement, and allow the narcissistic person to retain power and control in the relationship. This all happens against the backdrop of other narcissistic traits, such as validation seeking, which means that they still retain the charm they need to get that validation. While you experience hurtful patterns within the relationship, the world may still be seeing the charismatic mask, which leaves you feeling confused and conflicted.

In this chapter, we will break down the abuse that happens in these relationships.

# What Is Narcissistic Abuse?

Narcissistic abuse can be defined as the interpersonally harmful, deceitful, and invalidating patterns, behaviors, and alternation between disruptions of safety and trust and periods of normalcy and even enjoyment observed in any relationship with a person who has a personality style characterized by narcissism or antagonism. This definition is based on research, clinical practice, theoretical writings, and the thousands of people (including clients) I have talked with who have experienced narcissistic behavior in their families, intimate relationships, friendships, workplaces, and communities. These harmful behaviors allow the narcissistic/antagonistic person to assert control and dominance in the relationship and maintain a grandiose and distorted appraisal of themselves—which protects their vulnerability, insecurity, and fragility and suppresses their shame—while resulting in significant psychological harm to the other person or people in the relationship. The abusive behaviors alternate with periods of connection and comfort. In addition, there is typically the maintenance of separate behavioral repertoires by the narcissistic person (prosocial and gregarious in public while behaving in an antagonistic and manipulative manner in private, unobserved settings with partners, family, or others from whom validation is less valued). In other words, narcissistic people make you feel small so they can feel safe.

One way to understand narcissistic abuse is to consider the question, "What does the narcissistic person need?" The answer is control, domination, power, admiration, and validation. How they go about getting that is where the narcissistic abuse comes in.

Just as narcissism is on a continuum, so too is narcissistic abuse. Milder narcissistic abuse may feel like being taken for granted and being chronically disappointed, while at the severe end we may witness violence, exploitation, stalking, and coercive control.[1] The majority of folks affected by narcissistic abuse are not just dealing with the distraction and annoyance of a narcissistic adult who is obsessive about social media nor are they managing violence and coercion. Rather, they're dealing with moderate narcissistic abuse: systematic invalidation, minimization, manipulation, rage, betrayal, and gaslighting with periods of "normal" and "good" thrown into the mix. To the world your relationship may look fine, while you live in a confused and uncomfortable haze.

Let's look at some of the tactics, strategies, and behavioral go-tos that a narcissistic person uses to get their narcissistic needs met. You will also learn how these cycles play out, and the deep-seated patterns that can keep you stuck, even when you become aware that this is not healthy. Taken together, all of the patterns that comprise narcissistic abuse erode your identity, intuition, and sense of well-being.

## Gaslighting

Gaslighting is a centerpiece of narcissistic abuse and operates through a systematic pattern of generating doubt about your experiences, memory, perception, judgment, and emotions. Sustained

gaslighting causes you to question reality, and it qualifies as emotional abuse. Gaslighting can include denying events that oc-
curred, behaviors that were engaged in, experiences you are
having, or words that were said. A gaslighter may move objects
around the house and then deny having done so. Typical gaslighting statements include:

- "That never happened; I never did/said that."
- "Why are you always so angry?"
- "You are exaggerating; it wasn't that bad."
- "You have no right to feel that way."
- "It's all in your head."
- "Other people have it so much harder than you—stop
  being a victim."

Gaslighting is a gradual process. It requires you to have some
level of trust or belief in the expertise of the gaslighter, the way
we may have with someone we are falling in love with, a family
member, or an employer. The gaslighter capitalizes on this trust
and uses it to dismantle you, which keeps them in power.[2] The
gaslighter seeds doubt in you ("That never happened, you have
no right to feel that") and then doubles down by questioning your
mental stability ("You must have a memory problem, are you sure
you don't have a mental illness? I think I better step in and take
care of this, you certainly can't"). Gaslighting also allows narcissistic people to maintain their narrative and version of reality,
which serves an ego-protective function for them while harming

you. Over time you may accept the gaslighting as reality, making it more difficult for you to get out of the relationship.

For people who grew up with a narcissistic parent, gaslighting can mean that experiences of abuse within the household were denied and bullying by siblings was glossed over. Adding insult to injury, when people from gaslighted families grow up, their difficult experiences of childhood are denied even when they inquire about them in adulthood. To grow up in a gaslighted family is to not only have endured emotional abuse but also to have the experiences of your childhood fictionalized.

Gaslighting isn't a disagreement, nor is it lying. Anyone who has ever tried to show a gaslighter "evidence," such as text messages or video footage, knows that it doesn't lead the narcissistic person to take responsibility. Instead, they deflect the focus from the evidence to question your mental fitness, or they keep repeating the distorted narrative. The gaslighter may say to you, "I don't want to waste my time talking with someone who chooses to spy on me and look at my phone; you are a petty person." Or they may twist the situation by making it a reality smackdown. "Well, maybe that's your reality," they might say, even when you are holding the signed document or the email that undermines what they are saying.

If you stand your ground in the face of their questioning, the gaslighter might say, "Well, if you feel that way, maybe you really aren't committed to this relationship." Ultimately, for a narcissistic relationship to last, you must submit to their reality. When the narcissistic person implies that your desire to be acknowledged within the relationship means that you really don't want it, you may stand down, put the evidence away, and give in to keep the relationship afloat.

Another framework for more wholly understanding gaslighting comes from Dr. Jennifer Freyd, a renowned psychologist best known for her work on betrayal. She conceptualized the DARVO model to explain the response any abuser, but certainly a gaslighter, will engage in when confronted about their behavior. DARVO stands for *deny* (the behavior), *attack* (the person confronting them about the behavior), and *reverse victim and offender* (the gaslighter positions themselves as a victim—e.g., "Everyone is out to get me"—and the other person as the abuser—e.g., "You are always coming at me and criticizing me").[3] DARVO is a punctuation mark to gaslighting, and it helps people understand why they may feel not only confused and "crazy" but even like they are "bad people" after they have endured gaslighting for an extended period of time.

## SIGNS YOU MAY
## BE BEING GASLIGHTED

- Feeling the need to send long explanatory emails or text messages to the gaslighter.

- Providing an "evidentiary base" for feelings (e.g., showing them old text messages).

- Recording conversations either overtly or secretively so you have proof of what they said.

- Being overreliant on other people's feedback to determine how you are feeling.
- Giving long preludes before you say something.
- Feeling compelled to put all communication in writing as "proof."
- Giving in and going along to get along.

## *The DIMMER Patterns*

*Dismissiveness, invalidation, minimization, manipulation, exploitativeness, and rage*

These are specific behavioral patterns that encompass the devaluation you experience in narcissistic relationships. I use the acronym *DIMMER* to describe this set of patterns because the narcissistic relationship can be viewed as a switch that dims your sense of self and well-being.

To be in a narcissistic relationship is to have your needs, feelings, beliefs, experiences, thoughts, hopes, and even sense of self be *dismissed* and *invalidated*. This may be as simple as the narcissistic person not listening or contemptuously dismissing something you say ("That's just ridiculous, nobody cares about what you are saying"). Over time this can feel dehumanizing because anything you bring up is written off as unimportant or is simply not attended to, and it can slowly feel like you do not exist. The experience of dismissiveness and invalidation can occur gradually, and what initially may feel like a difference of opinion can evolve into a large-scale brush-off.

Dismissiveness often foreshadows contempt and an absolute disregard and disdain for you and anything that matters to you. Invalidation is not being seen, felt, heard, or experienced. Where the dismissiveness is a brush-off, invalidation is a negation. Dismissiveness is ignoring a concern or need you may be having; invalidation is having your needs chronically shamed and denied ("Don't be a baby and make me waste a day sitting at your doctor's appointments, I can't change your disease by sitting there, and I can't stand hospitals"). Over time the invalidation steals your voice and ultimately your sense of self. In the early days, you may furrow your brow and wonder, *Did they even hear me?* If you grew up with a narcissistic parent, invalidation is familiar to you; not only were you inconsistently noticed, but when you were, you were often shamed, scorned, or tossed aside. Over time it can feel safer to not be seen.

Minimization is when the narcissistic person plays down your experience to the point where they might outright deny it. Narcissistic abuse often entails having your feelings minimized with statements such as "It's not that big a deal" or "I don't understand why something so small is bothering you." It's a minimization not only of your feelings and experience but also of your achievements, for example, trivializing a promotion you received or the difficulty of completing your degree at school. There is a hypocrisy to the minimization: when something happens to the narcissistic person, they feel entitled to it being as big an issue or feeling as they want, but they will diminish the same experience in you. Minimization may even put you in harm's way, particularly when narcissistic people minimize your health concerns, which may result in a delay in getting support or treatment.

Narcissistic people use manipulation to control or influence you to achieve a desired goal that may not be in your best interest but is in theirs. Instead of being transparent about what they want or why they need your help, they play upon your vulnerable emotions—guilt, obligation, low self-worth, confusion, anxiety, or fear—to rope you into doing what works for them. Anyone who has ever been told by an adult narcissistic parent something to the effect of "Oh, I don't mind if you don't come to the holiday dinner, I may not be able to cook anyhow, my back is acting up, and each year I wonder if this will be the last year I can make the big meal, but I understand you have other, more important things to do" knows about manipulation.

*Exploitativeness* refers to the process of taking unfair advantage of another person. It involves playing on existing vulnerabilities or creating vulnerabilities, such as isolating you or making you financially dependent, and taking advantage of that situation. It may also mean taking advantage of the money, people, and other resources you brought to a relationship. Narcissistic people may imply that you "owe" them something, with parents even implying you "owe" them because they fed and housed you. The exploitativeness means that there will be a psychological debt that is created if you ever accept a favor, and in the future if you feel uncomfortable with something the narcissistic person is asking of you, they will remind you of what they have done for you in the past.

The narcissistic person's rage may be the most frightening aspect of narcissistic abuse. Narcissistic people feel entitled to their volatile and reactive rage, which is often activated by shame. If you trigger their feelings of inadequacy, they will often target you with either overt aggression (yelling and screaming) or passive-aggression (stonewalling, giving you the silent treatment, showing resentment).[4] They might then feel shame about their show of rage because they actually do know it's not a good look, so they'll blame you for it, and the whole cycle begins again.

The unwillingness of narcissistic people to control their impulses means they can be highly reactive, especially when they feel provoked, envious, or disempowered. Narcissistic people have high rejection sensitivity, and any experience that smacks of rejection or abandonment is met with reactive rage.[5] Narcissistic rage plays out in every possible communication platform—text messages, voicemails, emails, DMs, phone calls, in person—and through behaviors like road rage. Rage is the clearest behavioral manifestation of narcissistic abuse, and one that takes a tremendous toll on you.

## The Domination Patterns

*Domination, isolation, revenge, and threats*

Narcissistic abuse is about *domination*, which counterbalances the inadequacy and insecurity that are at the core of the narcissistic personality. Needing to control schedules, appearances, financial decisions, and the narrative is a classical part of narcissistic behavior. Their control may also feel spiteful and simply serves as a way to show you that they are in charge. This may happen when a narcissistic person refuses to go to an event that matters to you, which may mean that you don't get to go, either. They will use money to control you; for example, by paying your rent in order to keep you living nearby, or offering to pay a family member's medical bills so you then feel silenced and indebted. The control extends to *isolation*. Narcissistic abuse often consists of the narcissistic person criticizing your family, friends, and workplace, and when you are with those people, the narcissist will behave in a manner that is insulting and rude. A narcissistic person may also tell you falsehoods about people close to you so you question their loyalty and friendship. The result is that you slowly have less contact with people you care about, or those people just no longer come around. The more isolated you become, the easier it is to control you.

*Revenge* and vindication are another common feature of narcissistic abuse, and narcissistic people can be tenacious. Hell really hath no fury like a narcissist scorned. Their vindictive behavior may range from spreading damaging workplace gossip or stealing business leads to major things like quitting a job so they don't have to pay you spousal support or cutting you out of a family trust because you set a boundary. The challenging part about narcissistic vengeance is that narcissistic people are skilled at flying right under the radar, which may limit you from taking any substantive legal remedies—after all, being a jerk isn't against the law. Narcissistic abuse is characterized by *threats* big and small: legal threats, threats of exposing you to key players in your life, or financial or custody threats during a divorce simply to create a sense of menace. Grandiose statements like "Nobody messes with me" or "I will see you in court," or even behavior that leaves you looking over your shoulder, foster dominance.

## The Disagreeable Patterns

> *Arguing, baiting, blame shifting, justifying, rationalizing, criticizing, being contemptuous, humiliating, speaking in word salad*

This set of patterns reflects tactics that narcissistic people will often use to achieve the same goal as all narcissistic behavior—to control the narrative. Narcissistic folks love a fight, debate, argument, or any form of conflict. *Arguing* gives them another way to get supply, let out some steam, air their grievances, and remain dominant. It's like the aphorism "Never wrestle with a pig—you end up dirty, and the pig likes it." When you try to disengage from these relationships, it's not unusual that the narcissist pokes you and tries to provoke a fight. This is most commonly achieved by *baiting*. Sometimes it will be them twisting your words: "I thought you said you hated your sister's husband." You jump in there to defend something that is patently untrue, and the argument begins. Unfortunately, if you don't take the bait, they just keep upping the ante and will bring up issues that matter more dearly to you. Once you take the bait and get frothed up, they then calmly step back and paint you as the dysregulated and volatile one.

Narcissistic abuse always entails *blame shifting*. Nothing is ever their responsibility or their fault because for a narcissistic person to take responsibility or accept blame means having to accept that they are accountable and imperfect. The blame shifting allows them to maintain their grandiose and self-righteous conception of themselves as being better than you or as the victim of circumstance. In intimate relationships, it's your fault they cheated. With narcissistic parents, it's your fault they didn't get to achieve their dreams. With narcissistic adult children, it's your fault they can't hold a job. In narcissistic workplace relationships, it's your fault they missed all the deadlines and the deal didn't go through. There is no point in arguing because it will get you nowhere, as narcissistic people will hold firm to their assertion that it is anyone's fault but their own.

Blame shifting is frequently supported by justification. *Justifying* and *rationalizing* are key elements of narcissistic abuse and are related to patterns such as gaslighting, manipulation, and denial. For instance, the narcissistic person might say, "I cheated because you stopped paying any attention to me since the baby was born, even though I work all the time to keep us in this lifestyle. You never appreciated all the things I do." Over time you may begin to feel as bad as you would if you were the one doing something wrong, because you are being used as the justification for the narcissistic person's bad behavior. Narcissistic people can argue like lawyers, finding cold and logical justifications for behaviors that hurt you just so they can win the argument.

Other sparring patterns that characterize narcissistic abuse include *criticism* of just about anything you do. The criticism can reveal itself as *contempt* for you, your habits, your life, or your mere existence, and can also go a step further with *humiliation*. It may be framed as mockery in front of others, and downplayed as a joke, but it may also be indirectly communicated through non-verbals such as eye-rolling. Shaming and embarrassing you is an unconscious way for the narcissistic person to eliminate their own shame by pivoting it to someone else.

A classical element of the disagreeable aspects of narcissistic abuse is to overwhelm you with *word salad*. This is when a person says words that don't really mean anything (e.g., "I see my goals being me, and myself for growth and the world") or a bewildering barrage of words that come at you and bring up multiple random things from the past. For example, you ask a narcissistic partner why they keep working so late and they might come back at you with, "I am a striver, and you are a gold digger. I work hard to keep us going so we can eat, and I will strive. I give, you take, I strive, and I give. I don't know what you do all day. What do you do? Where does our food come from? I don't even know the password on your phone. I work and you play. What is his name? Maybe I should go down there right now."

Confusing, right?

### The Betrayal Patterns

*Lying, being unfaithful, future faking*

Narcissistic abuse can feel so devastating because someone who claimed to love you was able to deceive you and betray your trust.

Narcissists *lie*; it's what they do. They aren't quite as skilled as psychopathic liars, but they are in the ballpark. Narcissistic folks lie to maintain their grandiose narratives, get attention, and sell an image to the world and they lie as a hedge against their shame. The lying and the betrayal typically occur together. Narcissistic *infidelity* can be particularly painful, and the narcissistic person may be unapologetic, blame you, and quickly fly into self-preservation mode so they do not look bad to others. We often don't recognize how impactful and traumatic betrayal can be, but when someone you are counting on betrays your trust, it threatens your sense of safety and undercuts your ability to trust in the future.[6] For too long we have viewed betrayal as an unfortunate occurrence that can happen in a relationship, but that misses how devastating this common dynamic of narcissistic relationships can be.

Then there is *future faking*. Have you ever had that experience when the narcissistic person promises to change, or offers you that thing you wanted—whether it's to get married, move to a certain place, have children, go on vacation, repay you money, get into therapy, etc.—to keep you in the relationship longer, and then it never happens or the goalposts keep moving? Future faking is a particularly twisted element of narcissistic abuse. Narcissistic people know what you want, so they offer it to you as a manipulation to draw you back in and keep you on the hook. Most future-faked promises are tied to some date in the future: "We're going to move in a year," "I'll pay you back that money as soon as I sell the house," "I'll begin therapy once my work hours shift." You are left having to make a bet (a bad one). You can't expect you will get married that minute or in a week, or that you will move in a few days, or that therapy would change things overnight. So you wait, and you wait, and you wait. If you inquire about whatever was promised ahead of the future date, the narcissist will likely accuse you of being pushy. If you say, "I don't believe you" when they first make the offer, they'll say, "How would you know unless you give me a chance?" But when the year or whatever agreed upon time period passes, the promise is never kept, and you can't get that year back.

## The Deprivation Patterns

### Deprivation, breadcrumbing

Narcissism as a personality style is about transactional intimacy—narcissistic people give time or closeness only when there is a tangible payout (narcissistic supply). This means that narcissistic abuse is also about *deprivation*—of intimacy, time, closeness, attention, and love. The relationship consists of you perpetually dropping a bucket in an empty well, and every so often you bring up some water, but by and large it's a whole lot of empty buckets. Other times the relationship can feel like trying to survive on breadcrumbs. *Breadcrumbing* is a dynamic whereby the narcissistic person in the relationship gives less and less, and you learn to make do on less and less, and even express gratitude for it. This may be a gradual process, or it may simply have always been a dynamic in the relationship and you learned to make do with very little from the very beginning, which may be an extension of adjusting to the deprivation established in childhood relationships.

## The Narcissistic Relationship Cycle

On a night out with friends, Asha met Dave. Dave was charming and fascinating, and after the bar closed, they sat outside and talked until 3:00 a.m. Dave was an attentive listener, and he told her about his difficult childhood. As they started dating, he would text her frequently and remembered little things. She would find coffee and breakfast waiting at her desk that he'd had delivered for her. They traveled together frequently, and he whisked her to New York for her birthday four weeks after they met.

However, as time went on, Asha found it odd that there were two different versions of Dave. There was the attentive, generous, charming, and ambitious person, but then there was the sullen, resentful person who had a chip on his shoulder and behaved in an entitled manner. Dave would snap and throw tantrums then apologize on a regular basis. At first, Asha was confused, but she learned to be very supportive on those tough days. She slowly started to censor herself, not sharing her concerns or stresses because if she did, Dave would accuse her of burdening him or always making it about herself. She justified his behavior because she wanted their relationship to last. The good stuff was good.

One day, Dave received a promotion, and that meant a move. Asha gave up her beloved apartment and colleagues and got transferred to a different office. Then things shifted. Dave frequently accused Asha of not working hard enough or doing her part, of not keeping their apartment clean enough, of not being available when he wanted. The relationship became more and more about her defending herself and trying to be more and more perfect, simply to avoid his rage. She wondered what she was doing wrong, what she could be doing better.

Eventually, Asha started getting tired of it. She regretted the move, giving up her apartment, and leaving good friends, and the roller coaster of Dave's good and bad days made life incredibly unpredictable. Finally, she told him she was out. She would find a new place, get back to what felt like home. But Dave cried, begged Asha to stay, and claimed it was stress, promising he was going to go to therapy to deal with his demons. He was sorry. She didn't need to leave; he would change.

So Asha stayed. At first, things went back to the way they were when they'd first met. Dave was his charming, generous self, and even made an appointment with a therapist. Asha was hopeful they would make things work. But it wasn't long before the fights started back up, and Dave stopped following up with his therapist. Asha found herself walking on eggshells again, feeling stuck. Once more she felt the only way out was to end the relationship and move, and she even found a new apartment. This time Dave said, "I am so sorry, I can't lose you, I will move back with you, I know you wanted to be near your friends and family." She believed that with her supports around her, maybe it could be better, so she agreed, and they moved back to her old neighborhood. It felt like a fresh start in a safe place. It wasn't long before the tension started anew.

Narcissistic relationships follow a cycle. This cycle often begins with charm, intensity, idealization, or the patterns we call *love bombing* that draw us in. Then gradually, the "idealized" mask falls off and the expectable patterns of devaluation and discard kick in. While it doesn't always happen, typically the narcissistic person will attempt to pull you back in, and not just because the relationship ended or one of you left, but also in response to increased boundaries and disengagement on your part. If you grant a "second chance," the cycle invariably restarts.

These phases show up differently depending on the nature of the relationship, but the cycle is universal across all narcissistic relationships. For example, a narcissistic parent does not love bomb a child. However, the child will grasp onto idealized moments that will alternate with periods of devaluation and detachment, which the child will attempt to offset by being "better" so the parent will come back around. The idealization or love bombing is actually the deep desire of the child for a loving parent and the parent capitalizing on that willingness. When a narcissistic relationship begins in adulthood, the relationship cycle, and particularly the love bombing, are more transparent, with the seduction and idealization being an active process that hooks you and brings you into a confusing alternating cycle of both good and abusive patterns and experiences. These narcissistic relationship cycles can repeat for adult children of narcissistic parents, and set up a pattern of getting stuck in toxic cycles with a parent or a partner (or any narcissistic person) constantly pulling the other person back into a self-serving and invalidating process.

These toxic cycles are very difficult to break. Most of us have been raised on fairy tales and parables of irritable frogs turning into princes, relationships being "work," fantasies about being "chosen," and love that must be fought for. Narcissistic relationship cycles often embody these distorted narratives about love. For many of us, the cycle becomes a reenactment of trying to win over our unwinnable parent, so it feels familiar to be rejected and exciting and reassuring to be idealized. Or you feel a loyalty to people you love and don't want to impugn their character by labeling them or the relationship as toxic (so you end up blaming yourself).

The narcissistic relationship cycle is not always linear, where one phase occurs after the other. In the same week or even the same day, a person may experience both love bombing/idealization and devaluation. Or the love bombing may never happen again after the initial coupling, and it's devaluation all the time. Mini-cycles involving idealization, devaluation, and discarding can happen repeatedly. Some of you may be finding that every week is this same cycle. It's definitely not a one and done.

## The Love Bomb: The False Fairy Tale

In a relationship you choose, love bombing is the intense and overwhelming initial process that draws you in and distracts you from seeing any red flags. Let's say you meet someone new, have a captivating moment together, and exchange phone numbers. The next morning you receive a text: "Good morning, babe." It feels *so* good. You receive a couple more during the day: "Hey, just thinking about you. I can't concentrate on work. All I can do is think about last night." You feel giddy, can't focus. The evening comes and the person asks, "Hey, what are you doing this weekend? I'd love to see you again." You agree to go out and have dinner at a fancy restaurant. It feels like one of those perfect nights—and it feels electric.

You keep spending time together; you are seduced and courted. The gestures may start getting bigger, the attention more intense. Things are moving quickly; you may travel together or cancel other plans to spend time with this new person. You feel like you finally got your love story, the one you've been waiting for. You may even find yourself talking about a life together, marriage, names for children. This is a period of idealization.

Love bombing is an indoctrination into a controlling and manipulative relationship. It sets the tone for the justifications: *we had such a good time last night; this person is so attentive; everybody gets angry sometimes; they didn't mean what they said.* Love bombing is the "hook," and it creates buy-in. During the love bombing phase, you feel desired and seen and valued (which are good feelings!). Even toxic dynamics such as isolation may be romanticized as nesting and wanting to have a private love story, or to be together all the time. But one of the most pernicious elements of love bombing is that you slowly sacrifice your identity, preferences, and even aspirations to avoid losing the relationship, and you may barely notice you are doing it.

While all of this is happening—the excitement, connection, attention, and constant need to be with you—you may get distracted and take your eye off the prize, which is really getting to know someone and feeling safe expressing your needs, hopes, and wants. In getting dazzled, you may not slow down enough to notice the person, the patterns, or the subtle tells of narcissism. In the bait and switch that is the narcissistic relationship, love bombing is the bait that confuses you and plays on core wounds and hopes. Narcissistic folks are able to present themselves as what you thought you wanted for long enough to get you on the hook, and then the switch happens. The superficial nature of the narcissistic personality means that making things look good comes quite naturally to them.

During love bombing, a toxic approach-and-avoidance cycle may also get established. The narcissistic person may engage in lots of contact, then disappear. Or if you hold back from reaching out, they will keep trying to contact you, and then once you reach out, they'll go quiet for a while. This sets up a confusing game where you may find yourself starting to analyze every message, wondering how you should respond and what their messages mean, and you may feel relieved or excited when they finally do respond.

Of course, not all grandiose gestures at the beginning of a relationship are love bombing—even healthy relationships can be compelling and exciting in the beginning. The difference is that if you voice your needs, such as asking for more time or to slow things down in a new relationship, a narcissistic person may become angry and accuse you of not wanting a commitment. This may leave you feeling guilty, doubting yourself, and justifying the unhealthy or uncomfortable patterns. On the other hand, if you asked a healthy new partner to slow down, they wouldn't become sullen and resentful. True romance is respectful and empathic; love bombing is a tactic.

While classical love bombing is often depicted as more grandiose and enthralling—dancing until dawn, elaborate gifts, expensive dinners or nights out—it doesn't always look like that. With a vulnerable narcissistic person, love bombing may be about hearing their disappointment and wanting to rescue them; with a malignant narcissist it may be about constant contact, possessiveness, and isolation framed as "I can't bear the idea of anyone else having you"; with communal narcissists it may be about being inspired by their plans for saving the world or their spiritual "awareness"; with self-righteous narcissists it may be about the appeal of a highly organized, fiscally responsible "grown-up." Each of us is attracted by different things. Every fairy tale we are raised on ends with lovers walking into the sunset. The narcissistic relationship is everything that happens after that sunset.

One of the questions I get most often is "How can I identify a narcissist when I am dating?" The answer is that it's tricky. If you spend your early dates trying to spot red flags, then you spend that time in vigilance and miss the opportunity to be present with someone new. Many of us don't even have a template for what qualifies as healthy or unhealthy. The harder and more important work is getting yourself to a place where you are able to bring your authentic self into the situation and pay attention to how you feel in any kind of new relationship instead of treating dating as being about "having game" or following rigid rules. It's about holding standards for yourself and giving yourself permission to engage in a manner consistent with those standards.[7] Perhaps the hardest work of all is actually understanding who you are and giving yourself permission to show up as that authentic self. Part of this process is understanding the concept of what authenticity really means. To be authentic is to be genuine, honest, and comfortable in who you are and what you are about. That is hard for most people to do under the best of circumstances. It can feel painfully difficult for people in narcissistic relationships who have to go back to the beginning and figure who their genuine self actually is.

Keep in mind too that many people will say that the issues in their relationship did not even become fully evident until one to two years in, and there is no quick quiz that can unearth this in the first month. It can often take about a year to really start seeing the problem behaviors as patterns, and by then you may have become quite invested in the relationship. Hell, even a therapist needs a few months to definitively understand narcissistic personality patterns in a client, so be gentle with yourself as you unpack your relationship and wonder why you "didn't see it sooner."

The key to remember about love bombing is that enjoying it or even wanting it is not foolish or a bad thing. Do not devalue yourself for "falling" for love bombing; it is human to want to be desired and to enjoy romantic gestures. The harm of love bombing is that it gives you the ammunition for the justifications you make when the relationship becomes unhealthy.

## Can Love Bombing Happen in Non-Romantic Relationships?

We do not typically use the term *love bombing* when we talk about the relationship a child has with a narcissistic parent during childhood, but a similar experience can occur. For many children, all a parent needs to do is show up with a small gift, play a game, read a story, or just say hello. These crumbs of affection or fleeting attunement may feel like an idealized moment and set that child up to regard crumbs as sufficient in adult relationships. A child may also have an experience of an intrusive narcissistic parent who is constantly seeking out supply from or through the child (e.g., the child being pushed to excel at a sport the parent wants so they can get the praise), and if the child doesn't do the thing the parent wants, the parent detaches. This dynamic can result in difficulty maintaining healthy boundaries or in feeling you need to perform and be a constant source of supply to maintain a relationship with that parent (and may be a pattern that you fall into in future relationships as well).

A sort of love bombing may occur in adult narcissistic systems as well: family members can try to win you over so they can get what they need from you, a potential employer can entice you into a business partnership that is not advantageous for you, and friends can pursue you for connections or money.

## *The Gateway to Love Bombing:*
## *Welcome to the C-Suite*

If you are in the middle or end of a narcissistically abusive relationship, you may be asking yourself how in the world you were ever attracted to this person, why you took this job, or why you haven't completely cut off your partner, parent, sibling, or friend. Listen, if a narcissistic person opened with lack of empathy, rage, and entitlement, most of us would never have gotten into a relationship with them. Instead, narcissistic people roll up with something I call *the C-Suite*—it's the stuff that makes anyone attractive, and it's what draws us in and makes it hard to walk away. Let's take a tour of the C-Suite.

*Charm.* The narcissistic person is often the most charming and engaging person in the room. It's a grandiose and attentive mask that gets them validation. Charm is the psychological cologne they use to cover their insecurity, and it manifests in compliments, storytelling, short-term attentiveness, and impeccable manners.

*Charisma.* When the charm seems magnetic, compelling, or everyone is drawn to it, that is where you see charisma. Charismatic people may appear to be visionary, extremely attractive, or simply great performers.

*Confidence.* Narcissistic arrogance, entitlement, distorted self-esteem, and validation seeking can all combine to produce a person who seems very comfortable and self-assured about their abilities. Healthier people tend to be humble, so when you witness someone who is so demonstrative about what they know or have, you may erroneously (and understandably) assume they have the goods to back it up.

*Credentials.* Narcissistic people seek status and may pursue it through "credentials," such as elite educations, exclusive addresses, fancy jobs, great connections, intelligence, wealthy or powerful families, or just being really "hip." We can mistake these credentials for the quality of a person, and undervalue healthy "credentials" such as wisdom, kindness, respect, compassion, empathy, humility, and honesty.

*Curiosity.* Narcissistic folks may be overwhelming in how interested they are in you. In the early days of a relationship, they may ask lots of probing questions to get to know you when what they're really doing is getting information that will be useful for them down the line, like your assets, connections, vulnerabilities, and fears. For people who have rarely felt heard or seen, the narcissistic person's seeming curiosity can be a hook.

## Devaluation: The Unfolding of Narcissistic Abuse

The moment when you are all in on the narcissistic relationship, there's an almost audible click. Maybe you say "I love you." Maybe you agree to live together, take the job, attend the family get-together. Somewhere between four weeks and six months after the love bombing starts, the denouement begins, invariably once the narcissistic person believes they've "got you." You may have been resisting this relationship for a while, you may have been savvy enough to know that the love bombing might be too good to be true, and then just when you believe you have done your due diligence and settle in, the devaluation begins.

The transition from love bombing to devaluation may be gradual but it can nonetheless take you by surprise. The narcissistic person may start comparing you to, or casually mentioning, other people or bringing up what they claim others have said, for example, "My friends think you are too demanding." The red flags, which may have just looked a little pink before, are now unmistakable, but because you're fully in the relationship, escape is more difficult.

During the devaluation phase, the idealized version of the narcissistic person slips away. You might do everything—changing your appearance, trying to impress them with what you do or say, catering to their every whim, giving up things that matter to you, doing things for their family, or making more money—to recapture and maintain their attention. There is also a temptation to play hard to get in order to have the old chase back. One thing that I have observed in survivors of narcissistic parents is that some of them recall that once they were not as small, cute, portable, obedient, or photogenic as when they were younger, there was a shift toward devaluation in their relationship. Interestingly, for some clients, as they came up into early adulthood and could do things that their parent enjoyed (sports, travel, work in a family business), the parent became interested in them again, though the devaluing never fully went away.

With all this talk of red flags and cycles, you may wonder, "Why don't people get out once the devaluation begins?" Because you are confused. You aren't a robot who just processes red flags and runs away. You love or admire this person and want to maintain the attachment and connection. In a new relationship you may want to give it a chance; in a long-standing relationship there is history. Not only is the narcissistic person in your life seductive and compelling, so too are love and familiarity and hope.

## Discard: "This Isn't Working for Me Anymore . . ."

The discard phase is exactly what it sounds like: Either the narcissistic person is done with you or you are done with them. It doesn't always mean the relationship ends, but there really is no more *there* there. For example, narcissistic people may discard you by having an affair or doing things like having inappropriate text or DM exchanges without technically leaving you. They may take a job or an opportunity that does not take you into consideration, so you have to either leave your life behind to join them or be left behind. They may simply lose interest in you, cultivate a life that doesn't include you, avoid closeness and intimacy, and make you feel like a ghost. You may also find that you are disengaging. The discard phase may be when you have the aha moment—maybe you are in therapy or watching videos and reading books and wanting to step back. This can then create new chaos in the relationship as the narcissistic person not only may respond angrily to your perceived rejection, distance, and indifference to their baiting, but may also try to draw you back in (more confusion!).

During the discard phase you may experience an escalation of abuse, unmasked contempt, and more severe gaslighting. Narcissistic people are novelty seekers, so everyone's supply becomes stale over time. Keep in mind that it's not *you* who is boring; they get bored and contemptuous of everyone and live in a world that is never enough for them. They want life to be a kaleidoscope of perfect ease, validation, and entertainment. In your family of origin, the discard may have happened after a divorce, when your narcissistic parent met or married someone new and was no longer interested in you; or when you hit an age when they viewed you as a nuisance; or when new siblings were born; or when a parent had a career shift and disengaged from the family. During this phase, there may have been a palpable sense of your narcissistic parent not wanting to be bothered by you or anyone else in the family. Discard may also happen when the narcissistic parent no longer views the child as a source of supply.

If you try to hold the narcissistic person accountable for their behavior in the discard phase, they will likely gaslight you. For example, if you say you want to end it after learning about infidelity, they might say, "I didn't want this relationship to end and to break up our family, this was all you" and take no responsibility for how their betrayal was a factor. Narcissistic folks are invested in their public image and don't want to look like the jerk who left you for something or someone new (e.g., entering a new relationship almost immediately and insisting publicly there was never an overlap between their new partner and their relationship with you). They are also good at playing the role of victim and may expect you to do the dirty work of leaving so they can turn around and say, "You are the one who left me" or "You filed for divorce" or "You were just not responding to me."

During the discard phase, a note of desperation may enter the relationship. There may be apologizing, begging, and appeasing from either side. You may fight for the relationship because you feel as if you already put in so much time, effort, heartache, and money. You may try eleventh hour strategies like couple's therapy. But sadly, the time is already gone, and throwing more time and effort at the relationship won't get you back the time you already put in.

## Hoovering: "Hey, I've Been Thinking of You. Let's Give It a Fresh Start."

The devaluation and discard phases of narcissistic relationships are often followed by hoovering. Regardless of why a relationship with the narcissistic person ends, they will eventually try to suck you back in like a vacuum cleaner, thus the term *hoover*. Remember, for them, relationships are about control, supply, and regulation. Narcissistic people hoover to get back your supply, which may now seem fresh and new, especially if you called it quits for a minute or you are the one who disengaged.

Narcissistic people don't just hoover romantic partners; they also hoover adult children, extended family, former colleagues, and anyone they feel is out of their web of control or has something they need. If they are lonely or want companionship, they will pull you back in. If they see you happy or succeeding, they want to commandeer that narrative. Your happiness without them means they aren't controlling you, and hoovering is an attempt to regain their power. If you fall for it, the whole cycle begins again.

It can be seductive and easy to confuse the excitement of the hoovering with love, destiny, or being chosen. When narcissistic people try to suck you back into a relationship, it often works because they still have the arsenal of charm, charisma, and confidence. Or they use their own victimhood to play upon your guilt ("My mother abandoned me, and now you are leaving me, too"). They also use pseudoapologies ("I'm sorry you feel that way") that never reflect any acknowledgment of their role in your hurt. Because hoovering leverages hopes and narratives of being cherished and desired, a narcissistic person coming back for you can be even more seductive than the initial love bombing.

In narcissistic relationships, by the time hoovering rolls around, it's usually clear what needs to change. Maybe they need to stop cheating or invalidating you, stop insulting your friends and family, or just be more present and less arrogant and entitled. You may have tried asking them to change, to empathize, to just be aware, until one day you give up. And then the narcissistic person—with their sensitivity to abandonment, distaste of losing, and need for control and good optics—will make you the promise you have been asking for: "I will change." Maybe they offer to go to therapy or anger management or to let you look at their phone every night. It can be incredibly powerful to think that your words finally got through to someone. For a short while they may appear to have turned a corner, and then just as you exhale and shelve your ideas of splitting up or moving out, they slowly slide back into their narcissistic patterns. In other words, hoovering is where future faking is deployed as a tactic to draw you back in. The same red flags are there, the charm and charisma are front and center, but during hoovering you may feel avenged, as if you were finally "enough," worthy of being heard, and the exception to the rule of narcissistic relationships. And boom, you are back in it—except this time you feel more foolish and maybe even more likely to fall into the cycle of self-blame when things go south again.

Not every narcissistic relationship cycle ends in hoovering. Sometimes the narcissistic person finds new supply—a new relationship, job, living situation, or notoriety, for example—and therefore their needs are being met. (Once that new situation blows up, however, they may come sniffing around again.) If they betrayed you, they might avoid you to avoid the shame. The relationship may be at a standoff, and their ego may be waiting for you to reach out first. You may also be giving the narcissist enough supply if you remain in touch with them via occasional text messages or social media. Other times, hoovering can happen years after the initial relationship. I have heard stories of hoovering occurring ten years later. Mercifully, by then most people have moved on, but if you don't understand what hoovering is, you may get played by love bomb 2.0.

Remember, being hoovered isn't a statement on you being *enough* or an acknowledgment that the narcissistic person *needs* you. Hoovering is a reflection of narcissists and their needs—for validation, control, or whatever convenience you fill for them, or even to block you from moving forward into a new life. While you are healing, it is a blessing if you are not hoovered. Not being hoovered is like going cold turkey—it hurts initially, but it's essential to healing.

## Trauma Bonds: The Riptide of
## the Narcissistic Relationship

We often assume that people who are in a bad place, rebounding, or insecure are most at risk of getting stuck in narcissistic relationships. But this isn't necessarily true. Asha wasn't lonely, vulnerable, or needy when she met Dave; she was in a good place. She was drawn not only to Dave's grand and generous gestures but also to his seeming vulnerability. She saw red flags, saw two faces—mask on and mask off—and started slowly altering herself to manage his moods, win him over, and maintain the relationship.

Part of understanding why some of us get stuck in narcissistic relationships despite the abuse isn't just about unpacking the narcissistic personality but about acknowledging some universal responses to these kinds of dynamics. I am tired of people calling those of us who get stuck in these cycles "codependent" or "addicted" to the narcissistic relationship. It's not that. If you have any empathy, have normal cognitive functioning, and were shaped by societal and cultural norms and realities, it is not surprising that you would get stuck. The narcissistic relationship is like a riptide that pulls you back in even as you try to swim away. The intensity, attentiveness, and highs and lows are why you swim out to where the riptide is. The abusive behavior makes you want to swim away from the riptide, but the guilt and fear of leaving, the practical issues raised by leaving (financial, safety, cultural, family), as well as the natural drive toward attachment, connection, and love are what keep you stuck in the riptide's pull.

Narcissistic riptides are created by trauma bonds. The term *trauma bonding* is often misunderstood as the bond between people who have had similar traumatic experiences. It actually refers to the enigmatic bond that is created in relationships characterized by harm and confusion, and that is then mirrored in future relationships. In narcissistic relationships, the trauma bond is a deep and distracting sense of love or connection that blocks you from seeing the toxic cycles of the relationship clearly.[8] Nobody stays in a narcissistic relationship because it is abusive and uncomfortable, and describing survivors of adult narcissistic relationships as "masochists" or "gluttons for punishment" is an inaccurate and unfair characterization. The good moments are what draw you in and what you want to sustain; the bad moments are confusing and unsettling. The narcissistic person controls the "emotional thermostat" for the relationship, so if they are having a good run or trying to win you over, you may have weeks or even months of good days, and then when they don't feel validated or safe, the relationship falls into an abyss of invalidation, anger, manipulation, and gaslighting. Over time, the bad days become a signal that perhaps the good day is coming, and so even the bad days get paired with a sense of anticipation, keeping you even more stuck and less likely to see the bad days more clearly as alarm bells. Unfortunately, that also means that the good days are paired with a sense of dread, knowing that it is a matter of time before the other shoe drops.

Trauma-bonded relationships can have two different origins:

those that develop through childhood relationships and those that originate in adulthood. Childhood with a narcissistic parent means unpredictability, confusion, and conditional love. The narcissistic parent is simply not attuned to the child as a distinct person with needs, identity, and personhood separate from them, and these are not things a child can ask for directly. Children in trauma-bonded relationships learn to justify and normalize their parents' invalidating and unattuned behavior, can't process or acknowledge it as "bad," keep secrets, blame themselves, deny their own needs, and idealize their parents in order to survive (since children can't break up with their parents and can't survive without them). When children in narcissistically abusive parental relationships try to set a boundary or express a need, they will often find themselves feeling abandoned or guilty when the parent either gives them the silent treatment or behaves like a victim. Then these children find they are in the caregiving role of having to attune to the bruised parent's needs and silence their own.

Experiencing an invalidating childhood creates a relationship template that consists of hoop-jumping to earn love, feeling guilty for expressing your own needs, and believing that abuse and invalidation are a part of a loving relationship, as well as having the fear and anxiety that arise from not being able to foster healthy attachments. In addition, the alternation between good and bad days means that such cycles not only are normalized but also that self-blame for those cycles is carried into adult relationships. The trauma bond is the acceptance and normalization of these cycles in adulthood, and the sense that if these dynamics aren't present, the relationship lacks "chemistry"; this can result in a toxic déjà vu. When you are in a trauma-bonded relationship, there can also be a visceral sense of panic at the thought of the relationship ending or somehow losing them. You may have the physical and emotional sensation that you cannot live without them even when every rational cell in your body knows it is not good for you. Ultimately, the narcissist's charm and charisma and confidence are what get us in, and the trauma bonds are what get us stuck.

Of course, not everyone who experiences a trauma-bonded cycle in adulthood is replicating a childhood cycle. For many of us, an adult narcissistic relationship was our first time at this rodeo. The charm and charisma offensive, coupled with messages about fairy tales, about love needing to be intense, rescuing, sacrificial, amazing, passionate, "once in a lifetime," or overwhelming, can set a person up and can create a psychological buy-in to chaotic adult relationships. Trauma-bonded cycles that begin in adulthood are often more cognitive and less primal. You are invested in wanting it to work, you love the person, the relationship may tick some important boxes for you, and it becomes more of a slot-machine cycle—you stick it out thinking the big jackpot may come and subsist on the intermittent payouts for now. As a result, people whose first trauma-bonded experience was in adulthood find that education about these cycles can make a big difference in healing, whereas for those with trauma-bonded cycles that began in childhood, deeper trauma-informed therapeutic work is essential. The childhood cycles can create a tighter trauma bond that is more primal and difficult to break, but regardless of where it begins in your life, these are challenging dynamics.

## THE 10 COMMON PATTERNS OF
## TRAUMA-BONDED RELATIONSHIPS

1. Justifying abusive and invalidating behavior.

2. Believing the future faking.

3. Experiencing chronic conflict: breaking up and making up; having the same fights.

4. Characterizing the relationship as magical, metaphysical, or mystical.

5. Fearing what will happen if the relationship ends.

6. Becoming a one-stop supply shop for the narcissistic person.

7. Hiding your feelings and needs.

8. Rationalizing the relationship to other people or hiding the toxic patterns.

9. Feeling pity and guilt for having bad thoughts about the relationship.

10. Fearing conflict.

THE HARM OF narcissism is less about the narcissism and more about the behavior. People with narcissistic personalities engage in invalidating behaviors and defenses such as grandiosity and entitlement that offset their insecurity and allow them to feel a sense of power and control. And these behaviors alternate with patterns such as charm and charisma and even empathy that show up when they feel secure and validated. All of this results in cycles that confuse us. This is a relationship with someone you may love, care about, admire, or want to remain connected to who is unwilling to recognize your needs, your hopes, or you as a person separate from them, and is willing to use any tactic they can to maintain control and dominance. None of that feels good. Narcissistic abuse can leave you believing that there is something wrong with you. The reactions to narcissistic abuse are universal: anyone exposed to a partner, family member, friend, or colleague who engages in narcissistic abuse will experience and exhibit similar thoughts, feelings, behaviors, and impacts. Survivors of narcissistic abuse ruminate about similar things: *maybe they are right; maybe this is my fault; maybe it is me.*

It's not you. Keep reading to find out what happens to all of us when we experience a narcissistic relationship.

# The Fallout: The Impact of Narcissistic Abuse

*Pain is important: how we evade it, how we succumb
to it, how we deal with it, how we transcend it.*

AUDRE LORDE

Jaya had been living with Ryan for a year. In the early phase of their relationship, they had a great time together. But a few months in, she started spending most of their evenings listening to him berate his employer. He almost never asked her about her exhausting job as a physician in a busy clinic, because according to him "all she did was write the same prescriptions every day." When things did not go his way, even small things, Ryan flew off the handle, a pattern that terrified Jaya. He ended up losing his job, and while he portrayed it as an "unfair situation," he did not pursue litigation. She found out much later he was fired because he harassed coworkers, was rude to clients, and had repeated absences.

Jaya and Ryan had a cycle whereby they would get into intense fights and he would storm out. She would be relieved for a few days, then feel panicked, and when he would reach back out, instead of holding him accountable for his behavior, she would take him back on the basis of false promises. Jaya started feeling exhausted and like she was Ryan's mother more than his partner. She could not stop ruminating about the many lies he had told, the betrayals, how he kept asking for money and was still spending it on himself despite his debt to her. She wanted him to take some accountability for his actions; she wanted him to apologize. She found herself more distracted at work, second-guessing her judgment overall, and was so anxious that she sometimes had panic attacks on the way to her office.

Jaya would replay the relationship in her head, wondering how to fully separate their possessions but also having doubts about ending it. She got stuck thinking about how attracted she was to Ryan and how afraid she was to date again, and she held on to the hope that if his new business idea worked out, then maybe things would turn around. She was having trouble sleeping, her appetite had faded, she was getting sick more often, and she was becoming more argumentative at work, a pattern that was jeopardizing her job and her work performance. She was too embarrassed to talk with friends about the situation, so she felt she had nowhere to turn. She blamed herself: *Maybe if I was around more and wasn't so grumpy after work, he would be better. Maybe I should do more, I've let myself go. Maybe I'm not saying things the right way.* Some days, she wished they had never met and ruminated about the opportunities she had passed up to make this relationship function. On others, she could barely get up and work.

IF EVERYONE IN a narcissistic relationship were to grab a piece of paper right now and write out the top ten ways the toxic behavior has affected them and we put all those lists together, they would be similar. That constant anxiety or depletion isn't a weakness in you or coming out of nowhere—it's a result of the inconsistent and emotionally abusive behavior you have been enduring. The fallout of narcissistic behavior affects how you think and how you relate to the world. It sometimes overlaps with what we observe in people who have experienced trauma; it may manifest as shifts in your view of yourself and your abilities or even how you talk to yourself; and it influences your emotional reactions, behavioral patterns, and physical health and functioning. Every aspect of your functioning is impacted. The stress of narcissistic abuse changes you and your worldview in profound ways.

So much of the conversation about narcissism is focused on understanding the narcissistic person, and this does a disservice to you as a survivor. Identifying a narcissistic person is far less important than understanding what qualifies as unacceptable behavior and what it does to you. In my years of experience working with survivors, I have seen that most people improve significantly once they finally receive validation about the toxicity of the behavior in their relationship, at which point we can start to nudge away the self-blame and begin to heal.

Sometimes the in-your-face stress and strife and tension may dissipate once the narcissist is out of your life but the confusion, rumination, guilt, grief, and anger will often remain. A woman from a traditional culture in a fifty-year marriage with an older narcissistic man may say, "I can't leave, the guilt and the stigma would be too enormous." She even feels guilty when she feels better at the times he is not around. Can someone in a situation like hers actually heal? Absolutely, and a clarifying framework can be a game changer. You may even feel guilty about feeling bad or angry because of how someone close to you is behaving. That's how deep the trauma bonding can go—as though you are a bad person for being anxious because someone is raging at and manipulating you. The prevailing messages are to toughen up or get over it. But nobody can just "get over" this.

This chapter explains what narcissistic relationships do to you—from the anger and anxiety to self-blame and shame to despair and depression, all the way to panic attacks, substance use, and acute and even traumatic stress. Recognizing that your distress and confusion from enduring narcissistic behavior are expected and, dare I say, normal in these situations is an essential first step to recognizing that *it's not you*.

## What Does Narcissistic Abuse Do to Us?

Your experience tends to go through phases. These represent an evolution of how you may respond to these relationships. Early on, you may even assert yourself and behave as though there is balance and equality in the relationship. Then the slow devolution begins as you attempt to make sense of the relationship without a framework. Understanding this can help assuage self-blame and you will see that the healthy parts of yourself—empathy, accountability, and your drive for attachment and love—get undermined by the toxicity and control of narcissistic relationships.

## Phase 1: Standing Your Ground

Framing survivors as "shrinking violets" is a misconception—many of you come into these relationships strong and confident. During phase one you may not know what you are dealing with yet, so when your reality and experience are denied, you push back. You may call the narcissistic people out on their behavior or argue with them about taking responsibility. However, before long, confusion may start to set in. You may not be able to reconcile why sometimes you really enjoy being with the narcissistic person and other times it is simply treacherous and hurtful. You may start to blame yourself because they gaslight you and tell you there is something wrong with you, and it feels a tiny bit plausible that maybe there is. If you're dealing with a narcissistic family member, you may be having the same fights repeatedly but also feeling the confusion you had as a small child. The more invested you are in this relationship, the more you stop pushing back on their behavior.

## Phase 2: What Am I Doing Wrong?

The gaslighting and invalidation are starting to catch up, and you experience more anxiety but, most pointedly, you feel as though you may be in part to blame. During this phase you may spend more time ruminating about what is happening in the relationship, playing the narcissist's words over in your head and justifying their behavior. You may also try to change yourself to make the relationship work, largely by appeasing the narcissistic person, detaching from your own needs, and giving in. At this point, you may feel more isolated, confused, or angered by the discrepancy between the narcissist's public and private images. You may be getting through your life responsibilities, work, school, and caregiving just fine; many people may not notice what you are experiencing and, in fact, may think your relationship is fine because they see the "good mask" version of it. Some of us find it in ourselves to leave the narcissistic relationship at this point, but many of us may spend a lifetime in this phase.

## *Phase 3: Hopelessness*

At this phase you may have given up on yourself. You blame and doubt yourself, have difficulty making decisions, and may even find that depression and anxiety are now taking a significant toll on your life. You may have experienced major problems at work, at school, or in other relationships, and your health may be suffering. You ruminate to the point of distraction, and, sadly, other people may have pulled back their support or have fallen out of your life. You are very isolated in this stage, and even if you are spending time with people, you worry they may not understand the full truth of your experience. You may completely blame yourself or simply may not be able to see a path forward.

At this point, some of us may feel like we no longer recognize ourselves, or that whatever aspirations or hopes we had for the future are largely dashed. In this phase, you may be experiencing panic and other patterns we observe in post-traumatic stress, including avoidance, nightmares, and hypervigilance. Not all of us get to this point, and while therapy is useful at all these phases, by the time we get to this phase, therapy is essential.

## THE FALLOUT OF NARCISSISTIC ABUSE

### Thoughts and Beliefs

- Rumination
- Regret
- Euphoric recall (recollecting the "good stuff")
- Helplessness
- Hopelessness
- Powerlessness
- Confusion
- Perfectionism
- Guilt

### How You Experience Yourself in the World

- Loneliness
- Difficulties with trust
- Isolation
- Shame

## Severe Stress Responses

- Flashbacks
- Hypervigilance (being overly alert, constantly monitoring your surroundings)
- Hyperarousal (feeling on edge and jumpy)
- Difficulty concentrating
- Dissociating through numbing (e.g., mentally checking out, overworking, engaging in unhealthy behaviors)

## Your Sense of Self and Responsibility

- Fear of being alone
- Self-doubt
- Self-devaluation (putting yourself down)
- Self-blame
- Self-loathing

## Your Emotions

- Depression
- Grief
- Irritability
- Suicidal thoughts
- Anxiety
- Apathy (don't care about anything)
- Amotivation (don't want to do anything)
- Anhedonia (no joy from doing anything that has been pleasurable in the past)

### Things You Do to Manage the Relationship

- Appeasing
- Reassuring
- Apologizing
- Self-monitoring
- Self-denial

### The Ways This Relationship Affects Your Health

- Sleep difficulties
- Physical health issues
- Self-care deficits
- Fatigue/exhaustion
- Maladaptive coping

# Recognizing the 3 Rs

Narcissistic relationships get stuck in your head and pull you out of your life, and this is captured in the 3 Rs: regret, rumination, and (euphoric) recall. These are universal experiences of all survivors that can keep you feeling stuck in the dynamic, plague you after you leave the relationship, and play upon self-doubt and self-blame.

## *Regret*

Regret can be linked to self-blame (*Why didn't I pay attention to the red flags? Why didn't I try harder?*), to circumstance (*Why did I have parents like this?*), or to time (*Why did I stay so long? Why didn't I see it sooner?*). Common regrets include:

- That the relationship happened
- That it wasn't different
- Lost opportunities
- Missing out on a happy childhood
- Effects on your own children
- That you didn't get out sooner
- That you didn't do more to "fix" it
- That it ended

Intimate relationships or close friendships may result in more pointed regret because you feel responsible for choosing this person or not seeing it sooner. There is a bit of a regret catch-22. You may have a fear of potential regret if you stay and it doesn't change, and also a fear of regretting walking away from the relationship because of the possibility the narcissistic person will change and the next person will get a better version of them. You may be stuck between your fear of divorcing and regretting any harm that comes to your children and your fear of staying and regretting wasting more time, harming your children who are seeing an unhealthy marriage in which the narcissistic person's behavior never changes.

If you come from a narcissistic family, the regrets can feel insurmountable. You may regret missing out on critical developmental social and emotional needs. You may regret that you never stretched your wings because you felt as if you were not enough. You may regret never receiving the encouragement you needed to pursue your dreams or not having a safe, unconditional space to turn to, even as an adult. You may also regret never having had a template for a healthy relationship. In the workplace, there can be regrets about working hard for a narcissistic boss or mentor who held you back or derailed your career. You may regret giving the best of yourself for years and believing that your work would be noticed, and instead having your ideas get stolen or ignored, being replaced by the narcissist's enablers, and having your career and your earning potential harmed.

### Rumination

Narcissistic behavior is so confusing that you often get stuck in rumination "thought loops" or cycles to make sense of these relationships. A straw poll of the participants in my monthly healing program revealed that rumination was the issue they struggled with the most. The more gaslighting that occurs in a relationship, the more you ruminate about it when it ends, especially when there are significant betrayals. Regrets also contribute to the rumination because it is so common to remain steeped in

those regrets while you navigate these relationships. Because rumination pulls you out of your life, since you are basically always
in your head, you miss out on a lot. It's like getting punished
twice: Not only are you uncomfortably ruminating about an "un-
fixable" issue, but you are also distracted from the good parts of
your life, such as your family, friends, hobbies, and other meaningful activities. Rumination also blocks you from entering new
relationships and experiences. You find that you cannot talk or
think about anything else, and over time you may start burning
bridges with friends and family who are tired of hearing about it.

Ruminating in narcissistic relationships means replaying conversations, rereading emails and text messages, thinking about
different things you could have said or done, and focusing on
"mistakes" you believe you made. A narcissistic relationship can
feel like an attempt to outplay and outwit the other person, and
you may ruminate about "tactical" errors (*I texted back too soon; I
should have waited to call back; I wish I hadn't asked them about that*)
or about the good times in the relationship, wishing it could be
that way again. When it's over, it's common to get lost in an obsessive postmortem, turning over every event and trying to make
sense of the person's behavior. If the relationship ends and the
narcissistic person has moved on, your thoughts may focus on *What
did the other person have that I didn't?* and *Are they going to change?*

In your family of origin, the rumination may occur in two ways:
First, you may keep ruminating about the invalidation, rejection,
and neglect of your childhood. Second, if you still have a relationship with this parent or family system, then you may also
ruminate on current conversations and real-time gaslighting and

invalidation. You may wish that this event or conversation will be different, and then afterward ruminate about what went wrong. Workplace rumination can keep you up at night and distract you from life, friends, and family. You may get stuck in obsessing over the boss who plays favorites, the gaslighting, the triangulation, or the unfair promotion of a less-deserving colleague.

Rumination can contribute to the "brain fog" that you may be experiencing. This is very common and is a by-product of the confusing and chronic emotional stress you are experiencing because of narcissistic abuse. Just be aware that you do not "self-gaslight" and blame yourself for being the "problem" because you believe you are not thinking clearly.

## Euphoric Recall

The final *R* in the 3 Rs is recall, and more specifically *euphoric* recall, which is the cherry-picking of the good memories and events of the relationship. Even after years of invalidation, you still may be able to recall that one lovely dinner on a vacation long ago. Euphoric recall can make healing from narcissistic abuse difficult because it can impede you from seeing the relationship in a balanced manner, which can result in you gaslighting yourself and second-guessing your own reality (*Maybe it wasn't really that bad and I'm making too big a deal out of their behavior*). Euphoric recall is not only part of the fallout of narcissistic abuse but also the cement used by both parties to justify it.

In an intimate relationship, euphoric recall can play a role from the beginning. You may really want the relationship to work, so you focus on the good, ignoring the red flags and invalidating behavior. As the years go on and the narcissistic behavior accumulates, euphoric recall can make it difficult to see these relationships clearly, set boundaries, or get out because you get lost in the selective good memories. In families, euphoric recall occurs when you want to remember your family and childhood in an idealistic way, perhaps painting your family as close-knit, remembering childhood camping trips or one afternoon spent baking, and overlooking the manipulation and chronic invalidation. The euphoric recall becomes a sort of wishful thinking and a way of avoiding the grief and pain of seeing family relationships clearly.

Euphoric recall represents a hybrid of denial, hope, justification, and distortion. Recalling the good moments isn't necessarily a bad thing, unless it is keeping you stuck in toxic patterns and cycles of self-blame.

## Self-Blame

"Is it me?" is the mantra of almost everyone experiencing narcissistic abuse. In trying to make sense of the confusion caused by the narcissistic behavior, you wind up blaming yourself for your own abuse. Many of you may be experiencing lifetime and even intergenerational cycles of self-blame. Self-blame is a crossroads of many dynamics—an internalization of the gaslighting, an attempt to make sense of what is happening, and an effort to get some sense of control (*If it's my fault, I can fix it*). Self-blame means that you may get harmed twice: once by the narcissistic behavior in the relationship and then by believing that you are the one who did wrong. This can make it difficult for you to clearly see the situation and get the help you need, and it can allow the relationship to continue, since if it's your fault, you will keep trying to fix it. Self-blame can keep you stuck in a cycle of psychological self-harm that can persist for years.

Why do survivors blame themselves for what happens to them in toxic relationships? Is it a relic of childhood? Is it a way to stay in control? Is it the industry of relationship experts who push the rhetoric that both people are equally responsible for what happens in a relationship, and that date nights and relationship gratitude exercises will turn the ship around? Is it easier to believe that you are to blame than to believe that someone close to you—a parent, a partner, a spouse, or even an adult child—could be capable of such cruel behavior? Is it the guilt we feel when we know someone's backstory and believe that explains "why" they do the things they do?

The answer is yes to all the above. If you experienced childhood narcissistic abuse, self-blame was a survival strategy, a way to maintain an idealized image of the parent and meet essential attachment needs. The bulk of the "relationship industry" preaches that quick palliatives like looking at your partner when you talk to them are enough to set a straighter course. Hear that enough and you will start to blame yourself and ask whether you aren't communicating clearly enough. Self-blame is self-protective; by taking on the blame, you may dodge the conflict and the gaslighting.

You may also blame yourself for thinking negative or disloyal thoughts, such as *I can't stand my own father; my son is a horrible human being; I hate my husband;* or *I think my sister is a self-absorbed jerk.* You end up judging yourself for having such awful thoughts (*Yikes, maybe I'm the problem for thinking this, maybe they sense it and I'm the reason this relationship is so terrible. I wonder if I am the narcissist*). You internalize the dynamics of your narcissistic relationship and change how you talk to yourself (*It's my fault; maybe I am being too sensitive; I never get it right*).

A major piece of the puzzle to understanding self-blame in the narcissistic relationship comes from Dr. Jennifer Freyd's work on *betrayal blindness*, which she describes as the "unawareness, not-knowing, and forgetting exhibited by people towards betrayal."[1] Basically, a person experiencing betrayal blindness may see the incriminating text on a partner's phone, may even confront them and be gaslighted, and then just go back into life and not integrate that problematic text because to fully see and consolidate it means you have to shift your perception of them. This is even more pronounced in the betrayal trauma children experience, when seeing the parent clearly would be catastrophic for a child who must maintain a distorted and idealized view of the parent to feel safe and attached. We see it but don't see it, and this happens in order to preserve relationships, worldviews, and social and institutional systems.[2] In its simplest form, betrayal blindness allows us to maintain attachments and connections to people we love.

However, this convenient sliding of these inconvenient betrayals to the side doesn't come without a cost, and betrayal blindness can mean that even though we aren't consciously addressing it, the awareness of the betrayals is there in our minds. Cult expert Dr. Janja Lalich calls this the "shelf" in the back of our minds that ultimately collapses when enough terrible things happen in a relationship and we are forced to see the cumulative betrayals and emotionally abusive behaviors.[3] Before that collapse, people who are "blind" to the betrayal experience will blame themselves (*Maybe I am not an attentive wife; maybe I am a bad kid*) and alongside that will experience all kinds of other negative psychological patterns like anxiety, panic, isolation, and confusion.

One of the great traps of the narcissistic relationship is that the narcissistic folks actually believe they are nice people. They really do. It's part of their system of delusional grandiosity, self-righteousness, and moral rectitude. This would all be much easier if they walked around and owned it: "Hey, I am a jerk, and I believe everything should be all about me, so just deal with it." Then, when they behaved badly or in a manipulative manner, you may be a bit perturbed, but you wouldn't be surprised, and you'd be far less likely to blame yourself for their bad behavior. These are deeply asymmetric relationships, and you and the narcissistic person are playing by different sets of rules and expectations—where you are hoping for connection and attachment, they are working from control and selfishness. As a result, they are emotionally investing far less and deriving much more.

Narcissistic people are often so resolute in the belief of their goodness, warmth, empathy, and all-around awesomeness that if you already have a devalued sense of your own worth, you are more likely to take the blame (*They are saying they are awesome, and I don't see myself as awesome, so maybe it IS me?*). And just when the relationship seems untenable, narcissistic people will often pull a rabbit out of their hats: a vacation, getting something done you had asked about for years, helping someone you care about. Alas, this only magnifies the self-blame, and you may feel you are being ungrateful and should be recognizing how "lucky" you are.

The dynamics of these relationships set us up for self-blame, especially the trauma bonding. In childhood situations, the parent exploits the child's attachment needs and willingness to internalize the parental guilt and shame (*It's my fault, Mommy, I'm sorry*), and over time the child detaches from their own needs and becomes a de facto babysitter of the narcissistic parent. From there on, internalization of shame and blame and taking responsibility for others become reflexive in all relationships.[4] Children cannot divorce their parents, so they must adjust to the antagonistic conditions, and that adjustment looks like self-blame.

## SELF-BLAME STATEMENTS
## AND BEHAVIOR

**What you say:**

- This is all my fault.
- How can I be better?
- Maybe I am not saying things clearly enough.
- I am not trying hard enough.
- I always say the wrong thing.
- I need to be more careful.

**What you do:**

- Constant apologizing.
- Appeasing the narcissistic person and walking on eggshells.
- Taking the blame for actions and occurrences that are clearly not your fault.
- Overpreparing or taking on responsibility for every detail in a household, workplace, or family.
- Creating and giving people multiple options (e.g., multiple meal choices).
- Attempting to read the narcissistic person's mind and anticipate their needs.
- Changing yourself or the environment to please the narcissist (e.g., obsessive housecleaning).
- Denying your own needs or wants.

# Shame

Shame leaves us feeling damaged, broken, and sometimes even irredeemable. Shame is the self-blame being made public, the belief that the world is judging us for what we are already judging ourselves for. If you came from a narcissistic family where "not good enough" becomes the family motto, secrets and lies proliferate, and isolation is common, shame sets in at a very early age. Children from these systems may exhaust themselves by weaving false stories or trying to portray their family as "normal" to the rest of the world. They may feel isolated, embarrassed to bring friends around, and ashamed when witnessing the healthier systems of peers or neighbors. The shame narrative places the onus of being "damaged" on yourself rather than on the family member(s) causing the issues. The narcissistic relationship can work only if you internalize the narcissistic person's shame and make it your own. In essence, you become the storage unit for the narcissistic person's shame.[5]

This shame dynamic can also play a role in how you get trapped in adult narcissistic relationships. There is the shame and subsequent self-blame about the relationship not working, the shame of staying in a relationship that is so dysfunctional, and the shame of leaving and divorce. The dynamic of shame (*I am in something broken*) can translate into *There must be something wrong with me.*

# Confusion

Most of you have probably asked yourself *What is happening to me? I feel crazy.* When you don't know what narcissistic behavior and abuse are about, confusion will become your new normal. The confusion largely stems from not being able to conceive of another person having so little empathy; of going from telling you that they love you to invalidating you or disappearing; of taking advantage of you even when you had their back; of good days and bad days all mixed together; of understanding their histories and having compassion for them but still having them rage at you; of simultaneously struggling with duty, loyalty, and disliking people you believe you are "supposed" to like, such as your parents and family. When you are narcissistically abused you are told how to feel and what to think, so you lose all sense of who you are and what you are about, which magnifies the confusion.

There is a complicated dance of denial that you must perform in these relationships. You may find that you have become good at behaving as though all of what is happening around you is normal, and the narcissistic people and enablers expect that from you. In part this is the slow indoctrination and distortion of reality, but also the confusion about what constitutes normal or healthy behavior. You were flexible enough to make this work, but the dark side is that this expectation or your ability to show up like everything is "fine" means that even the good people around you often have no idea how bad it was or is for you.

Gaslighting and future faking both contribute to confusion.

You may find yourself poring over old messages, making sure you heard them right and feeling confused that maybe you didn't. Their lying also contributes to your confusion. Then there is the confusion that comes from triangulation, which is a form of manipulation that involves pitting people against each other and using indirect communication, such as talking behind people's backs instead of communicating directly with someone. For example, your narcissistic mother tells you that your sister said you are greedy. This makes you mad at your sister, and you may not invite her to a party. Your sister never said this and is hurt and confused about being left out. Triangulation fosters confusion and cultivates mistrust in families, friend groups, and workplaces.

## Despair

To slowly realize that the person you love or believe you were supposed to love doesn't have real empathy, doesn't appear to care when you are hurt, and will always put themselves first is a bleak realization. Despair is experienced by almost everyone navigating narcissistic relationships, and it is a mix of sadness, helplessness, hopelessness, powerlessness, fear, and sometimes even suicidal thoughts. There is no way to fix the situation, make it better, be seen, or receive empathy. No matter what you say or do, nothing changes. Regardless of the type of narcissistic relationship, the recognition that it cannot change creates a sense of dread and unfathomable grief.

If you try to exert your wants, aspirations, or needs in one of these relationships, those attempts will not be tolerated by the narcissistic person, and over time, you will no longer feel that you are a meaningful player in your own life. Narcissistic relationships are often not just about you—they may affect your children, jobs, friendships, or relationships with other family members. Your sense of powerlessness within your narcissistic relationships can extend to a sense of helplessness in your other relationships as well, and you may feel despair about not being able to protect other people. You may experience some (or many) of the patterns observed in depression, including sadness, irritability, changes in appetite, problems sleeping, feelings of worthlessness, being distracted and unable to concentrate, tearfulness, and social withdrawal.

A major challenge is figuring out whether you are depressed or if this is a by-product of the narcissistic abuse. Some of you will say that some areas of your life are fine—you laugh with friends, enjoy time with your children, work is going well—and that your sadness and despair are restricted to the narcissistic relationship; you may dread seeing the narcissistic person and enjoy seeing everyone else. However, if these depressive patterns are starting to breach into other areas of your life, and you feel you can't function well at work, at school, or in caregiving responsibilities, or are just not interested in life anymore, then this may have escalated to clinical depression and requires mental health care as soon as possible. If your feelings of despair and depression have escalated to suicidal thoughts, you're not alone. It's critical that you seek out help right away; resources are included on page 311.[6]

# How You Experience Yourself in the World

Experiencing narcissistic abuse can be very lonely. Until you recognize that your situation is not unique, it is like living in an alternate universe where the world views your relationship and the narcissistic person very differently than you do. That loneliness may persist if you decide to end the relationship or no longer remain in contact. After an experience with narcissistic abuse, you may feel that you will never trust yourself or others again and become suspicious of everyone. As a result, you may miss out on building future friendships, collaborations, relationships, and opportunities. If you grew up in a narcissistic family, trust was either distorted, misplaced, or never developed. The second-guessing can also mean that not only do you not trust the world but you do not trust yourself. It can be exhausting to regard the world with chronic mistrust and suspicion.

The loss of trust you experience as a result of narcissistic abuse can also extend to a fear of relying on other people. This can create an exhausting "you versus the world" pseudoautonomy in which you may feel safer doing everything yourself so you cannot be let down by others. But narcissistic abuse may also make you very inefficient because you never know when you can count on other people. You may have become very good at making allowances for the narcissistic people's unpredictability. The good-bad shape-shifting means that the narcissistic person may happily drop you off at the airport on a good day and then rage at your selfishness when you ask for a ride the next time. These experiences and perceptions about asking for help may become generalized, and you may grow to believe that asking anybody for help will result in disappointment or anger.

## Mental Health Challenges in People Experiencing Narcissistic Abuse

If you are experiencing the fallout of narcissistic abuse, many of the feelings and patterns overlap with or may be occurring alongside other mental health issues. Keep in mind that the fallout of narcissistic abuse is not a disorder and is an expectable reaction to the stress of a toxic relationship. Mental health issues such as panic, anxiety, and depression may co-occur with the fallout of narcissistic abuse. These may be issues that predated and were then worsened by the narcissistic abuse (for example, you had a preexisting history of depression before you got into the narcissistic relationship), or issues that may have been activated by the narcissistic abuse (for example, you develop an anxiety disorder after experiencing a narcissistic relationship).

If you have an existing history of trauma, post-traumatic responses can become even more pronounced as a result of being exposed to narcissistic behavior. Social anxiety may also come into the mix because after so much gaslighting, you believe you are reading social situations incorrectly or have been told by the narcissistic person that you sound foolish when you are with other people. If you are experiencing any of the patterns listed here and find that they are interfering with work, caregiving, school, social relationships, or other areas of functioning, please see a licensed mental health practitioner for further evaluation and treatment.

## Can Narcissistic Abuse Make You Physically Ill?

Ask yourself if you notice your health getting better or worse depending on your contact with a narcissistic relationship. Being in one of these relationships is stressful, and stress affects your health in a variety of ways, such as headaches, muscle tension, and diminished immune function, which can make you more vulnerable to illness. If you have preexisting chronic health conditions, like autoimmune conditions, asthma, or diabetes, stress can exacerbate your illness. It has been suggested that suppressed trauma can be experienced as physical pain,[7] and the chronic pain and other similar physical discomfort reported by long-term experiencers of narcissistic abuse are consistent with that observation.

Doing the kind of research required to substantiate this narcissistic abuse–illness connection is not easy. In an ideal world we would follow groups of narcissistically abused people for many years, monitor their health, measure their relationships and stress levels, and observe what unfolds. From my observational perch, I have witnessed otherwise healthy people who are experiencing the fallout of narcissistic abuse develop illnesses that didn't make sense given their age, genetic history, and physical condition, or whose illnesses had a much more complex course than expected. Anecdotally, many health practitioners are seeing the negative impacts of toxic relationships on health.

Your body is a more honest scorekeeper of the toll of narcissistic abuse than your mind. Your brain and mind are engaged in the trauma-bonded justifications and rationalizations, while your body feels and holds pain, grief, trauma, and loss with less censorship. I've also witnessed many of these health problems begin to remit once a person distances themselves from a narcissistic relationship. I recall one woman who had numerous health issues, including headaches, gastrointestinal issues, and chronic pain, and her narcissistic partner passed away unexpectedly after a brief illness. She told me that her physical symptoms remitted within a month of his death, even though his passing and the debt he left put her in a financially precarious and stressful position. She felt guilt that she was relieved about his passing and the end of his psychological torment of her, and even felt guilty about the improvement in her health when she knew the world expected her to be a grieving widow. All to say, none of this is simple.

The physical effects of narcissistic abuse also occur through indirect pathways. You don't take care of yourself. You may be so exhausted or preoccupied that you forget to refill prescriptions or take your medication properly, you may sleep and eat poorly, not exercise, or not follow through on preventive medical care with potentially tragic consequences, such as neglecting to get regular cancer screenings. In addition, narcissistic people are terrible caregivers, and while you may stick out a narcissistic marriage with the hope that one day your narcissistic spouse will take care of you in your old age, that is not likely to happen. Narcissistic folks are more likely to feel inconvenienced by your health issues—they do not like infirmity or other reminders of human frailty or mortality, and they are too selfish and impatient to engage in compassionate and sustained caregiving. I have heard far too many episodes of narcissistic people dropping spouses or family members at the curb for chemotherapy appointments or urgent care visits. If you held on to the hope that someday perhaps your toxic partner or family member would care for you when the need arose, their disappearance at your vulnerable medical moments not only leads to despair but can be quite dangerous and expensive, as you may have to scramble to find caregivers or live without sufficient assistance. In so many ways, narcissistic relationships take years off your life.

NARCISSISTIC ABUSE ISN'T just hurt feelings. When you are exposed to narcissistic behavior, you will experience a series of psychological reactions to it. This is a pattern that happens to almost every person in a narcissistic relationship, which is a reminder that *it's not you.* You aren't having a strange or dramatic reaction; this fallout is happening to everyone and anyone in one of these relationships, and even money, privilege, and power don't fully protect people.

It's time to talk about recovery, healing, growth, and thriving. As difficult as this is, I have observed many people come out the other side of these relationships wiser, more courageous, and infused with meaning and purpose. We can't change our backstories but we can move forward. You can heal whether you stay or leave, whether you see the narcissistic person every day or never again. You will shift from focusing on managing the narcissistic people in your life and blaming yourself to your own growth, self-understanding, reality, and clarity. Instead of focusing on mere survival, it's time for you to put your energy, bandwidth, and time into thriving and flourishing.

PART II

# Recognition, Recovery, Healing, and Growth

*We delight in the beauty of the butterfly*
*but rarely admit the changes it has gone*
*through to achieve that beauty.*

MAYA ANGELOU

For many of you, simply hearing the term *narcissistic abuse* is the first time your pain received a name. This is no ordinary broken heart, and for many it is a shattered spirit that began in childhood or a series of invalidating relationships that shaped you, wounded you, changed you, and stole reality and your sense of self from you. Some of you may have showed up to therapy and been told that you were just anxious, that all relationships are difficult, and that you should find better ways to communicate, which made you doubt yourself more. Others of you may have felt shamed for being "estranged" from family members. When you are actively experiencing the fallout of narcissistic abuse, you can't imagine coming out the other side, and even when you are out of the relationship, some wounds remain—the grief, the loss of trust, and a permanently changed worldview.

What does healing mean to you? You may believe that healing would mean being at peace; no longer doubting or blaming yourself; not ruminating; feeling whole; trusting your instincts; and forgiving yourself. You want the narcissist to be held accountable, to be unmasked, to take responsibility for what they did, and you may feel that to heal, you need justice. You want to see that the narcissistic person doesn't just get to move on while you struggle with anxiety, grief, regret, and doubt. Sadly, we don't always get justice and accountability, or even an apology. Is it possible to heal even if the narcissistic person doesn't face any consequences?

Healing isn't just about crying it out. It is about grieving and clearing out space, and in the new space, building a new life, finding your voice, and feeling empowered to articulate your needs, wants, and hopes, and finally feel safe. This is a process of evolving from surviving and coping to growing and thriving.

There is no schedule to healing. It takes as long as it takes, and it varies depending on the nature of the relationship, whether you stay or go, and your own life history. Healing means being kind to yourself, even when you get hoovered back in or burned after giving the narcissistic person a second chance. It means wisdom, discernment, and a willingness to step away from toxic people, even when other people are shaming you about forgiveness. It is about radical acceptance and living with the painful realization that narcissistic patterns do not change. It is about no longer blaming yourself and wondering if you are enough. It is about finding meaning and purpose and learning to breathe after years or a lifetime of walking a tightrope of appeasing and validating them while censoring yourself.

I wouldn't have written this book if I didn't think healing was possible. Every day I witness people appreciate simple joys they couldn't have while they were in narcissistic relationships, pursue goals they were once mocked for having, reconnect with people they lost. I've also seen people finally come into their own and experience an identity separate from the narcissistic people in their lives. I've seen people fall in love again . . . and tentatively learn to trust.

But healing is only part of the destination. Your goal is to get to thriving and living in synchrony with your authentic self (and figuring out who that authentic self actually is), to retrieve those wings that have been clipped by the narcissistic relationship and finally fly. Once you push back on the rumination and regret, protect and liberate the trauma-bonded child within yourself, and switch up your self-talk and stop gaslighting yourself, you will shift to unpacking your true self, as well as the goals and aspirations you silenced, and allow yourself to live into them.

As you use this next part of the book, be active. Journal, record your thoughts and feelings, and track your progress. Try the techniques and reflect on how they are working. Take some chances and pay attention to how it feels. Healing is an active process.

Narcissistic people are noisy storytellers, and they tend to infect you with their limiting narratives for you. Ultimately, healing is about taking yourself back, revising the stories you were told, and rewriting them on your own terms.

# Understand Your Backstory

She had an inside and an outside now and
suddenly she knew how not to mix them.

ZORA NEALE HURSTON

W hen Sarah moved to Los Angeles, it was jarring and exciting. She had recently come out of a toxic relationship and wanted a fresh start. Her employer offered her a transfer, which was also a blessing since her prior manager had made life difficult for Sarah and her team. She also welcomed the respite of moving farther from her family. Trying to take care of everything for them felt like its own part-time job.

Sarah was not looking for a relationship when she arrived in LA. So when she met Josh, her guard was down. After her last relationship, she had taken the time to learn all about narcissism and narcissistic relationships. She knew the architecture of a narcissistic relationship, love bombing and all the rest of it, but since Josh was just a friend, she didn't think any of that was relevant. Over time, she found herself looking forward to seeing him around. Because he was a "friend," she opened up more, sharing about her own invalidating family, how she often felt like she wasn't enough, how she was always trying to fix everything for everyone, and the difficulties of her relationship with her ex-partner. He listened intently. In turn, he shared more about his life and told Sarah about a project he had been struggling to get off the ground. She felt terrible that he didn't have family support and empathized with that.

A few months after meeting, Josh told her that he was planning on moving from their apartment building to sleep on a friend's sofa to save money and pursue his dream. Sarah hated the idea of losing the person who had become an oasis in the city, so she offered her couch to crash on. Living in the same place, a more intimate relationship unfolded, and it was comforting for her since she felt she already knew him. It was nice to have someone to share simple pleasures with, like dinner at home or their mutual love of anime films. She liked waking up next to someone and having intimacy back in her life.

Sarah soon found out life wasn't always perfect with Josh—but who's perfect anyway? He didn't help with household chores that often, but she didn't question it since she was accustomed to doing it all, plus he was busy with his new venture. He would sometimes "help" around the apartment by making adjustments that benefited him (e.g., moving some furniture to accommodate a work nook for himself), and while she was a little put off by it, she was glad he was making himself at home and hoped all of this would foster the success of his business. He would often ask her detailed questions about where she was going and who she saw but was quite cagey about his own comings and goings. "It's nice that he even cares about where I am. My last boyfriend was so selfish he didn't even ask," Sarah thought. She felt bad about how difficult it was for Josh to launch his new business, and at the same time felt guilty because her career was going quite well. That's why she felt she had to give him a pass whenever he would go on long-winded monologues about his day, his frustrations, and his work. Or whenever he would respond to her advice with "Stop acting like you understand anything about running a business. It's easy to punch a clock." Or when he refused to contribute financially to the household. Sarah believed that fixing things for people was a way of showing love, so instead she tried to comfort him and introduce him to colleagues who could help him.

IF NARCISSISTIC PEOPLE are so bad for us, why are we drawn to them? Why don't we run away at the first sign of red flags? This is a tricky question, and one I often struggle with when I am talking about healing. I remember hearing an interview with a woman who had been in a very narcissistically abusive relationship. The uninformed interviewer asked her, "Why didn't you just leave?" I cringed at the question because it felt like she was blaming the woman for staying. The woman had a sharp retort: "Why aren't you asking the question of why he is an abuser?" It was a fair ask, but even that still doesn't cut to the core of healing. The man who abused her was deeply narcissistic, has and continues to abuse people, and likely always will. That is why *healing cannot be contingent solely on addressing the behavior of the abuser.*

To heal means not only addressing our existing wounds but preventing future wounds to the greatest extent possible. Almost all of us have traits or backstories that make us vulnerable to entering and staying in narcissistic relationships. Addressing these vulnerabilities is not about "blaming" yourself for a weakness. It is about helping you understand how some very healthy, good parts of yourself (your empathy, compassion, and kindness), as well as complex elements of your history (trauma, narcissistic families), can make it more difficult to disengage from these cycles.

It is easy to understand this when we have a physical vulnerability: I twisted my ankle, I can't take the stairs. I have asthma, I can't go into a room full of dust. Similarly, to heal from the fallout of narcissistic abuse and help prevent future abuse, we must first know our whole selves, including our vulnerabilities, belief systems, and histories. Even if you come from a happy family, are content in a good job, and have plenty of friends, narcissistic relationships may still play on your belief systems.

Understanding your backstory and vulnerabilities to these relationships can help you heal and protect yourself in the future. This chapter will lay out these risk factors at multiple levels: you as an individual, the experiences you had in your family of origin, the cultural messages you received, and the messages from society at large. We will also explore the idea that "finding red flags early" is actually a fool's errand, and that it can take a minute to determine what is happening in a new relationship.

# What Makes Us Vulnerable?

The magnetic characteristics we often observe in narcissistic individuals, such as charm, charisma, and confidence, can explain the attraction, the draw, and some of the justifications we may make for their behavior. Thus, while *all* of us are vulnerable to narcissistic relationships, there are characteristics, situations, and histories that can magnify that susceptibility. The more of these that populate your backstory, the more vulnerable you may be to the narcissistic person's charms or to getting stuck in one of these relationships. Trying to heal and shift without acknowledging this is analogous to pulling out only the top of a weed, leaving the root to take hold and eventually overtake your garden. I am frustrated when people dispense quick and easy "change how you think" guidance without recognizing that you bring a complicated history that unfolds in a complicated world. Trying to simplify such nuanced and individualized processes often just ends up shaming you. There is no easy five-step healing hack for narcissistic abuse.

I once spoke to a group about their backstories and vulnerabilities and they asked ruefully, "Based on your list of risk factors, who isn't vulnerable?" We had a laugh about it, but there is some truth in that statement. Most of us, whether due to our histories or our innate traits, are at some level vulnerable to narcissistic relationships. Managing these vulnerabilities means understanding our backstories but also understanding what narcissism looks like, being clear on unhealthy interpersonal behaviors, catching yourself in the justifications and reflexive behaviors, and being aware of when reality is hijacked. Above all, it also means not seeing your vulnerabilities as weaknesses but rather as valuable and integral parts of you. Healing means acknowledging all parts of yourself but also giving yourself permission to be discerning, self-protective, and aware.

## *Empathy*

Empathic people are magnificent, and I wish all of us lived in a world full of them. (We don't.) But the narcissistic folks often exploit this goodness. Your empathy makes you extremely vulnerable to the narcissistic relationship cycles of idealization, devaluation, apologies, and justifications, and positions you as a great source of narcissistic supply. Empathic people give second chances, forgive, and always attempt to see the other person's point of view.

If you are empathic and do not understand narcissistic behavior, you might keep offering that empathy, as well as empathy-adjacent behaviors such as forgiveness, and the narcissistic person will take it without reciprocation, resulting in an asymmetric empathic reversal (all empathy out, none coming in). If you are empathic, you may keep making excuses and see the narcissistic person through a lens of compassion until you are exhausted. Empathy may be a vulnerability not only for getting in but also for getting stuck for the long term, even when the toxic patterns are firmly in place. Earlier in the chapter, for instance, Sarah's empathy for Josh's struggles made her a great source of supply for him and made her vulnerable to listening to his one-sided rants without complaint or concern.

## *Being a Rescuer*

Rescuers are people pleasers who fix, problem solve, and try to make things better. You may feel compelled to cheer up and praise other people all the time. You may even offer them a place to live, a car, money, or help with getting a job. But as a result, you may end up placing yourself in precarious positions in the name of rescuing, like spending money or time you don't have, or even putting yourself in legally or ethically questionable positions. This can be perilous when dealing with a narcissistic person who will let you twist in the wind with little regard for what it is doing to you.

Narcissistic folks, especially vulnerable narcissists, come out early with their victimized narrative and a sullen sense of entitlement ("Everyone else gets special treatment. Nothing is fair to me"). This may leave you feeling guilty and driven to make things "right" for them. You may even try to do what you wish had been done for you at a time of need, so the act of rescuing may be a working through of your own wounds. Or you might try to gain a sense of control within the relationship by rescuing and doing more and more to make it work. But the narcissistic person is a rescue mission that will never end. No matter how much you do—no matter how much money, opportunities, contacts, or time you give them—it will never be enough. You may believe you can make the relationship better by "fixing" everything, but short of cordoning off the narcissistic person from every possible disappointment, it doesn't work. Rescuers are at risk not only for falling into these relationships but for remaining in them with the illusion that "If I do enough, then it will be okay."

When we look back at Sarah, her fixing and rescuing were not only an early hook but one that kept her focused on what to "do" within the relationship rather than being present with what was happening.

As Sarah's story shows us, there can be overlap between the empathic folks and the rescuers. However, the empathic folks may not always feel compelled to "fix," as their empathy is usually a feeling that contributes to guilt and justification. On the other hand, rescuers may feel empathy and be motivated by the need to please in order to stay safe, be connected, and feel useful.

## Optimism and Positivity

You find the silver linings, turn lemons into lemonade, and see those half-full glasses. You genuinely believe everyone has potential and anyone can change. You believe in fairness, justice, and everything working out. You may also believe that if you just give someone another chance, then maybe they will change. But if you are very optimistic and positive, it can be challenging to get your head around the idea that narcissistic people don't change.

Belief systems are core to who we are, and it can be devastating to give up on your worldview. Clinically, I have found that healing work with optimistic and temperamentally positive survivors initially takes longer, because there is such resistance to the concept of unchangeability. When it was finally clear that the narcissistic person's behavior really won't change, that was a moment of devastation and depression. (On the plus side, this optimism is often harnessed after the initial grief and may foster resilience.) Optimism can be a two-way street of attraction. Optimistic people may be drawn in by the magnetism and charisma of the narcissistic person, and the narcissistic person may be attracted to the positivity and validating encouragement that come from an optimist. Optimistic people may also get stuck because of the chronic willingness to hold out hope that things can get better.

While Sarah wasn't a clear optimist, her willingness to hold space for Josh's grandiose plans and big ideas reflected an openness to his ideas, even as they were showing no sign of launching. In the same way, your positivity and optimism may also fan the flames of the narcissistic person's grandiosity and make you a prime target for a narcissistic person's future faking.

### Being Forever Forgiving

Do you forgive everyone? Do you give lots of second chances? There are many reasons you may forgive: because you believe it is the right thing to do, it is part of your religious or cultural teachings, you hope that once you forgive the person they will change, you believe everyone deserves a second chance, you think maybe it was all a big misunderstanding, or you are afraid of what will happen if you don't forgive them. Forgiveness in and of itself is not a bad thing. It just doesn't work with narcissistic people. If you are a committed forgiver, that raises tremendous vulnerability because instead of embracing forgiveness as a call to be better, narcissistic people view it as a sign that there will not be consequences for their behavior. Because they lack empathy, a narcissistic person's concern for you won't be what stops their behavior. In the absence of meaningful consequences and with the assumption they will be forgiven, a cycle of betrayal and bad behavior will persist. Remember how Sarah kept letting Josh's behavioral transgressions go? While she wasn't actively forgiving them, she was justifying them and not questioning them. Forgiving may result in making allowances for early red flags, and it contributes to getting stuck in these relationships.

## Narcissistic, Antagonistic, or Invalidating Parents

Growing up in a narcissistic family system is a form of indoctrination. These family systems leave you feeling deflated, self-blaming, self-devaluing, and as if you are not enough.[1] The message in these families is that you need to earn love or be a source of narcissistic supply to your parent to keep their love, or you are judged on the basis of what you can do for the narcissistic family member. As a result, you learn to push down your own needs, enable the narcissistic family member, and become accustomed to being gaslighted, manipulated, and subjected to the silent treatment. Over time, narcissistic families normalize narcissistic behavior, which makes you much more vulnerable to the narcissistic people who wander into your life in adulthood. These family systems instill in you the idea that you need to "settle," and that you have no right to hold standards for other people's behavior. Children in these families find themselves in different roles that are designed to benefit the narcissistic parent(s) and keep the children limited and defined by the function they serve in the family. We will do an in-depth exploration of these roles later in this chapter.

There is a risk that someone who superficially offers whatever it was that your toxic system lacked—financial stability, affection, intense interest, or attention—can feel like an offset to the toxic patterns of childhood. This might cause you to miss other toxic patterns that may be unfolding, such as invalidation. For example, Sarah had moved away from her family and had empathy for Josh because he also came from an invalidating family. This played upon her inner rescuer and her sense of empathy, and she may have been addressing her core wounds by being there for him. It's quite likely she didn't take note of how unhealthy his behavior was because it had become so normalized for her, and this may have not only made her less discerning in the beginning, but also kept her stuck because it was so familiar.

## Happy Families

Yep, the happy family vulnerability is real, even though this may seem paradoxical. Some of you grew up in happy families where your parents had a respectful, loving marriage; your family is genuinely close-knit; there is empathy and compassion; everyone has each other's backs; people listen to your dreams and see and love you; when you're sad they soothe you; and no one is yelling, fighting, or hurting each other. So what is the downside? You don't learn how to walk the mean streets of narcissism. With this as your origin, you may have a hard time believing that people can be invalidating, manipulative, dismissive, and cruel. You were taught that any relationship bump in the road can be addressed through communication, forgiveness, and love. You may believe that love will ultimately conquer all because that's what has always worked in the happy relationships you've seen while growing up.

Your happy family may believe in redemption, but as a result they may also unwittingly enable your narcissistic relationship situation and suggest loving the narcissistic person even more and sticking together. I remember talking with an older couple who had an adult child who was in a narcissistic marriage. The parents had been married for forty-five happy years, and the family system was close-knit. When their daughter was in a relationship with a malignant narcissist, they didn't quite understand it, and they tried everything, including loans, lavish vacations, and babysitting the grandchildren to encourage the marriage to sustain and improve. When that didn't work, they watched their daughter psychologically wither, and her marriage ultimately dissolved. The couple believed in justice, and that the court would grant full custody to their daughter because the dad was a "mean guy." Both parents were shattered when they realized the actual machinations of the divorce process with a narcissistic co-parent.

The upside is that if you did grow up in a happy family, the social support and resilience that derive from coming from a place of secure attachment and having a soft place to land can fortify you once you start to make sense of your narcissistic relationship.

## Difficult Transitions

Many of us, when we are going through a period of transition, are not on our game. I have witnessed many people enter narcissistic relationships soon after ending a prior relationship or while going through a divorce, but also after moving to a new city or while dealing with the death of someone close to them. Transitions can be traumatic (loss) or they can be aspirational (new job, a move), but either way, they can be destabilizing. Your attention is drawn to the new things happening in your life. You're dealing with acute crises or logistics, and you do not have your typical touchstones like your routines, support networks, or even the luxury of autopilot that comes from familiar landmarks, commutes, and people. The new and unfamiliar can also raise anxiety or a sense of incompetence, which can make you feel vulnerable. Your bandwidth is occupied with this process of acclimatizing to the new situation, leaving you at risk of missing toxic patterns that may be unfolding in front of you. Recall how Sarah had just moved to a new city, had recently ended a toxic relationship, and was working in a new office when she met Josh. While she wasn't actively looking for a new relationship, she welcomed connecting with a new friend in an unfamiliar place. Being in a transitional phase may make you more vulnerable to getting into a narcissistic relationship.

## *Rushed Relationships*

Many narcissistic relationships get their momentum from a sense
of pressure. Biological clocks, social pressure, or even a time-
limited opportunity can mean that you aren't looking at red flags
because they may be an impediment to getting what you want. I
have had clients who are in narcissistic relationships sit in front of
me and say, "I know this relationship is bad for me, but I don't
have time to go back out there, find someone new, get married,
and have a child before it is too late." Under those circumstances,
the devil you know becomes the devil you keep, and the long
game will show that the rush resulted in messy, painful, and expensive divorces or unsatisfying and abusive relationships. The
reality is, we rarely make our best decisions under pressure.

Narcissistic relationships often unfold too quickly. You may
move in together too fast, get engaged too fast, or invest your
money into a business venture too fast, and the love bombing
means that relationship milestones like big vacations or meeting
families happen a little too quickly. If that fast-forwarding inter-
sects with life goals that you are rushing to achieve, then it's easy
to get too deep into a relationship by thinking you can deal with
problems later without acknowledging how toxic it is now.

Circumstances pushed Sarah's hand; as she juggled multiple
transitions and wanted to hold on to a new person, her rescuing
tendencies pushed fast-forward on a pivot from friendship to romantic relationship, as well as on moving Josh into her apartment.

## *History of Trauma, Betrayal, or Significant Loss*

The experience of trauma or significant betrayal changes us. It shapes our inner worlds and makes us more vulnerable to self-blame, self-doubt, negative emotions, shame, guilt, and difficulties with close relationships.[2] Betrayal can also be quite traumatic, whether it is an unfaithful spouse, embezzling business partner, or thieving relative. These *betrayal traumas* are psychologically very painful because a person or system we trusted deceived us or broke our sense of trust and safety in the relationship and can often have worse and longer-lasting psychological fallout than other forms of trauma or loss.[3] This combination of self-devaluation, self-blame, and distortions in discernment and trust that come out of betrayal trauma renders you more vulnerable to narcissistic people and narcissistic abuse. Many trauma survivors, especially those who experienced complex trauma in childhood, have never received adequate trauma-informed therapy, and healing can be a lifelong process. If you have had a history of trauma, you may judge your reactions and gaslight yourself (*I think I am overreacting to a person yelling at me*) instead of recognizing that the way the body and mind hold trauma and emotional pain means that the rhythms of a narcissistic relationship can take an even more profound toll on you. Because many people have histories of untreated trauma, a lack of awareness about how trauma works creates a risk for entering and staying in future abusive relationships.

As you examine your backstory and the vulnerabilities it creates, notice how they overlap and feed into each other. Your positivity may feed rescuing. Your narcissistic family and history of trauma may diminish discernment. You can't change your backstory, but you can harness it to better understand when to slow down, pay attention, be kind to yourself, and let go of self-blame.

## The Narcissistic Family System

In the Smith family, the narcissistic matriarch, Isabelle, was about appearances and status above all else. Emotion was an afterthought, and it was as though everything and everyone in their home was a piece on a chessboard or a role on a stage. The eldest son, Andrew, often found himself trying to protect his siblings and checking in with his father, who was constantly enduring Isabelle's criticism for not advancing high enough in his career. The next sibling, Sheryl, looked just like her mother and was a ballet prodigy. Their mother focused on ensuring Sheryl was studying at the best dance school and got coveted roles in *The Nutcracker* every Christmas. She was a near-perfect student, and Isabelle would often travel with Sheryl, taking her to ballet performances around the country.

Diane, who was two years younger, had a sweet and gentle temperament, was not a strong student, and struggled with her weight. Isabelle often greeted Diane with contempt, put her on numerous diets, and on bad days would blame Diane for anything that was going wrong, calling her names, and saying, "Please tell me you found a friend to play with this weekend so I don't need to deal with you. Sheryl and I are busy." Martine was just thirteen months younger than Diane and was almost forgotten by the family system. Few of Martine's interests were cultivated, so it was either figure it out herself or go without. She had researched an after-school program, and even got a scholarship that allowed her to attend, but her parents regularly forgot to pick her up afterward. Martine slowly figured out the local bus system and would walk the two miles home from the stop.

The youngest was Thomas, who from a very young age almost seemed to "get it." He didn't say anything and was very helpful; by the age of four he would be sure his room was clean and would implore his siblings to do the same. By the time he was twelve, and especially since his mother was increasingly focused on Sheryl, he would sometimes ensure dinner got on the table. Despite how helpful Thomas was, something about him put Isabelle on edge. She needed him, but it was as though she felt shamed by his presence. Thomas would soothe Diane, who struggled under the cruelty of their mother. Diane would ask Thomas, "Why doesn't Mom like me?" and Thomas, with a wisdom that belied his years, would say, "Diane, it's not you."

The fixer/peacekeeper eldest son Andrew exhausted himself trying to be a human shield and a therapist.

Golden child Sheryl was often oblivious, but over time felt terrified about how she was going to tell her mother she wasn't interested in pursuing ballet as a career.

Diane, the scapegoat, developed patterns consistent with obsessive-compulsive disorder, would go on dangerous crash diets to lose weight, and struggled with depression and anxiety. Martine, the invisible child, was left to her own devices and made some suboptimal choices as she approached adulthood with little guidance.

Helpful and truth-seeing Thomas burned out on keeping the household running and—hard as it was to leave Diane, whom he wanted to protect—moved away on his eighteenth birthday, never to return.

In healthy family systems, while preferences, differences, and temperaments are recognized, a child may not necessarily be defined by them. In narcissistic family systems, the tendency for the parent or parents to use children within the system to regulate, to view them as either supply or inconvenience, and to harness them to get their needs met means that children in these systems are defined and cast in roles that work for the narcissistic parent with little regard for who the children are and what they need. These roles allow the narcissistic parent to retain unquestioned power and control within the system as well. Children may not always be placed in these roles, but the child may detect that taking on the role and behaviors may keep them safe in an attempt to remain attached to an invalidating parent. Not all of you grew up in a narcissistic family, but interestingly, you may observe these roles in toxic workplaces or in a partner's or spouse's family. Understanding these roles may not only illuminate how you repeat cycles within a family of origin or another system, such as a toxic friend group or workplace, but can also help inform your healing, because these roles can limit the process of individuation that is so essential to healing.

If you come from a narcissistic family, you may see yourself in at least one of those roles.

Were you the repository of abuse, bullying, and insults? Were you running around trying to make sure everyone was okay and acting as a pint-sized diplomat? Were you aware of the problematic nature of your narcissistic parent's behavior, an awareness that threatened their ego? As you read about these roles, you may notice that some of them overlap—you might be both a truth seer/teller and a scapegoat, for example. Or if you are in a blended family, you may take on one role in one family and another role in another family. Your roles may also shift with age—you may be the golden child when you are young, only to be replaced by a younger sibling or be dethroned because you are no longer cute enough or aren't bringing adequate narcissistic supply to your parent. The larger the family, the more likely all these roles may be represented; in smaller families, siblings may take multiple roles, while other roles are simply not represented in some systems. You may also take on roles in an extended family system of cousins and aunts and uncles.

Unfortunately, if both of your parents were narcissistic or antagonistic, these roles can become cemented to your identity and become the only way you can get your needs met. These roles get you stuck into inauthentic identities that can persist in your adult relationships, and it's important to be aware of them so you can slowly grow away from them. The more roles you had, the more work is needed to break out of them and into your true self.

Let's go through these one by one.

## *The Golden Child*

In the Smith family, Sheryl may have received the disproportionate share of her mother's attention, but she still has the overwhelming anxiety of facing her mother's rage and disappointment
if she attempts to pursue her own interests. The *golden child* is the
favored child, the narcissistic parent's favorite familial source of
supply. Golden children represent something their narcissistic
parent values: they may resemble the parent; are very attractive,
obedient, and compliant; or are a brilliant student or athlete. The
golden child's success, appearance, or behavior is supply for the
narcissistic parent, and golden children get their attachment and
affiliation needs met by being what the parent wants. Sometimes
the golden child receives more or better resources (their own
room, a car, tuition) than their siblings. But the golden child lives
on a conditional and perilous pedestal, knowing that if they no
longer perform or deliver, their stock may drop.

Empathic golden children may feel a sense of guilt, grief, or
even shame about being the "chosen one" instead of their siblings. Golden children who are not empathic may be bullies and
may evolve into narcissistic adults. If you were a golden child, you
may be in the prison of wanting to retain that status by continu-
ally pleasing the narcissistic parent, and that can curtail your
freedom to pursue your own interests or life path. As a golden
child, in adulthood, you may remain in this beholden role, still
reliant on your narcissistic parent's validation. You may also feel
that you must step up and coordinate life for your narcissistic

parent as they get older because your siblings may have cut bait. However, even into adulthood, if you step out of line, the narcissistic parent may take back any validation.

If you were the golden child in your dysfunctional family, be aware of how this role has affected your siblings and may still be playing a role in tense relationships with them. Don't gaslight them when they share their experiences of your parents or their childhood, which may be different from yours. There may also be survivor guilt if you were well provided for and your siblings or other parent were not; therapy to explore that guilt and grief is also essential. Also be mindful that you do not perpetuate this intergenerational cycle by anointing one of your own children as a golden child.

## *The Scapegoat*

Narcissistic people use and abuse other people to regulate their behavior and emotions, and that is where the *scapegoat* comes in. If you were the scapegoat, you received the bulk of your narcissistic parent's wrath and took the hardest psychological blows. You were probably blamed for behaviors you did not engage in, were given a disproportionate burden of chores, did not receive resources in the same manner as your siblings, and experienced all the aspects of narcissistic abuse from a very young age, including the worst of any physical abuse. All of this can result in psychological harm. For example, Diane, the Smith family scapegoat, was facing numerous issues that may have long-term harmful impacts, including disordered eating, and obsessive-compulsive patterns that may have represented an attempt to stay safe in or cope with the family system.

There are multiple reasons for scapegoating. The narcissistic parent perceived you as weak or undesirable, as a threat, or as vulnerable. The scapegoat becomes the primary repository for the narcissistic parent's projected shame. Or the scapegoated child may not "be" the way the parent wants or is an insufficient source of validation: a boy with an athletic narcissistic father who decides to pursue the arts or isn't physically strong may be a scapegoat, or it may be a child who does not conform to gender roles and expectations. Scapegoating can also be part of a larger dynamic called *family mobbing*, in which the entire family system targets the scapegoat and siblings may go along to avoid the narcissistic parent's wrath.

As a scapegoat, you may enter adulthood feeling deeply distanced, experiencing low self-esteem, and lacking a sense of belonging. You face one of two paths. The more problematic path leads you to continue to struggle with identity, self-esteem, and anxiety. Not only might you fall into trauma-bonded cycles in your adult relationships, but you may also remain stuck in the vortex of the family and eternally try to win over the narcissistic parent. The better path allows you to set boundaries or distance yourself from the harmful members of your family. (You may also be a hybrid who got away but still struggle with identity, self-esteem, and anxiety.)

The role of the scapegoat can carry a lot of pain and even complex trauma, and that's when trauma-informed therapy becomes essential to address these impacts. If you were the scapegoat of your family, work on finding your voice separate from your family system, cultivate new sources of support, develop a chosen family, and engage in activities that are self-affirming and allow you to develop as a person, independent of the invalidating system.

## *The Helper*

If you had the *helper* role like Thomas, you kept yourself safe by ensuring your narcissistic parent's needs were met. This could look like anything from cooking meals, cleaning the house, looking after younger siblings, or even soothing and reassuring your narcissistic parent. You may have derived some sense of control or safety because you could "do" something to maintain the narcissistic parent's attention, but you may have also become exhausted, struggled in school, and missed out on friends and normal childhood stuff by having to "serve" the narcissistic parent. Keep in mind, there's a big difference between being placed in the helper role and having an "all hands on deck" supportive mindset. In healthy larger families, families with single parents, or families in financially precarious situations, helping out may be required, but it may also be recognized and appreciated, with the child feeling safe, loved, and supported, instead of feeling they must do these things to be loved.

If you were a helper as a child, you may find yourself always being the helper in adult relationships or overextending yourself in work settings. Narcissistic parents are entitled enough to believe their children are a means to getting their needs met, and although the helper child is co-opted into that role, some helper children may recognize that it is the only way to be noticed by the parent, while others may do it to appease the parent, avoid their wrath, and keep the family system functioning. If you don't begin to detangle yourself from the helper role in adulthood, you may find yourself still assisting your parents and stymieing your own life while your siblings, if you have them, look to you, the helper, to take care of everything.

If you were a helper as a child, start practicing saying "No" and don't feel like you always must help with the dishes, drive people around, or get it all done. I recognize that not "doing" may raise anxiety, but that is simply the process of letting go of the identity of this role. Start with small *No*s and slowly work your way up.

### The Fixer/Peacekeeper

The *fixer/peacekeeper* role is the child who is the de facto diplomat in the narcissistic family system. For instance, as the mediator of the family, Andrew was always trying to negotiate the peace or soothe his father, but also trying to ensure his siblings were not in the psychological line of fire. As a fixer you may have been motivated by anxiety, self-protection, fear of abandonment, or protection of others. You were acutely aware of the narcissistic parent's short fuse and were constantly trying to keep the peace. You may also have been protective and attempted to shield the non-abusive parent, the scapegoated sibling, or anyone else in the family system (including pets) by trying to de-escalate conflict. In a way, you were the resident rodeo clown, trying to distract the narcissistic parent and get ahead of anything that could enrage them by redirecting the conversation or even taking the fall yourself. This is an exhausting role, and over time you become vigilant and on edge, monitoring for anything that may set them off. Unfortunately, you may also become an unwitting enabler, trying to soften the blows by appeasing everyone, including the narcissistic parent, and in the name of peace, may cajole everyone to sign off on the narcissistic parent's behavior.

In adulthood you may retain the role of the fixer, continuing to insert yourself into family dramas, acting as a referee, reassuring everyone on the dysfunctional family group text, and trying to make everything seem more functional than it is. Outside of your family, you have a real risk of getting into narcissistic relationships, always trying to mediate and find a solution. You may also be conflict averse, a pattern we often see as part of trauma bonding. Fixers may often capitulate to what the narcissistic person wants and avoid setting boundaries, because of the tension and conflict that would come from those boundaries.

Working through the fixer role you acquired in childhood means allowing yourself to experience the anxiety that surfaces when you don't fix or keep the peace. A great place to start is to give yourself permission to set small boundaries with your family of origin; for example, take a break from that group text where everyone looks to you to continue ironing out the conflict and managing your narcissistic parent.

## The Invisible Child

Martine may have spent all night at school if she hadn't figured out how to get home. It was as though her parents couldn't be bothered. She was literally just unseen. If you were an *invisible child*, you too got lost in the shuffle. Your interests were not cultivated and your needs were overlooked. Your narcissistic parent rarely noticed you, asked about you, or addressed you. The invisible child is almost entirely psychologically abandoned. The anguish for the invisible child is that you may have had siblings who were "seen," especially the golden child, so the contrast of your experience against theirs can foster the "not-good-enough-ness" that characterizes children from narcissistic families. You are in a uniquely painful position because even the scapegoat is being seen (though obviously to their detriment). In some families, the invisible child may also become the *lost child*—a child who may be adrift with little direction and may waft in and out of the family system.

If you were an invisible child, you may have been left to figure out a lot on your own, from major life decisions to issues at school. Not being seen can leave you feeling unworthy, diminish self-esteem, and limit your ability to advocate for yourself. This places you at risk for entering and remaining in adult relationships where you are unseen or being preyed upon by narcissistic people who initially do pay attention to you. The one consolation here is that when you do drift away from the family system, it may go relatively unnoticed. The risk, however, is that you may spend a lifetime trying to get the family to notice you, an effort that unfortunately does not usually bear fruit. This keeps you locked into the toxic system, denying your true self to try to be what they need you to be to be seen, and missing out on the opportunity for developing your identity outside of this system.

Moving beyond the invisible role means being very discerning, because not all attention is good attention. Find your way of being seen that is authentic to you. Stop sharing your achievements, joys, and experiences with your family of origin; it dampens the joy of these experiences to have them unacknowledged and risks replaying that cycle of wanting to be noticed by people who can't see you.

### *The Truth Seer/Teller*

There is almost always an insightful and wise child in every narcissistic family system who, with tremendous insight and wisdom, sees the narcissistic patterns as toxic and cruel (even if they do not know the words to describe it). This is the *truth teller* or the *truth seer*. If this was you, then you have a gift, but it can also put you at risk. Your mere presence, without you even saying a word, may evoke shame in the narcissistic parent. Maybe you dropped a zinger like "Mom doesn't like it when people don't think she is smart," and it quickly made you into a scapegoat. While the narcissistic parent will often attempt to silence your truth telling, they can't stop you from seeing what is happening. You may have soothed siblings who are hurt, you may have gotten into it with the golden child who benefited from the system, and you may have silently or overtly called out the narcissistic parent as the naked emperor. But as you get older, you may become the proverbial "black sheep" who sees the family dynamic with clarity and whom the narcissistic parent will be glad to discard.

If you were the truth teller, you may have been biding your time, waiting for the chance to get out of the system. In the Smith family, for instance, Thomas may have been the helper, but he was also the most truth seeing of all, and he got the hell out of Dodge as soon as he could. However, despite your wisdom and because you may have grown up in a narcissistic family, you can still be plagued with anxiety regardless of your resilience. You may lack the self-confidence or sense of self-worth to activate your plan to get out, or you may feel guilty about leaving siblings or your non-narcissistic parent behind. You may also struggle with a permanent sense of grief because you recognize that you did not have a safe space or family who loved you unconditionally.

However, you may also thrive. You may be quite good at boundaries, have good instincts, and be able to see unhealthy situations, step back, and not engage. If your family discards you at the behest of the narcissistic parent, there can be tremendous grief, which is when therapy to manage these feelings as well as cultivating healthier sources of social support (a "chosen family") becomes essential. You have a gift. Value your ability to see toxic patterns and act accordingly.

## Making Sense of Your Backstory

Protecting yourself in light of your backstory can feel so overwhelming. It is recognizing how some of the most beautiful parts of yourself may have paradoxically put you at risk while still having to protect yourself in a world, workplace, or family that doesn't recognize or care what is happening. As a psychologist, I struggle to balance how I talk about the importance of knowing your backstory, vulnerabilities, and past family roles while ensuring that I don't prop up a narrative that places the responsibility solely on the survivor—for example, that you got into a narcissistic relationship because you are a fixer. This is why we must also understand how people, families, and society at large enable narcissism and magnify our vulnerabilities and self-doubt.

In narcissistic and invalidating family systems, the dynamic is often "see something, say nothing." If you call out a narcissistic family member, you are viewed as the problem or are silenced, gaslighted, or ostracized. Workplaces also foster narcissism by promoting cultures that protect the golden goose and reward high performers, even when their conduct in the workplace is harmful. Whistleblowers may feel silenced or gaslighted if they try to raise awareness of bullying or other abusive behavior. Whether through encouragement of or applause for unapologetic narcissistic behavior, or by silently ignoring the issue, the world is in on the enabling game. All of this has taken this narcissism problem and blown it up, with these cycles repeating intergenerationally and intersocietally. Even if you are aware of your backstory and the associated vulnerabilities, systems at large continue to reward these narcissistic patterns, which means that you have to heal in a context that may not provide a healthy ecosystem for healing. If moving forward seems difficult, it's not about you not trying hard enough; it's about trying to heal while you remain in broken systems.

That said, you can do this. In its simplest form, healing is about reaching out to the vulnerable child in you who needed someone to say, "It's not your fault," "This isn't your responsibility to fix," and "Your voice is important." You may find yourself experiencing multiple vulnerabilities culminating in a nuanced backstory that explains not only why you got drawn in but, more importantly, why you got stuck. For instance, you may have grown up in a narcissistic family system, have a history of trauma, be very empathic, and experienced a transition at the time you met a narcissistic person. The presence of multiple vulnerabilities magnifies your likelihood of trauma bonding, self-doubt, and self-blame. Healing means understanding this.

You can't go backward and change your backstory, but you can remain attuned to and aware of these vulnerabilities and histories. Healing is often simply just opening our eyes and seeing these situations more clearly. These strategies are a way to integrate your vulnerabilities and worldviews in a manner that accounts for the risks and dynamics of narcissistic relationships, and a way to protect yourself.

## Remain Mindful and Slow Down

Your vulnerabilities can manifest as reflexive responses, such as jumping up to fix something or always stopping what you are doing to listen to other people's issues. The only way you can even begin to shift these deeply etched patterns is by being mindful of them in the first place. Start by slowing down, talking to yourself, and being aware of how you respond. If you are in a stage of life where you feel rushed, find ways to foster mindfulness by breathing, meditating, and slowing your mind down. Take ten minutes and do an activity that you need to accomplish—empty a dishwasher, fold some laundry, go to the grocery store, fill in a spreadsheet—but do it slowly and pay attention to what it feels like to be more deliberate. Moving and doing things quickly means we often aren't intentional or discerning, so finding ways to practice slowing way down may also help you with discernment or paying attention to when your backstory may be quietly drawing you into something unhealthy. Your higher-order goals and aspirations like marriage, children, and career matter, but rushing into a relationship or opportunity and missing unhealthy patterns can mean that those goals get distorted.

### *Learn to Discern*

Mindfulness is an essential foundation to the next step, which is discernment. Discernment has two elements: how you assess new people and how you manage yourself with the existing people in your life. Being discerning with new people means watching their behaviors unfold and learning how they respond to stress, receive feedback, and respect your time, then acknowledging that data instead of justifying unhealthy and unacceptable behavior. Use an old hack I learned in graduate school: the first time something happens is a blip, the second time is a coincidence, the third time is a pattern. That rule of three can allow you to give someone a chance and then give yourself permission to recognize and step back when something is revealed to be a problematic pattern.

With existing folks in your life, it's never too late to take an analytic eye to their behavior. It can be difficult to think of discernment as it applies to people, so think of it as it applies to food: you wouldn't eat spoiled or unpleasant food. To be discerning is to be willing to step back from people who are not good for you. Discernment serves another key function—it can keep you from getting stuck once enough red flags and uncomfortable patterns have piled up.

Checking in with yourself is a great discernment exercise. Pay attention to how you feel after you spend time with narcissistic people in your life—emotionally, mentally, physically, even energetically. Do the same after you spend time with healthy people. After time with a healthy person, you may find that you feel energized, inspired, happy, and clearheaded. After time with a narcissistic person, how do you feel? My guess is fatigued, frustrated, disgusted, or angry. Then reflect on how you feel about yourself after an encounter with someone. After a healthy encounter we often feel a little better about ourselves (I often say that we feel about two inches taller after we spend time with a good person). However, after time with unhealthy people, you may feel bad about yourself, self-doubting, depleted, or somehow "less than." These check-ins can teach you something useful that you can take into new interactions and can help you remain attuned to how you feel. You know what healthy feels like. You just need to slow down and pay attention.

None of us get discernment right all the time—you would have to be a cyborg to pull that off. If you are empathic, you will get burned again, and that's okay. It doesn't mean you will always be stuck in toxic relationships, and it's better to get burned or singed a little rather than lose the human, beautiful, and compassionate parts of yourself that are open to new people. Discernment is a lifelong process of calibration and a willingness to see narcissistic behavior patterns as consistent, unchanging, and not good for you. Discernment doesn't mean that you have to run away from people, either; it may mean you just take a few steps back and continue to monitor how you feel. If being forgiving is who you are, then pay attention to whether your forgiveness leads the relationship to grow and the behavior to change or whether you keep pardoning the same sins and errors. If someone keeps behaving badly and you keep forgiving them, then bring discernment into your forgiveness cycle. You may have had the belief that to forgive is divine but have come to learn that to discern may be transcendent.

## *Practice Contrary Actions*

Your backstory and roles can set you up for reflexive behavior that can be harmful in a toxic relationship and set precedents that can be difficult to break. Hard as it may be, try to break these instincts by doing the opposite of what you usually do. For example, sitting on your hands and not fixing things or forgiving or giving a second chance. Practice in other relationships in your life as well. When someone seems to be angling for help but is not asking directly, don't sweep in and fix it. Reflect on the origins of your rescuing behavior. If you are meeting a new person, consider a three-to-six-month period before you do any of your usual fixing or saving.

## Cultivate Safe Spaces

Having spaces in your life where you feel safe and don't need to worry that your backstory and vulnerabilities will be exploited, whether that's among friends, safe family members, therapy, or support groups, is crucial to healing. If you were a scapegoat or an invisible child, you simply want to be seen and accurately heard, and these safe spaces can help you break through the rigidity of your roles and allow you to experience and express yourself more fully. Toxic relationships are so time-consuming that you may not be able to easily foster and cultivate healthy spaces while in them. Start small by simply staying in touch with healthy people, then slowly start prioritizing these relationships and intentionally put time with these folks ahead of the rescuing, fixing, and forgiving you are often doing for the narcissistic people in your life. You can just phone it in to your toxic relationship and bring your A game to your safe spaces.

## Get Educated

Get educated about narcissism, and if you are from a happy family system, you may be able to educate them as well so they can be a supportive space for you (though you do not want to do this in a narcissistic family system!). Flip back through the early chapters of this book and recognize that this isn't about labeling a person as narcissistic and walking away, but about identifying unhealthy behaviors that are simply not good for you, and realizing that these patterns don't really change.

## Have Some Rules

After a surgery we are given rules—no weight on the leg for six weeks, no bending for a month, no driving for two weeks—and we follow them so we can heal. Because of your various vulnerabilities and backstory, strong rules and boundaries can serve as a protection, like not entering a new relationship during a significant transition, building up a support base before considering dating, or turning off your notifications so you don't interrupt your work to keep addressing the entitled needs of the narcissistic person. These aren't arbitrary rules; they can be guardrails that connect you back to yourself and remind you to "stay off that leg" a little longer until you feel stronger.

## Consider Therapy

Depending on your history of trauma or narcissistic relationships, trauma-informed therapy can be essential. A central tenet of this work is to recognize that you are not defined by your trauma and have an identity apart from what happened to you. People who have histories of betrayal trauma often swing between deficits in trust, excessive trust, and misplaced trust. Therapy also becomes a place to explore your relationship with trust, to practice your capacity to make choices that are healthy, and to simply recognize that you have the autonomy to make a choice, something that is often co-opted by trauma and by narcissistic family systems.

## Be Open

Your backstory often limits and closes you off to the idea that things could be different, but your life and relationships don't have to stay as they are. Curiosity can be a powerful motivator. You may find it overwhelming to explore other paths that may touch on unpleasant feelings like regret. If you can even plant a mental seed that your life could be different, it can significantly shift your perspective. You don't have to change a thing right now but being open to other possibilities can plant that tiny seed. Being open is not just about the conditions of your life but about you and the possibility within you. It's a loosening of a rigid script and a detaching from the idea that there is only one path for you. There are infinite paths within you, remember that.

## Identify Your Favorite Justification

Your vulnerabilities and roles drive your justifications, and even your denial, in narcissistic relationships. But once you can see your justifications clearly *as* justifications, you are in a better position to catch yourself. Write down and reflect on the justifications you most often fall back on (*She didn't mean it*; *I may be asking too much; maybe I am being silly in expecting people to be polite; he doesn't know better; I am overthinking it—that's just how she communicates; he is getting old*). You may notice patterns, such as using different justifications for family members compared to friends, or find that your justifications tend to be more self-gaslighting (e.g., justifying narcissistic behavior on the basis that you are always being too sensitive). Perhaps you are making justifications differently based on gender, age, how long you have known someone, or the situation. Also consider how your backstory and vulnerabilities may drive your justifications. Those of you who are very empathic may have empathy-driven justifications (*They may just be having a hard day*), while a rescuer may justify by saying *They just need someone to help them out*. Once you have written these down, be mindful, catch your justifications, and see your relationships more clearly.

## Work through Your Guilt

Guilt is an uncomfortable emotion that is evoked when you believe you have done something wrong. But guilt is subjective, and you may feel guilt at setting a boundary, expecting other people to do their job, or not showing up to an event even though you know you will be treated badly there. Years of working with survivors of narcissistic abuse has taught me that survivors spend a lot of time feeling guilty. My question to them is "What did you do wrong?"

When you feel guilty, ask yourself, "What *did* I do wrong?" And then the follow-up question is, "If someone else did this, would I feel they were doing something wrong?" Journaling about this can be useful, and reflecting on how your backstories and roles may magnify this sense of guilt and how it plays out in your different relationships can help you to start pushing back on it. You may find out that these "bad things" you are doing are simple pleasures, like taking a day off for your birthday, sleeping late one rare day, or no longer engaging with someone who chronically gaslights you.

### Remember Your Strengths

Identifying strengths may be one of the hardest things for a survivor to do, but in fact, it was your strengths that not only drew a narcissistic person to you but kept you safe in the relationship. These are also part of the model of how you get in and get stuck. You may recognize that you are actually very flexible, a great planner for all kinds of contingencies, an expert problem solver and solution seeker. The things that may have drawn the narcissistic person to you—creativity, laughter, intelligence—are all still there, perhaps more hidden now, but there. Write out the strengths that you developed to survive and the strengths you have always had. This is part of your process of identifying that your experience in this narcissistic relationship wasn't you just passively going along but actively surviving.

IDENTIFYING AND UNDERSTANDING your backstory, vulnerabilities, and the limiting roles you have been placed in by narcissistic relationships can make you more aware and discerning.

But your backstory, vulnerabilities, and roles aren't happening in a vacuum, and as you make shifts and draw boundaries within yourself, there will be resistance from others who may shame or doubt you. By digging deep and exploring these patterns, you start excavating your authentic self—not the version that was shaped to cater to the needs and preferences of the narcissistic people, but the actual you. Healing doesn't mean that all narcissistic relationships magically fade from your life. Instead, healing means that you continue the process of growing yourself outside of these narrowly defined toxic spaces while preparing for the other narcissistic and manipulative people you will inevitably meet as you move forward. Growth and individuation mean facing the core of healing from narcissistic abuse, and that is radical acceptance.

# 5

# Embrace Radical Acceptance

Pain reaches the heart with electrical speed, but truth
moves to the heart as slowly as a glacier.

BARBARA KINGSOLVER, *ANIMAL DREAMS*

You may know the story of the scorpion and the swan. The scorpion charms the swan, asks for a ride across the river, promising not to sting her, and against her better judgment the swan acquiesces and gives the scorpion the ride (the scorpion future faked the swan, and love bombed her, too!). No surprise, when they get to the other side, the scorpion stings the swan, despite their promise. Ultimately, no matter how persuasive they are, a scorpion is going to sting. It's what they do.

The scorpion and the narcissist have a similar ground game. Despite the charm, flattery, promises, and false reassurance, the narcissistic person will not change, and they will sting you. Even more important than understanding narcissism is acknowledging how the associated unhealthy behavioral patterns have played out in your relationship. There is a lot of intense analysis about why narcissistic people do what they do, but when it comes to healing, it really doesn't matter. It's less about the "Why did they do that?" and more about the "They did that, it's not good for me, and they are going to do it again." Radical acceptance is acknowledging this consistency and unchangeability to help you move forward.

Understanding acceptance means understanding both what acceptance is *and* what it is not. Acceptance doesn't mean you are signing off on what happened in your narcissistic relationship, and it is not submission or capitulation. Acceptance doesn't mean you are a doormat. Radical acceptance is acknowledging the reality of the narcissistic relationship landscape and, above all else, that *their behavior is not going to change.* Radical acceptance gives you permission to heal, because you stop channeling your energy into trying to fix the relationship and instead focus on moving yourself forward. The alternative is to remain stuck in the unfounded hope that it could get better and stay in these invalidating cycles in perpetuity.

## The Power of Radical Acceptance

Luisa finally got it. After twenty-five years in a narcissistic relationship, working in therapy, meeting with support groups, she got it: her partner was not going to change. This was the penny-drop moment: it was about the hundredth time she'd prepared an elaborate dinner and he'd claimed to be "working late" after promising to be there on time. Like the proverbial straw that broke the camel's back, there was nothing special about that one evening.

She wasn't even angry when he said he wasn't coming, and she was oddly calm when he finally got home. She didn't try to do the usual scrutiny of asking where he was or rushing about to set the table and warm up the meal. Instead, without getting up and without getting snarky, she pointed out the plates and the microwave, then un-paused her TV show and went back to it. She'd fought this moment hundreds of times, to avoid the grief of knowing this was how it would always be. She felt a mix of sadness, clarity, and lightness.

Similarly, Costa had been enduring the insults of his wife for twenty-five years. He was always doing either too much or not enough. He supported her career, focused on the children, and tolerated the jabs from his in-laws about how his brother-in-law was more successful than him. Nobody in his family had ever been divorced, and his children were his life, so he couldn't bear the thought of spending half his time away from them. His friends saw how his wife treated him, but he usually responded with "It's hard to be a woman in her industry; she brings her tough persona home."

When Costa's sister showed him a video about narcissism, he pushed it away and felt it was disloyal for a man to think this way about his own wife. However, his health had declined and he was exhausted from his competing responsibilities and the ongoing invalidation and gaslighting. He didn't want to go to therapy, but when he talked to his sister, he owned up to the idea that he just didn't really want to explore this idea of narcissism—because he was afraid of what he might learn.

All roads are hazardous when navigating narcissistic territory, but only one pathway will get you to a better destination, and that's the one of radical acceptance. Of course, as Luisa's story shows us, accepting a narcissistic situation for what it is can lift the curtains and allow you to see it so you can finally stop jousting at windmills. There is grief in having to accept that your relationship cannot improve, that there will be no phoenix rising from the ashes, and that the narcissistic person will never really attempt to see and understand you. This can be devastating and cement the loss you may have been trying to avoid mentally and emotionally.

However, not only does acceptance open the gateway to healing and growth, but it can give you a sense of relief. In some ways, it's like learning that there was no right answer to the test question, so you never could have gotten it correct. You can ultimately let go of the erroneous belief that there is something you can do to "fix" the relationship, and then you can stop wasting time and invest those hours into yourself and the relationships and pursuits that are actually good for you.

Most of us do not like the loss of power, efficacy, or hope that radical acceptance creates. We don't want to expose ourselves to the grief about a situation not changing; we want to avoid conflict; there is relief at maintaining the status quo. Do you have to leave the relationship for radical acceptance to happen? No. But is meaningful healing in the absence of radical acceptance possible? Not really. If, like Costa, you still believe the relationship can change, or that there is something different you can do to make things better, it means that the ongoing cycle of abuse, self-blame, and disappointment will persist eternally, and this is also a difficult way to live.

## Radical Acceptance
## Is the Gateway to Healing

I remember working with a client who coordinated a large staff. Although he managed one hundred team members, there were three people who took more time, effort, and energy than the other ninety-seven. Because of the hassles raised by these three, he was burned out, anxious, distracted, and exhausted. When he was able to see the commonalities in the three people's behavior (a laundry list of narcissistic behaviors) and understand narcissism, he was able to work toward radical acceptance. He stopped viewing himself as a bad manager and instead changed his hiring and evaluation procedures. He recognized that until he was no longer their supervisor, he had to keep figuring out the work-arounds. He admitted that it still wasn't easy, but he felt a little less exhausted when he realized that he couldn't manage them better. He just had to get to the place where he could fire them or hope that they would quit.

Healing is a difficult enough journey as it is, and healing in the absence of radical acceptance is like trying to walk on a broken leg the day after you broke it. Seeing the narcissistic relationship and behavior clearly, not being surprised by the gaslighting and invalidation, and being resolute even as the narcissistic abuse continues but with realistic expectations and the benefit of knowing this is not going to change allow you to slowly cut the trauma bond, ease up on the self-blame, and clarify the muddy waters of confusion. However, radical acceptance is not a magic pill—you also need to accept that even if you do radically accept that they won't change, their ongoing hurtful behavior, even if you are prepared for it, still hurts.

When I guide people through healing from narcissistic abuse, we work on the issue of "surprise"—the agitation they experience after looking at yet another toxic text message, email, or conversation and saying, "I can't believe this is happening. How could he do this?" Having radical acceptance means you are less surprised and, in fact, would actually be surprised if these things *didn't happen*. When these toxic patterns unfold, not being surprised doesn't mean you are okay with it, or even that it doesn't hurt, but rather that you knew it was coming, and you get better at being prepared for it and experiencing your feelings about their behavior without judgment.

Finally, radical acceptance is critical because it allows you to stop framing your assessment of your life based on how things are going in this relationship. Once you accept that the unhealthy patterns in the relationship are a constant, you can shift your focus to you and the people and activities that matter to you. The day you stop waiting for the narcissistic situation to change is the day you take back the psychological resources and time that you expended on hope, avoidance, trying to make sense of it, and trying to change yourself to make it work.

# The Barriers to Radical Acceptance

Acknowledging the reality of the narcissistic relationship is not easy. Recognizing and living with the emerging recognition that this person will never change and the relationship will never get better means moving into a very different reality than the one you had hoped for, may still want, and molded yourself to fit for so many years, sometimes a lifetime. The greatest barrier to radical acceptance is hope. Hope for change. Hope that the promises will be kept. Hope that things will get better. Hope for the genuine apology or accountability. Hope for the happily ever after. Hope that it is actually a normal and healthy relationship. In a narcissistic relationship, hope takes a long time to fade. The challenge of acceptance is that it squelches that hope, and evokes grief, guilt, and helplessness.

When hope gets extinguished, many people feel pressured to make a decision they are not yet ready to make, because radical acceptance begs the question "If it is really this bad, and it is not going to change, I can't really stay in it, can I?" It can also raise tremendous guilt, as though you are a bad person for having a "defeatist" mindset about someone you are supposed to love. To avoid having to make a difficult decision, you might erect barriers to acceptance such as justification, rationalization, denial, and personal narratives that frame your story in a more palatable manner (*It isn't that bad, we found love despite our tough childhoods; Relationships are hard, and one day once things are settled, it will all*

*be good; Families are complicated; We work hard and we fight hard*).
All of this allows you to remain in the relationship and not face
the more frightening issues raised by acceptance, such as giving
up hope, setting boundaries, being alone, distancing from family,
starting again, or being wrong.

But radical acceptance isn't necessarily a call to leave a relationship or situation. It is a shift in expectations regardless of what
you choose to do. It means that if you stay in the situation, you see
the relationship and the behavior within the relationship clearly.

Acceptance doesn't just mean seeing that the person's personality and behavior are not going to change, but also that this will
not be a safe space or a relationship you can rely on. That is not
easy to do, but the pathway to radical acceptance begins with the
simple acknowledgment that this is how it is and it is not going to
change. Initially, no actions need to be taken—you don't need to
break up or file for divorce or go no contact. In fact, in the early
days of radical acceptance, letting it breathe for a minute is essential, because your entire reality must integrate this seismic shift.
After this first step, you are in a better position to make decisions
that are protective and informed.

This is a major shift in how you have been thinking about your
relationship, sometimes for decades, and it may feel pessimistic
or even cynical to "give up" on another person. This alteration in
your thinking can feel like a barrier because you may not view
yourself as a person who gives up on anyone. But radical acceptance is not a disavowal of a narcissistic person; it's a rejection of
their behavior and a recognition that this unacceptable behavior
will not shift. When we are in the throes of a narcissistic situation,

we are already struggling with self-devaluation, and radical acceptance may magnify those feelings if you think you are giving up on another human being. That mental trap of "I need to be forgiving, I know they don't mean it" or "I am as bad as them if I give up on them" can keep people stuck and impede the process of healing. Instead, focus on framing narcissistic abuse as behavior, because it can feel less dehumanizing than viewing it as "This is a bad person."

What's so unfortunate about radical acceptance is that sometimes it requires scorched earth to finally see it. The subtle elements of narcissistic abuse may not be enough. A betrayal or harm so profound that you cannot unsee it may need to happen, such as infidelity, placing a child in harm's way, getting arrested, having a colleague share confidential information about you with a supervisor or boss, or destroying the family's or a business's finances. It could be the day their anger and rage continue to escalate and they finally physically threaten you or abuse you.

Other times, it's difficult to see the harms of abuse, especially in childhood. A child cannot radically accept that a parent's behavior is toxic. Children with narcissistic family systems learn to justify and rationalize seamlessly.[1] To break through those enduring patterns and finally see parents clearly in adulthood is no small task. It's only through radically accepting that your parent or family won't change, and also that your childhood cannot be different, that you can start to heal.

Sadly, some of us view ourselves as tarnished or even damaged because of these affiliations and histories. Avoiding radical acceptance means that you can avoid grappling with those difficult feelings in the short term. But you aren't damaged just because you were in a narcissistic relationship, and you aren't somehow less than because your parent was a narcissistic person or you are with a narcissistic partner. Seeing the narcissistic behavior doesn't make you "bad" but rather quite courageous. To clearly see and accept a pattern that is painful to acknowledge yet be willing to make realistic choices and protect yourself is the height of fearlessness and resilience.

## Radical Acceptance If You Stay

Emma spent years trying to communicate with her husband, make her needs known, and point things out clearly, and she was typically met with rage and manipulation. She tried everything with her mother, remembered special occasions, visited her as often as she could, but just when she thought they were having a good day, *bam*, her mother would bait her, Emma would defend herself, and it would fall apart again. Emma tried to work on herself, went into therapy, and assumed it had to be her fault because she was the only common denominator in both relationships. Emma struggled with depression, exhaustion, guilt, and anxiety, and both her husband and her mother told her she was being manipulative and had no reason to be struggling.

After she had children, her husband often complained about having to balance work and fatherhood, and her mother criticized her mothering and told her that she wasn't spending enough time with her. Emma kept thinking there had to be a way to keep her husband and mother happy, or at least mildly satisfied, and when she recognized that there wasn't, she acknowledged, *I am not going to get a divorce because we can't afford it. I am not going to cut out my mother because I am an only child. But I recognize that I'm in a marriage with a guy where we sometimes get along but more days than not it is manipulation and disappointment and tantrums. I have a mother who is so egocentric that she wondered why I didn't call her while I was in labor.*

After Emma really accepted that her husband's and mother's behavior was not going to change, and that she did not feel able to separate from either of these relationships, she was hit with a tidal wave of grief. She felt that she could accept that she wouldn't have a perfect relationship with her mother, or that her marriage would be rocky. But accepting that it wouldn't change felt like a loss of hope; she may not ever get a loving, patient partner or a safe, compassionate mother. Letting go of those hopes and narratives was like a funeral in her mind.

Now Emma no longer takes the bait, and she has developed some new interests. Her friends and her therapist are her sounding board now, and she puts time and effort into cherishing her friends and enjoying her children. She has figured out workarounds on household issues and knows that turning to her husband for help just raises more conflict (the workarounds are more work but less anguish; it's easier to bring the trash cans in herself). She has set dates with her mother and recognizes that what her mother wants—24/7 access to her—is impossible. On her hardest days, Emma feels her life is a sham. On most days, she is grateful that the number of conflicts has dropped, and she is less disappointed on a daily basis. As time goes on, she recognizes that in many ways radical acceptance has set her free, and while the echoes of grief are always there, they are getting quieter.

The vast majority of us stay in at least one narcissistic relationship. That is why advice that only encourages you to get out doesn't help. Radical acceptance does not mean you have to end the relationship; it simply means you must see it for what it is. Our reasons for staying, even after we understand what the narcissistic relationship is really about, include financial realities, family relationships we want to maintain, religion, societal and cultural expectations, fear of losing social connections, fear of post-separation abuse, and even love. However, radical acceptance does topple other reasons for staying, such as hope.

When you first accept the narcissistic person for who they are, it's normal to grieve the relationship or situation you'd hoped for. You may start wondering, *What is supposed to keep me going now?* Radical acceptance requires you to rather surgically examine why you are staying in the narcissistic situation. Is it practical factors like children or money? Is it trauma-bonded factors like guilt or fear? Being honest with yourself is a crucial piece of this daily process of acceptance. It may be a harsh reality check that can also break through the shame of staying in something you know is invalidating and unhealthy, and it places "staying" within a context (and acknowledges the lack of other viable choices or options).

If you choose to stay, radical acceptance may make you less likely to give in to the narcissistic person's baiting, and since you know nothing is going to change, you may be less likely to fight and more likely to find workarounds. Boundary setting becomes a little easier. You are no longer trying to scrimmage with, gain advantage over, outplay, or even win over the narcissistic person. You may even be willing to flex your "No" muscle a bit more because you're no longer playing their game.

Ultimately, radical acceptance can set you free even if you remain in a narcissistic relationship. You are no longer looking at the eastern horizon and searching for the sunset. You can divest your psychological investment and put it into other areas of your life: healthy social support and relationships, meaningful pursuits, or other interests. There can be a complicated relief that comes from no longer living in suspended hope and waiting for the future-faked better someday. Instead of it being resignation, acceptance can be framed as an opportunity to finally settle into and bring your authentic self to your healthy relationships. It's such a difficult balance—when you bring your authentic self to the narcissistic person, they often shame and rage at you, and yet it is central to your healing that you cultivate your true self and share it with others. I have talked with people who said that once they really accepted, they no longer waited for empathy, compassion, or respect from the narcissistic person. Their reasons for staying were varied, but they said that with acceptance, they could now disengage and yet remain authentic to who they were. Some who didn't feel comfortable going no contact with an elderly parent shifted to only providing practical support. Others who didn't want to share custody of children counted the clock down to eighteenth birthdays before filing for divorce. Yet others stayed in toxic workplaces until a job search was successful or benefits and pensions got figured out.

The goal of radical acceptance while staying in a narcissistic situation is to have realistic expectations, check in with yourself, ensure you do not fall into the trauma-bonded justifications, and remain true to yourself (which I recognize is not easy as you are also navigating the process of figuring out who you are separate from this relationship).

## Radical Acceptance If You Leave

Narcissistic relationships don't just end neatly. Dynamics such as hoovering, smear campaigns, manipulation, guilt, and post-separation abuse mean that you have to manage the fallout of the narcissistic behavior whether you are still in the relationship or not. That's why radical acceptance if you leave or end the relationship is a two-step process: First, you must accept the unchangeability of narcissism and narcissistic abuse. Second, you must accept the process that will unfold after you leave.

Narcissistic people do not like being left. They are highly sensitive to rejection, so as a result, if you leave, they may become punitive, vindictive, manipulative, and rageful. They also don't like giving up control. Radical acceptance encompasses the awareness that this post-separation abuse will happen. Whenever I sit with a client who is in or is about to enter the process of a divorce from a narcissistic person, I warn them that this will get so bleak and abusive that they will doubt their decision. Some folks will share that the abuse got so much worse after a relationship ended that they almost wanted to go back in just to make it stop. This is why radical acceptance is so crucial—to end one of these relationships also means having your eyes open to what is about to happen, so you can prepare and not lose your resolve. Even with a moderately narcissistic person, the post-separation landscape is dismal. Radical acceptance is likely what pushed you to leave the relationship, so in some ways the bad behavior that may persist after the relationship ends should be reassuring, as it is confirmation of your perceptions and experience. But it certainly doesn't feel that way while it is happening.

For some of us, the radical acceptance may not commence until we actually leave the relationship. This is particularly true if the narcissistic person is the one to end it. Radical acceptance becomes a critical tool for processing the aftermath of the relationship. Recognizing the patterns that were consistent both before and after the breakup and noting the narcissistic person's post-breakup behavior—like quickly moving into a new relationship or ongoing harassment—can round out the picture and predictability of their narcissistic behavior.

Divorces or other relationship endings that require dividing assets or distributing money can protract the narcissistic abuse, and radical acceptance is critical to navigating these situations. The narcissistic person's patterns will persist at least until the logistics are settled, and may even get worse if they can't control the process and outcome the way they want. Many survivors of narcissistic relationships are stunned that, even years later, the narcissistic person still seems as angry and aggrieved as they were at the time of the breakup. Simply put, radical acceptance, done correctly, should fortify your resolute expectation that all of this would happen, even if it still feels stressful after all these years. However, the harm of post-separation abuse may magnify the fallout of narcissistic abuse that you are already experiencing.

## Don't Burn Your Umbrellas: What Are Realistic Expectations for a Narcissistic Relationship?

Whether you stay in or leave a narcissistic situation, realistic expectations are the core of radical acceptance and are essential to coping with and healing from narcissistic abuse. These relationships are strangely consistent. Even the hot and cold, good days and bad, charm mask and rage mask are actually predictable to the extent that you know they are going to happen. That makes realistic expectations rather straightforward. And once you become proficient at realistic expectations, you will be close to crossing the finish line of radical acceptance.

The best way to understand realistic expectations is to go back to the laundry list of qualities that comprise a narcissistic person and the behaviors and patterns we observe in these relationships: variable empathy, entitlement, grandiosity, invalidation, dismissiveness, rage, manipulation, and gaslighting. Plan on these things happening. I tell folks in narcissistic relationships, "Don't burn your umbrellas." The good days in narcissistic relationships can undercut your realistic expectations and radical acceptance. When a day comes when they are bringing the charm, charisma, and some performative empathy, enjoy it for the sunny day it is, but don't burn your umbrellas—it will soon rain again. You will need them soon enough, and many a survivor of narcissistic abuse will say, "Damn, we had two good days, and I got cocky and started teasing them like I would any friend, and my fun little ribbing turned into a reactive two-hour tantrum."

Having realistic expectations also means not succumbing to the narcissistic person's excuses, justifications, and future faking. When a narcissistic person says they won't lie or cheat or show up late or cancel at the last minute again, don't believe them. Radical acceptance is not engaging with them or trying to point out the evidence of why you know they will cheat again. It's the knowing without the engaging.

It's also about the workarounds. Because you know the narcissistic person won't remember the groceries, will cancel at the last minute, will insult your friends, or will show up late, plan around it. Don't entrust them with important groceries, have a plan B, visit with your friends alone, and make reservations at places that don't require your full party to be present before being seated.

Realistic expectations are also about information management. This means not sharing good news with them because they will minimize and take the joy out of it or behave in a victimized and passive-aggressive manner. It also means not sharing bad news with them because they may rage and criticize and make it worse. What's left? Indifferent topics: the weather, the neighbor's cat, the taste of the chocolate cake. Is that a relationship? It's not a deep one, but there never was the possibility of a sustained and close relationship with them. Realistic expectations mean knowing what will happen if you try to engage or wait for a different outcome. Radical acceptance is living it.

Finally, having realistic expectations is necessary to weather the storms that continue to roll in even if you do end the relationship. Some of those storms may be from the narcissistic person themselves: ongoing nasty messages, protracted custody battles, passive-aggressive barbs, and gossip and rumors about you. The other storms are about how challenging healing can be. Some of you may find that things improved for you quickly once your relationship ended and the narcissistic person was no longer in your life. Others may find that the scars of the narcissistic abuse persist deeply, even with the relationship gone. Many if not most of us who leave may find ourselves surprised by missing the narcissistic person, wondering if they would be "proud" or impressed if they saw all we were doing, and that healing is harder than you expected. Realistic expectations mean acknowledging that healing often looks like two steps forward, one step back.

## Tools for Fostering Radical Acceptance

When you're trying to incorporate radical acceptance into your life, it's not as simple as saying, "Okay, the narcissistic person isn't going to change." It takes your mind a minute to catch up. There are a variety of techniques that can help you accelerate and solidify the radical acceptance.

## Entering the Tiger's Cage:
## A Pathway for Radical Acceptance

Entering a tiger's cage has an inevitable outcome, but if you really want to pet the tiger because you think it's just a misunderstood cat, go in and see how it works out for you. Over the years, many clients who aren't at the point of acceptance have shared the narcissistic patterns in their relationships with me. By this point, the client has largely stopped communicating their needs or is doing it sparsely. This *need avoidance* is a self-protective and trauma-bonded behavior that avoids conflict, but it also keeps them from seeing the toxic patterns—and from getting their needs met. We do an exercise called *entering the tiger's cage*. I never like sending someone into harm's way, but sometimes it is the only way to cement the acceptance about the consistency of the invalidating patterns. This exercise consists of communicating a need directly to the narcissistic person in their life. It may be a need for closeness, for something to get done around the house, for a change in how the business is run or how that person communicates with you, or even feedback on their behavior and how it affected you.

Then I tell the client to pay attention to the response from the other person. If they receive an empathic or non-defensive acknowledgment of their need, and then a real attempt to address it, then maybe this isn't a narcissistic abuse situation, especially if the person goes into the tiger's cage a few times and keeps getting the same self-aware response from the other person—it turns out that it was a sweet cat after all. If, however, the response is gaslighting or manipulative, rageful, or abusive words or behavior, it is further confirmation that what my client is suspecting and don't want to fully see is in fact narcissistic abuse.

If you do this exercise, remain mindful of the justifications you make for any invalidating responses so you can witness your own trauma-bonded cycles. This exercise is meant to be intentional—most relationships with narcissistic folks are a daily entry into the tiger's cage, but this time you are entering with eyes wide open and a willingness to really see and feel their response. Making a need known is a clear and painful way to witness these patterns. Unfortunately, folks often need to wander into that cage a few times to confirm that the tiger indeed has some sharp claws. The goal is to get to radical acceptance before the tiger destroys you.

## Don't Hit Send

We've all written that text or letter or email where we explain ourselves to a narcissistic person: the long, meandering email, the text that goes on far longer than a text should. You probably wrote that letter because they never listen to you while you speak, and they gaslight, interrupt, or confuse you so much that you get tongue-tied. Maybe you thought if you wrote it out carefully, then they could see your point of view clearly. But it never works. They read it and either respond with an obscene emoji, send an eviscerating and scathing response, or gaslight you (again).

Now, take a different approach to writing that email or text or letter. Write down the stuff you are always trying to explain to the narcissistic person in your life—your point of view, your hopes, your feelings. You may write exactly what you think of them or how you feel about their behavior. Just lay it all out and get it down. Let it be a catharsis and a clearing out of all the things you want to say. *But do not send it to them!* You may want to share it with a trusted friend or a therapist just to have someone bear witness to your experience. I have read countless numbers of these letters, texts, and emails over the years, and they are usually painful, poignant, and poetic reflections on a survivor's pain. Sharing it in a safe space such as therapy allowed them to receive empathy for their experience, empathy they would not have received if they'd shared it with the narcissistic person in their life. These letters also became a place to share other strong emotions such as anger that they could have never safely shared in the relationship.

When you're done, destroy the letter. Make the destruction ceremonial. If it's safe, burn it, or write it on something biodegradable and drop it in a pond or the sea, toss it off a mountaintop, or bury it. If you can't do any of those, run it through a shredder. Or just write it into your phone as a note and then delete it. The point is to give yourself an opportunity to vent and clearly lay out all of your thoughts and feelings about this relationship. Then by destroying it, you acknowledge that the narcissist will never hear your words, which fosters acceptance.

### The Lists

Euphoric recall and a lifetime of denial mean that survivors almost reflexively "forget" the patterns in a relationship. On the good days it's easy not only to forget all the toxic stuff that happened but also to lose sight of how much of ourselves we give up for these relationships. Writing down the patterns of harmful behavior can keep us from gaslighting and doubting ourselves, and research suggests that there is a real power to writing things down and seeing them, not just thinking about them.

You can make these lists alone or with the help of others. They should be living documents that you continue to add to. You can keep them in your phone or in a journal—just be sure they are private and easily accessible for you. Gentle reminder: Never keep these lists in a place where they can end up in "the cloud" or some other shared drive and be seen.

## The Ick List

One of the most helpful lists in your radical acceptance tool kit is what I call the Ick List. This is a list of all the awful stuff that happened in the relationship. Write down the terrible things this person did: cruel things they said, insults, invalidations, betrayals, lies, manipulations, special events they ruined, and all the gaslighting. This process can take days, weeks, or even a few months or years, and the recollections will keep coming to you. If you have close friends or family who saw it, they can add to it as well. I have helped many a client and friend construct an Ick List based on the episodes and behaviors they shared in our sessions or what I witnessed them experience.

I get pushback from people on this exercise, that it's somehow petty or keeps people stuck. It may even feel kind of gross and mean-spirited to make such a list, or it can feel psychologically unsettling to have to even think about these experiences again.

But when euphoric recall takes over or fear kicks in and you start thinking about the great sex or that perfect night in Miami or, in the case of other relationships, fun memories of baking cookies, taking fishing trips, or going on a trip with a friend, you can look at the list. Radical acceptance requires calibration. It is obviously easier to write this list on a day when everything has been awful, and on the good or confusing days when you are having a lapse in recall, the list can get you back on track to keep you from doubting and blaming yourself; it shows you how consistent the narcissistic patterns have been. As a therapist, I have often been the memory storage for clients navigating narcissistic relationships and have gently reminded them of events from the past when they doubted themselves. Nearly all of these clients have been grateful for these recollections that they have forgotten, and since many people do not have a therapist whose job it is to do this, the Ick List can serve that function.

This list is equally important if you are going to stay in the relationship. The slippage away from radical acceptance is more pronounced for people who stay. While it may be painful to catalog all that is bad about something you are staying in, this list can help stave off self-blame and fortify the realistic expectations and radical acceptance so you don't find yourself falling for the manipulation. A few folks have shared with me that creating a list like this was overwhelming and set them back. That's understandable, as this list can bring up strong negative emotions. Take your time with this. Healing means always honoring your rhythms and comfort level.

## *"Biscuits in Bed" List*

Maybe the narcissistic person in your life would throw a tantrum when you would cook with garlic, or they refused to watch films with subtitles, or they made fun of you for wanting to make crafts during the holidays, or they berated you for having soda in the refrigerator. Now, do those things—cook up a storm with all the garlic you want, have a personal French film festival, get a glue gun and have a ball, or buy cases of soda. (My little pleasure is eating biscuits in bed while reading and playing games on my phone, thus the name of the exercise.) Seeing it all written down is a reminder of how many little things you gave up for the relationship—and likely faced their contempt and rage for. Once you start living as yourself, it can put the toxic patterns in starker focus and make radical acceptance more sustainable. If you didn't leave the relationship, this list can focus on things you will give yourself permission to do, and then it's important that you take the time to do them, perhaps when the narcissistic person isn't around, in order to avoid the fight. The doing, even if it is just making a pom-pom cat ornament, is part of the healing.

## *"It's My Turn" List*

Maybe you've always dreamed of going to graduate school, redecorating the house, traveling, or writing a book. But whether it's due to a partner whose wants and needs always came first, a parent who negated you or demanded so much attention that you never had time for that class you wanted to take, or a toxic workplace that paid a salary but kept you from your genuine ambitions, you have likely placed your dreams on the back burner. Make a list of the larger-scale aspirations you gave up for this relationship. Some people get overwhelmed by reflecting on all the experiences they sacrificed in the name of their narcissistic relationship, and this list can even foster grief because of your unachieved or unpursued aspirations. But you don't need to go get a PhD. Perhaps those graduate school dreams may manifest as taking interesting classes at a local university. Maybe that book you wanted to write winds up being a series of blogs.

After you make this list, pick a goal and once a day or once a week do one small thing toward achieving it. Put a few bucks aside for the trip, move furniture around a room, look at the website of a local school, write a paragraph about something that matters to you. If you stay in these relationships, you may still feel stifled, but you can still do one small thing toward a goal. This process can foster radical acceptance because you witness the contrast between the potential that lies in you and the limitations that the narcissistic person placed on you.

### *Lean into the Rumination*

Rumination may be one of the most vexing barriers to recovery from narcissistic abuse and can undercut radical acceptance. But trying to fight rumination is like trying to sidestep gravity. There is no thought-stopping exercise, hypnosis, or memory eraser that can make it go away. If you try to fight the riptide of rumination, you may drown. So don't fight it. Talk about it instead—in support groups, in therapy, with trusted friends (but be mindful of not burning them out), by journaling, and in any way you can express yourself in an appropriate and safe manner.

Think of talking out and leaning into your rumination as the "hair of the dog" for a hangover. My clients worry about telling me the same story about what happened in their relationship a hundred times, but it isn't the same story. By telling it over and over, they are learning from and releasing it. Holding these painful thoughts within your mind is what makes rumination so uncomfortable—it's like needing to throw up and not being able to get to a place where you can. Express whatever you've been ruminating over, because believe it or not, that expressed rumination will slowly help you digest your experience and ultimately step away from it.

After one of my personal experiences with narcissistic abuse, a friend of mine listened to me constantly talk about it for two weeks. She didn't judge me or try to solve it or make me feel better. She just listened and encouraged me to keep talking and talking. After two weeks I had released much of it, and by getting it out of my head, my thoughts and confusion had lost their power.

## The Toxic Cleanup

Most of us don't have just one toxic person in our lives. Once you pull back the curtain on the more compelling or demanding narcissistic people in your life, you will see that there are more people like this in your world than you initially recognized. If we do not see them clearly for who they are, we run the risk of enabling or minimizing their impact. By setting boundaries, ending relationships, disengaging, and radically accepting what narcissistic relationships are really about, you can start extending those boundaries to the other unhealthy people in your life. If cleaning out a closet is supposed to bring joy to a person's life, cleaning out toxic people should bring ecstasy.

First, go through your list of contacts in your phone—and this is going to sound a little childish—and put a little symbol or emoji next to the names of the people who aren't good for you. They may not be as toxic as the more demanding narcissistic people in your life, but they may still be taking a toll on you and leaving you depleted. When any of these less-than-healthy folks text you and you see that little toxic symbol, that reminder may be enough to stop you from engaging. It may also be a reminder to say "No" to that phone call you know will be a one-sided time suck. This extends to not falling into the "birthday trap"—reaching out on the birthday of a narcissistic person from your past—which may place you at risk of being sucked back into the narcissistic relationship cycle. You can expect to feel guilt, fear, and anxiety when you begin to eliminate or distance from these difficult people, but you will also feel relief. And you will augment the radical acceptance because you are more broadly able to see that your life is better without engaging in unnecessary invalidating exchanges with people.

Purging your social media feed is also part of this cleanup. Engineer the settings in a way that keeps you from seeing victimized or passive-aggressive posts from your more toxic followers and friends. Block selected folks from seeing aspects of your life you don't want them to know about. Consider unfollowing people who are linked to the more challenging narcissistic relationships in your life, especially if your relationship is over, so you don't see references to that person in their posts. Find a way to change settings so you don't get the "12 months ago" or "5 years ago" photo montages sent to you. And in an ideal world, spend less time on social media. Something about the validation seeking, the rants, the comparisons, the cruel clickbait, and the egocentricity of social media just isn't good for healing, so try to reduce your exposure. Once again, the less of this you are dealing with, the better you will feel, and this fosters radical acceptance.

Finally, consider either throwing away, giving away, or permanently archiving photos and documentation from the relationship (if these are family photographs, consult with other family members who may want them as a part of their history and offload them that way). If you need some of these items for divorce proceedings or other litigation (e.g., old text messages or emails) or want to keep them as part of the archives for the Ick List, hold on to such items. But old photos can be placed in storage. Removing these items from your life can feel like getting the ghosts out of your house—and out of your heart.

## Stacking Multiple Truths

The core of radical acceptance is the acknowledgment of multiple truths. Look back at the story of Emma in this chapter: *I can't get divorced, my husband is never going to change, I still love my husband, I love my mother, I can't cut off my mother, my mother is selfish, my husband will never help, my mother will never be happy with the amount of time I spend with her, I have to do most of the parenting.* In Emma's story, all those things are true, and they do not fit together well. Radical acceptance becomes about listing out the multiple truths, not just the bad stuff (you already have this from the Ick List) but also the good stuff, and ideally saying it out loud. Write it out, good and bad. It feels odd and uncomfortable (*I love my mother, I never want to see her again*), but once you say it all together, it can be a big step in breaking through the denial and dissonance and fostering the acceptance. I do this exercise with clients, and it can sometimes help to do it on separate pieces of paper (like index cards) so each of your "truths" isn't contaminated by others you have listed. Doing this can help break through something called *cognitive dissonance*, the tension that comes up when we encounter emotional inconsistency (*I love him, he cheated on me*). Typically we attempt to resolve the tension of cognitive dissonance by justifying something so the pieces fit (*He cheated on me, but I've been distracted with the baby and it was just a one night stand*)—and narcissistic relationships raise constant cognitive dissonance (good and bad days). This exercise forces the dissonant truths to be simultaneously tolerated so you see your situation holistically and don't rationalize what is happening. This stack of inconsistent truths is a lesson on why this has been so difficult and allows a person to simultaneously hold space for loving someone and also recognize why they may need to disengage from them.

Life is complicated and multiple things can be true. You do not, and actually should not, view these relationships through a black-and-white lens. To do so discredits your process of healing and simplifies a process that is anything but. You loved these people; in some cases you still do. You may have compassion for their histories and gradually recognize that their behavior is not good for you. This is some of the hardest work of radical acceptance but it also gets you to a place where you realize that radically accepting does not mean that you have lost your empathic recognition of who this person is and who they have been to you.

## Radically Accepting Yourself

Radical acceptance of a person or situation that won't change is key to healing, but we should also be applying this to ourselves. Do you radically accept yourself? Do you accept your foibles, gifts, quirks, personality, and preferences and recognize that they make up who you are, and that you can change what you want but keep what you like and stop judging yourself? Some folks arrive here as they get older. They see enough, live enough, and finally realize "This is me."

There is no reason to wait for the wisdom of age to get you here. A narcissistic relationship, especially with a parent, often steals the opportunity to radically accept yourself because you were never able to be seen or heard or valued. You learned to silence yourself, and certainly couldn't dare to radically accept yourself. You also learned to modify yourself to appease the narcissistic person, to suppress your real self to survive in the relationship. Discovering who you truly are and accepting yourself may be the strongest radical acceptance tool you have, because the more you know and accept who you are, the more you don't sacrifice and subjugate yourself.

This isn't about rigidly holding a position. This is about being able to take note when another person is asking you not to be yourself. You aren't likely to cut off your own arm because a narcissistic person asks you to, yet most of us have cut off sizable parts of our souls in the name of narcissistic "love." Radically accepting yourself means that you are kind to yourself on the bad days.

Recently I had someone with whom I have had a complicated relationship send me a mean-spirited email mocking my work. I felt the usual reaction rise up in me: the discomfort in my gut, the dry mouth, the tightening of my throat. I know that when this person pokes me professionally it leaves me feeling not enough, something that he has made me feel throughout my adult life. But I genuinely enjoy my work, and in that moment, I allowed myself to acknowledge that. I felt sad that his behavior never changes, but I also saw what he was doing. This time I didn't critique myself for being "too sensitive." And instead of responding, I leaned into my work harder. In the end, I never responded, which was a real shift for me, and it felt so much better. Radical acceptance of myself and of the situation gave me a new way of responding and healing. *I love what I do, he is always going to bait me, I don't need to respond.*

Much of the misery of our world is rooted in all of us not accepting ourselves, comparing ourselves to others, and feeling we are not enough. Radical self-acceptance is giving yourself permission to become acquainted with and accept yourself, then working from there. It is practicing self-compassion, not judging yourself, and recognizing that anyone in a narcissistic relationship is probably having the same experience you are. Try asking yourself the following questions:

- What do I like about myself?
- What don't I like about myself, but really can't change or don't want to change?
- What don't I like about myself and can change?
- What am I about?
- What matters to me?

In that process of radical self-acceptance, you may recognize the vulnerabilities in yourself—you crave romance, you don't like being alone, you are sensitive about your work. And that's okay. Just recognize it as a potential vulnerability, not a weakness, but a beautiful part of yourself that you can safeguard. When you devalue yourself or deny who you are, you aren't doing the most fundamental radical acceptance of all: the acceptance of yourself.

BUILDING RADICAL ACCEPTANCE can be a soul- and eye-opening process. You're letting go of the hope that the narcissistic person will become kind, empathic, and interested in your life and you are recognizing that the invalidation, hostility, and carelessness are here to stay. It's not about giving up or giving in or agreeing with the abusive behavior, but about seeing a situation clearly. While this may initially make you feel hopeless or cynical, radical acceptance is an essential gateway to healing and to separating from their reality and upholding your own. Radical acceptance raises tremendous grief, a unique grief that can overwhelm us and keep us stuck. In the next chapter, we will learn how to process the sense of loss and grief that these relationships can evoke.

## 6.

# Grief and Healing from Narcissistic Relationships

*Healing doesn't mean the loss didn't happen. It means that it no longer controls us.*

DAVID KESSLER

Maria's mother, Clare, was volatile, manipulative, and fiercely egocentric. Maria was the golden child in her family, and Clare would bask in her daughter's successes and cruelly cut her down when she didn't "shine." Maria struggled, because her mother always reminded her how much she sacrificed for her, which Maria felt was true since her mother had always supported her and paid little attention to her siblings. Maria lived in fear of disappointing her and blamed herself for Clare's down days. She felt that she owed her for all she did and remained aware of her mother's difficult life story of immigration and poverty. So she withstood her mother's rage, believing it would improve if she was simply "enough."

When Maria graduated from college, Clare expected her to be her best friend and include her in everything she did. She would frequently call, expect Maria to spend hours on the phone with her, and would use guilt to induce more time and visits ("I gave up so much for you, it's so sad you can't do a little thing for me"). If Maria missed a call or couldn't make time to see her mother, she would feel guilty about her mother's ensuing meltdowns. It was a tricky balancing act of her career in finance, her mother's demands, and wanting to create a life for herself.

When Maria met her future husband, she started spending less time with her mother, which resulted in rage, disappointment, and Maria needing to calm her down regularly. Because she was unable to balance the needs of her mother and be present for her husband, who was also quite demanding, entitled, manipulative, and sporadically and superficially empathic, Maria ended up walking away from her career. When her husband had an extramarital affair, she blamed herself for letting him down and ruminated about how she could have been a better wife. Clare was of little support during this time and blamed Maria for not being more attentive. When Clare developed cancer a few years later, she told Maria it was caused by the stress of having an ungrateful daughter. At that point, Maria devoted herself to her mother's care because she didn't want to face the regret and aggravation of letting her mother down again. Maria felt she had lost out on so much—a healthy marriage, a normal mother-daughter relationship, her own independent interests and career. Accepting her situation raised a new set of problems . . .

THE NARCISSISTIC RELATIONSHIP is an intricate dance: the narcissistic person projects their shame onto you, and you, because you're an empathic and accountable person, may receive it, integrate it, blame yourself, and ultimately take responsibility for all the toxicity within the relationship. Only with this structure can these relationships persist. The day you finally accept that the narcissistic dynamic will not change and that it has nothing to do with you is the day these cycles shift—and the day the relationship stops "working."

The grief raised by a narcissistic relationship is quite unique, and these relationships are about the loss of opportunities, hopes, aspirations, narratives, instincts, and sense of self. Ultimately, not running away from the grief but making the brave and painful journey through it is essential to the healing process. There is a real risk in denying the process of grief, ignoring it, or minimizing it. As Robert Frost once wrote, "The best way out is always through." You must process the losses in order to create the space in which you can cultivate yourself and healthier relationships and life. This chapter will help you do just that by giving you the tools to begin to work through your grief.

## Grief after Narcissistic Abuse

Lauren was in her mid-fifties when one of her closest friends unexpectedly died. Her death was a wake-up call to the reality that life can end at any moment, and looking back, Lauren was saddened to realize just how many opportunities and dreams she had passed up due to the fallout of narcissistic abuse. Lauren grew up with a malignant narcissistic father, and she spent most of her life trying to please him. She paid off her parents' house, delaying purchasing one for herself as a result, and would do anything so they would see her as "good."

The grief for Lauren hit home when she recognized that she had never received the life lessons that many people get from their families of origin: being seen, witnessing a loving and respectful marriage, feeling safe enough to ask for guidance, and feeling valued. Without those experiences, she didn't feel able to pursue an intimate relationship and instead had a string of invalidating and narcissistic partners. She blamed herself for being socially unskilled, emotionally unintelligent, and incapable of intimacy, when in actuality she is warm and has a lovely sense of humor and deep empathy for others. Despite taking more chances in her life now, Lauren grieves never having been married, never having a family, never traveling, and remaining in an unrewarding job.

Lauren is grieving the loss of time; a childhood marked by fear, invalidation, and anxiety; wasted hope on her father and a series of toxic partners; a financially successful but spiritually empty career; and waiting for her family to see past themselves and actually see her. She grieves not having learned about narcissism earlier so she could have made better choices.

In essence, she grieves herself.

The grief raised by narcissistic relationships is an experience you cannot outrun. It doesn't follow a schedule—you can't rush it or slow it down. It's a process, one you may cycle through for years, and it takes as long as it takes. At some point you can get to the other side and put it down, but you may also carry some of it with you for a lifetime. In some ways, grieving the living is far more difficult than grieving the dead. It isn't simply about grieving your dream of a happy intact family, growing old with someone, or giving your child a more stable home than the one you grew up in. It's grief for your life, the life you hoped to have, and moving through that takes time.

There are many reasons we grieve a narcissistic relationship. You may be grieving what you never received. If you had a narcissistic parent, you may grieve the loss of a healthy childhood, which can become magnified when you contrast your childhood with what you may be trying to give your own children. If you disengage from your family of origin, you may grieve that you never had a safe space, a sense of belonging, a soft place to land, or unconditional love. You may look back at your life and ask the question: *How would my life have been different if I hadn't been through this relationship?* It's a complex mix of rumination and regret, as well as reflecting on loss of identity, love, and opportunity.

There is also grief about that significant developmental window that was harmed. You can remarry after a narcissistic marriage and have the experience of a healthy adult relationship, but there is no second attempt at childhood. In adulthood, decisions around maintaining relationships with your narcissistic parent can get complicated, because their presence can elicit the grief of your lost childhood. And since your narcissistic parent has not changed, you may reexperience the grief every time you see them.

If you are in an intimate relationship with a narcissistic person, you may grieve the loss of a marriage and family as well as the loss of your own pursuits or path, a career, identity, reputation, and financial freedom. You may grieve not sharing a life and growing old with a loving and kind partner. There may also be the grief of losing what you believed was love, and the idea that a long-term committed relationship can be safe and trustworthy. You may also grieve what your children will not get, and the confusion and anxiety they may experience by having a narcissistic parent. If you are divorcing a narcissistic person, you may grieve time spent away from your children, and their loss of the experience of a functional family.

While in the relationship, you may also experience ambiguous loss,[1] described as loss that is ongoing, unresolved, and unclear. It's akin to the loss a person experiences when they have a family member or loved one with dementia—the person is there, but they are not *there*. In the same way, the narcissistic person is there but they are not really there as a companion or with empathy— and they are emotionally abusing you.

The grief evoked when a narcissistic relationship ends can be confusing because there is the sense you should be relieved, yet you still feel sad. The sadness and loss may snap you into thinking you made a mistake, and you may go back into the relationship. Leaving a narcissistic relationship may mean grieving the hopes you had for the relationship and the good days that were very real, as well as the time and parts of yourself you lost in the relationship. If the relationship ends, the narcissistic person is still alive. That means they can move on, enter new relationships, get remarried, or continue to lash out at you, and that can also result in a cascade of grief and fear (*What if they change for the new person? Did I make a mistake?*). Dead people do not move on to new lives, but narcissistic exes can. It can seem as though they are flowing into their best lives while you as a survivor are navigating a landscape of pain, loss, and regret.

A narcissistic relationship is also a loss of innocence. Many survivors feel that they grieve that belief in goodness, and that it has been replaced with cynicism. Cynicism is not a bad word, and in fact it can help protect you if it makes you more discerning.

The grief of narcissistic abuse is consistent with something called *disenfranchised grief*,[2] which is grief that is not acknowledged by others or socially sanctioned and supported as a loss or grief experience. Imagine that someone close to you dies and the people around you deny that the person is dead and say there is no need for you to be upset. It would be unsettling to say the least. But that approximates the experience of a person who is enduring narcissistic abuse or the end of a narcissistic relationship. People may deny that you are experiencing a loss, especially if you do not end up leaving the relationship. The ambiguity and the marginalization of your grief experience or hearing that you are simply having "relationship problems" only magnifies the experiences of shame, grief, guilt, and self-blame. Because the people around you may not recognize what you are experiencing as "grief," you may feel completely alone. If you remain in your relationship, single friends may say to you, "Hey, at least you are in a relationship." If you leave, coupled friends may say, "Look, now you have your independence, how fun that you can start dating again!" Family members may minimize your parent's behavior and say that at least you had a better childhood than your parent. If your partner or parent had passed away, folks would be

around supporting you. But since you are experiencing psychological and existential losses, it can feel as though the word *grief*
has been annexed so that only people experiencing "permissible"
losses are allowed to use it. Unfortunately, this leaves you feeling
as if you are not granted the right to use the language of grief and
instead can only use the language of a person who has messy or
dysfunctional relationships.

## Grieving the Death of a Narcissistic Person in Your Life

So far, we have largely focused on the losses that result from being in a narcissistic relationship—time, self, money, childhood,
hope, innocence, trust, love, children, and family. However, the
grief following the death of a narcissistic person can be complicated. Over the years I have worked with many survivors who
used the confidential space of therapy to share that they were relieved after the death of a narcissistic person, and that relief
brought a cascade of emotions, especially guilt, shame, and even
the sense that they were a bad person for having those feelings.

The death of a narcissistic person may bring up the same spectrum of grief reactions we witness after any death, but complicated by a sense of relief plus regret, anger, self-doubt (*Did I do
enough?*), and fear. Even after the narcissistic person passes away,
their voice can linger within you for a lifetime. Healing means
you still need to do the mindful work of facing that distorted
voice down, whether the narcissistic person is living or dead.

## BLOCKS TO GRIEVING

Grief, especially the grief of a narcissistic relationship, can be very uncomfortable, and like most things that are uncomfortable, you may attempt to avoid it. It's important to be mindful of some of the blocks to grieving so you can understand they are normal. These are actions or activities that prevent you from fully engaging in the grief process so that you can move forward. These behaviors are often self-protective but working through grief means being willing to take some steps into an uncomfortable space.

- Staying busy and distracted
- Using drugs and alcohol
- Denying the reality and your feelings
- Being falsely positive
- Using social media
- Engaging with too many people who are still connected to or enable the narcissistic person
- Trying to be a healer of others too soon
- Blaming yourself

# Navigating Your Grief

You need strategies to navigate the complex landscape of narcissistic grief, and many people find that traditional grief strategies don't address these complicated losses. This becomes even more complex when you are staying in the relationship (if you are going through a narcissistic divorce, at least people will recognize divorce as a loss, but if you remain in a relationship, the losses are as profound but not as recognized). It's crucial to remain aware of some fundamental tenets of narcissistic grief recovery.

1.  *Call it what it is.* Despite people telling you that this isn't really grief, or just treating it as family or relationship issues, it is real. Identifying this experience as loss helps you understand and experience the profound impact it is having.

2.  *Engage the process.* Navigate your grief through therapy, support groups (ideally ones for survivors of narcissistic abuse), mindfulness, meditation, and meaningful activities. Also don't rush it—grief takes as long as it takes, so give yourself permission to experience it without judgment.

3.  *Stay with your feelings.* Grief, sadness, and anxiety are all uncomfortable emotions, and because narcissistic relationships and the associated losses may persist in our lives for a long time, be prepared for these painful feelings to revisit you. When this happens, stay with these feelings. These emotions are a signal from your body and mind to slow down and be gentle with yourself. This may mean rest, moderate exercise, meditation, breath-

ing, or being in nature. Disconnecting from feelings can keep you stuck in them, so think of them as a gentle wave you are riding back to shore, and don't try to jump off.

4. *Journal.* Writing down your experience allows you to track the small shifts in yourself as you slowly release this relationship or process the losses of being in the relationship. There will be good days and bad days, but over time you can witness the improvement, and it can substantiate your commitment to growth and individuation.

5. *Focus on you outside of this relationship.* After defining yourself by the narcissistic relationship for so long, the hard work is experiencing yourself outside of it. Work on understanding your values, preferences, joys, and wants outside of the narcissistic relationship. After any kind of loss, it can be difficult to plug back into life, and this is magnified after narcissistic abuse because you may be not only trying to get back into life, but also trying to discover or reclaim (or claim) your sense of self outside of this relationship.

6. *Remain mindful of anniversary dates, reunions, or anything that may pull you back in.* Dates such as actual anniversaries, birthdays, and relationship milestones can be unsettling and heartbreaking, and can magnify your process of grief. Attending events such as weddings or other gatherings

where people from your past will be assembled may also be taxing. Be prepared for those days. You may deliberately plan alternate activities, spend time with friends, take a quiet day by yourself, or build in rest on the back end of these days. If you aren't prepared for the psychological pullback, it can surprise you and be quite destabilizing.

## Recovering from the Lie

Have you ever looked at pictures from your narcissistic relationship, pictures where you are smiling, days you remember as fun, and wondered, *Was any of it real? I was smiling, but was I happy?* Having to recover from the lies and betrayal complicates narcissistic grief. You may start to ruminate about the lies and wonder why you didn't see them or why people who knew didn't tell you. You may think, *Why was I so stupid? Why did I fall for it?* Doubting your feelings does a number on your grief and recovery.

So how do you deal with this? By processing the stacks of multiple truths that these relationships contain. The rumination that is such a common fallout of narcissistic abuse and a central piece of the grief is often about what feels like the "big lie" of these relationships. By laying this out more clearly, you recognize the complexity of what happened to you and can develop self-compassion that can help detach you from a cycle of feeling foolish or deceived. Instead you can visualize this as a situation that you entered in good faith and that slowly revealed itself to you, then, framing it as grief about what you had once believed to be true and lost.

Recollections of special experiences, especially those that are documented with images and videos—a trip, the moment in the delivery room, your wedding day—can distort your reality, so I will often use them as a tool to help survivors navigate grief and the disconnect between what was happening, what they feel now, and what they felt then. The betrayals and distortions that can keep you stuck in rumination call for you to dissect those experiences. My guidance is to divide these experiences and recollections into *episode*, *context*, and *feeling*.

Let's say you took a trip to Italy with a narcissistic partner. During the trip you had a beautiful time. However, some errant text messages came in at strange hours that made you suspicious. When you asked your partner about them, he said that it was a work thing that was unresolved before he left, so you felt silly at bringing negative energy into the trip and put it out of your head (betrayal blindness!). A few months after you returned, you learned that he was having an affair.

The fact that you went to Italy is real—that is the *episode* part. But when you look at the smiling photos and recall that your partner was having an affair at that time, it doesn't take away the episode (you *did* go to Italy), but it does change the *context*. The trip was real, the smiles were real, but the circumstances were not what you thought at the time those smiling photos were taken.

Then there is the *feeling* part. You believed you had gone to Italy with a loving partner, and you remember being happy that day. All of that was real. Your feelings are different as you look at the picture now, but the feelings on that day were based on what the story was at that time. However, as you look back, it's easy to feel like the entire relationship was a scam and that you were played. In the landscape of grief, we look back at all of this and doubt how we were feeling or even what was happening. Yes, you went to Italy. Yes, he was having an affair. No, you didn't know. Yes, he gaslighted you about it. Yes, you were happy. And yes, now you are devastated. Once again, holding space for multiple truths, painful as it is, is essential to moving through this process of grief.

## Grieving the Injustice

In my experience as a psychologist working with people recovering from narcissistic abuse, I have observed that it is the injustice raised by these relationships that has the most profound impact on healing. The process of grief can be facilitated by some sense of closure, fairness, or meaning—and none of that is happens when you are grieving these types of losses, especially in the acute phases of grief. The injustice can also feed the rumination process. Narcissistic people rarely genuinely apologize, face meaningful consequences for their behavior, take accountability or responsibility, or meaningfully acknowledge your pain. As a result, narcissistic relationships can feel deeply unjust—you get hurt and psychologically wrecked, and they get to move on with their lives with little insight into the damage they wrought. A core belief for you may be that life is fair, so when these relationships repeatedly show that it is not, it can be unsettling and uncomfortable. You may then blame yourself, which is a manifestation of the internal experience of injustice, and this can make it more difficult to let go and heal.[3]

Healing in the absence of justice is difficult. It may not hurt less, but it can feel easier to move forward if we know there were consequences or some form of accountability for someone who harmed us. To get past this sense of injustice means to focus on the path of differentiating from the narcissist. The longer you focus on the injustice, the longer you remain in the narcissistic person's abusive system and frame your healing around them (*If they suffer, I will feel better*). (But do show yourself some grace; it's common to get lost in revenge fantasies for a minute, and some survivors even find it helpful, just don't get stuck there.) Detaching and differentiating means that your healing takes primacy over their comeuppance. But it takes time to get there. Many of you may find that, for years, reading or seeing news stories and documentaries of injustices that aren't even related to you can bring up negative emotions. Cutting back on doom scrolling, avoiding social media (especially posts that feature the narcissistic person), and reading the news less can be useful. If you do read or watch something that leaves you with that familiar feeling of dread, give yourself a minute. Radical acceptance of the injustice is part of this process—*it is not fair, I cannot change it; I can, however, chart a different and authentic course forward and learn from this.* Be kind to yourself, take a breath or a rest, and recognize that with time your growth and healing will supplant this injustice, but for now it needs to be grieved.

## *The Importance of Therapy in Processing Grief*

I acknowledge that not everyone has access to a therapist who understands narcissistic abuse, or access to therapy period. A good therapist will allow you to talk out the grief and contextualize it as part of the process of letting go of a toxic relationship. Processing the losses incurred by these relationships is like releasing toxins and it can help you break the cycles of rumination. For many clients I have worked with, our grief work was about repeating the same stories over and over until one day they were able to get past them. Support groups are invaluable as well because they provide the opportunity to be with other people who get it and can validate your experience and reality.

Therapy is also important if the process of grief is developing into more pronounced issues with mental health and disruptions in social and occupational functioning. If you are finding that grief is negatively impacting caregiving/parenting, self-care, work, or daily functioning, mental health intervention is essential.

## *Grief Rituals*

When people die, rituals and practices such as funerals, wearing black, covering mirrors, periods of confinement, and other rites provide structure to the process of grief and may help us cope with loss. In the same way, some form of ritual to acknowledge your experience of loss can be part of your healing experience. These can be enacted alone or include other people. Rituals may help you manage the pain raised by the losses you have incurred in this relationship. Here are some ideas for rituals you can adapt and make your own.

- Have some sort of "funeral" or ceremony to release or let go of the relationship, regret, or other losses such as the loss of time, love, or safety. Consider burying something from the relationship to let it go or writing regrets on a rock and dropping it in a lake or ocean. Ensure this is intentional; feel yourself letting go of this person, their words and behaviors, or whatever else it is you perceived you lost.

- Have a "birthday" for yourself—for the new you that is emerging from this relationship. It doesn't have to be on your actual birthday, but should be some sort of commemoration of you coming into yourself. Whether you are leaving or staying, celebrate yourself as you put down the weight of the loss and regret and allow yourself to come out of the shadow of the toxic relationship. This may involve cake, candles, or an evening out with friends who get it.

- Switch up your space. If you are letting go of a narcissistic relationship in some way, changing up a space in your life can feel like a reinvention. This may involve painting the walls, getting rid of objects that remind you of the relationship, rearranging your office, or literally moving.

- Toss the items that remind you of the toxic relationships, people, or situations. The ticket stub from the concert where they wouldn't talk to you all night—toss it. The piece of jewelry you were gifted after finding out about an affair—sell it. The sweater a narcissistic parent gave you knowing it wouldn't fit you—donate it. Again, the key to these rituals is the intention and mindfulness that go along with them. This isn't about tossing the clothes in a bag and running them down to the donation center, but rather breathing and feeling the sensation of releasing these items and the feelings attached to them.

- Take back important places. You may feel you have "lost" your favorite places because they were ruined by a fight or a particularly cruel evening or some other invalidating experience. These can be restaurants, bars, beaches, parks, even entire cities. Take them back. Get some friends together, dress up, and fill these spaces with laughter and joy, or go with one trusted friend and take it slow. This can feel difficult to do alone, but let your laughter replace the abusive memories that may fill these special spaces.

- Create a grief box. Get a box—it can be a cigar box, shoebox, whatever works. Write down the losses from the narcissistic relationship on little pieces of paper—things you gave up, parts of yourself you lost, experiences you missed out on, hopes you sacrificed—and put them in the box. Consider it a strange coffin of sorts. Knowing these losses can be put somewhere can be a practice that intentionally pushes you to let them go and make space for your evolving sense of self.

THE GRIEF EXPERIENCE following narcissistic abuse is quite different from what we typically think of as grief, but that doesn't make it any less real or less painful. Envision grief as a tunnel you must navigate through as the first part of the healing process. However, we live in a world where narcissistic personalities proliferate, and grief, shame, self-doubt, and self-blame can be magnified if you fall into a toxic relationship again. How do you stop that from happening? Can you become more "narcissist resistant"?

# 7.

# Become More
# Narcissist Resistant

There is nothing like returning to a place
that remains unchanged to find the ways in
which you yourself have altered.

NELSON MANDELA

**L**in had endured a narcissistic mother as an only child. Years of trauma therapy allowed her to set better boundaries, and while her mother didn't always honor them, she felt less guilt about it. Lin's second marriage to a narcissistic man ended in divorce and an expensive and painful custody battle. She continued in therapy, joined a narcissistic abuse survivors support group, read books, watched videos, and even left a job with a narcissistic boss and took a new job with a lower salary but greater empathy, with a team who recognized her skills and contributions. Now that she was in a better job and her youngest child had moved on to college, she felt ambivalent about ever dating or getting into a new relationship.

Lin, however, was very lonely, and her friends were pressuring her to find someone: "Hurry up, Lin, we are all already too old to be dating. If you wait any longer you will end up alone." But so far, her online dating experience was like a tour through a swamp of narcissism. She ended up meeting someone at a professional convention. She found him attractive, they had similar interests, and he lived twenty minutes away. On her third date with him, she again listened to his professional struggles and his frustration with the world. The mix of loneliness, the desolation of online dating, his attractiveness, the excitement of meeting someone interesting, his monopolizing conversations, his grievances, their shared interests—Lin may have gotten her life in order, but once again she was in a relationship that was confusing. She'd worked so hard to heal from her narcissistic mother and her narcissistic marriage—and now what? Does healing from narcissistic abuse mean that she was going to end up spending the rest of her life alone? What should Lin do?

HEALING IS AN act of resistance, defiance, and rebellion. It requires a commitment to breaking out of long-standing cycles of self-blame and away from the existing narratives from the world at large. It means ending intergenerational cycles of trauma and toxic relationships. Healing is not just about getting past a broken heart, a toxic divorce, parental estrangement, or a narcissistic boss. It is about a shift in your psychology, worldview, and perceptions.

Healing is about discernment and spotting a gaslighter before they dismantle reality. It is about giving yourself permission to say "No," and not just to the narcissistic folks who already riddle your life, but *to the ones you still haven't met.* It means healthier boundaries all around: with the narcissistic folks, enablers, and even the healthy friends who may unintentionally be annexing more and more of your time. Healing means you see narcissistic and antagonistic patterns clearly and don't think that this time will be the exception. You learn to gracefully end the conversation and disengage. Radical acceptance becomes reflexive. You cut the trauma bonds and trust in your own subjective world— your thoughts, feelings, and experiences. You recognize that the more you engage with the narcissistic person, the more you end up disengaging from yourself. Healing is the attempt to extract lessons from the suffering, taking what you learned and paying it forward into the rest of your life.

As you attempt to recover and heal, the looming fear is: *What if this happens to me again?* The truth is it *will* happen again. The ubiquitous nature of the narcissistic personality style and the fact that society rewards it means that you will continue to encounter it—in potential partners, friends, colleagues, acquaintances, or parking-lot bullies. As you heal and collide with these patterns again, it can reactivate the fallout of the narcissistic abuse. The key to healing is to grow and flex the psychological muscle that helps you recognize these toxic people and patterns as they come up, and instead of trying to change them, you manage them. You listen to your instincts and establish protective boundaries.

This chapter is focused on helping you become more narcissist resistant. It will explain why your sympathetic nervous system is better than your rational mind at detecting narcissistic people. We will unpack the differences between going no contact or firewalling the narcissistic person, so that you can choose which method is best for your situation. Finally, it will include a blueprint for a twelve-month narcissism cleanse, a period where you embrace your own company, foster your autonomy, and become reacquainted (or acquainted!) with yourself.

## What Does Narcissist Resistance Look Like?

What does it mean to be narcissist resistant? It is to be knowledgeable, self-aware, self-forgiving, wise, courageous, discerning, rebellious, and realistic in your relationships. Think of it as a tunnel. The entry point to the tunnel is when you first meet a new person, the middle is when you are in the relationship or situation, and coming out the other side is the ending or distancing from the relationship. Narcissist resistance looks different depending on where you are in the tunnel. In the beginning, during the gatekeeping, getting acquainted, and discernment phase, narcissist resistance means taking the time to notice behavior that makes you uncomfortable. It means not getting caught up in the rhetoric of *Let me give them another chance* and instead trusting your instincts. Of course, this is harder than it sounds. Good gatekeeping is often thwarted by lifelong narratives that show up in thoughts like *Who do I think I am?* for holding a boundary or *Maybe I am asking too much* for simply wanting respect, or, despite knowing what constitutes unacceptable behavior, not feeling you have permission to acknowledge it and step aside.

When you have no clear plans of ending or leaving the relationship, the "middle of the tunnel" may be the most difficult place of resistance. During this time, it's essential to develop radical acceptance, avoid taking the bait, not fall for the future faking, and recognize the gaslighting when it happens. To limit the narcissistic person's impact, it also helps to not take responsibility for their bad behavior.

As you come out the other side of the tunnel, the liberation from the confusion and devaluation may still be complicated. Narcissism resistance at this phase means seeing the toxic patterns and behaviors clearly, catching yourself in the distortions of euphoric recall, steering clear of the enablers, and journaling the hell out of this relationship so you have a point of reference and cannot trick yourself with denial.

## Become Gaslight Resistant

Celine's fiancé was entitled, arrogant, and manipulative, but they had a long history—they traveled together, their families knew each other, they shared the same religion. She couldn't imagine anyone else. But their relationship had always been bumpy. Early on, her fiancé had been unfaithful, and when he was finally caught, he framed it as her not being supportive enough and he never really apologized. He also shamed her for not having enough faith, and even mobilized their religious community to talk to her about respect within marriage. Celine's self-doubt grew over the course of the relationship.

Despite the chronic invalidation of the relationship, Celine pursued a leadership position in her company, and much to her surprise, she got it. The job meant more money, but also a steep learning curve and more hours. Her fiancé, who was already very competitive, said, "You sure you can handle a job like that? Are they aware of how anxious you are?"

Celine held her ground. "Yes, I am. It will take a minute to get up to speed, but I love the job. I can do this."

Her fiancé then responded, "Okay, not sure you can plan a wedding and do all the other stuff you need to do if you are trying to learn a new job, and you are already so disorganized."

Celine stayed strong. "I am not worried, my mother is offering to help with the planning, and I actually think I will do better since I will be happier."

Her fiancé pushed further. "I don't know, seems like work is winning out here, and your career is the most important thing. I thought marriage was about our commitment to the divine. Maybe we should take a break while you figure that out . . ." Celine wondered, was she committed? Would she be sacrificing their relationship for a job? Aren't love and faith more important? Her mother and some friends and even people from their religious community weighed in and said, "Yikes, are you willing to be single again just because you want to work all the time?"

*Gaslighting* is a buzzword these days, and many people don't understand it. As we learned earlier, gaslighting is a form of emotional abuse that involves the gaslighter denying reality and dismantling a person's sense of self by denying their experiences, perceptions, emotions, and, ultimately, reality. Gaslighting isn't lying, nor is it just a difference of opinion. It's designed to confuse you and undermine your autonomy and sense of who you are. It is a process that is present in every narcissistic relationship I have witnessed, and it is one of the most harmful interpersonal dynamics. To become more narcissist resistant, you also need to become more gaslight resistant.

The best way to turn off the gaslights is to avoid them in the first place by owning your reality, recognizing it as reality, and not sacrificing your experience and perception in the process, even while acknowledging that someone can have a different experience from you. Resisting gaslighting early on in a new relationship can result in the gaslighter becoming frustrated and moving on to a target they can more easily dominate. If you're currently in a relationship with a narcissistic person, your resistance may result in the person escalating the gaslighting and rage. But simply knowing what gaslighting looks like can help you know when it's happening and remain aware of your subjective reality instead of capitulating or falling into self-blame and self-doubt.

If you have been or are currently in a narcissistic relationship, you have been told how you feel, whether you are hungry or not, or even that "You can't be cold, this room is warm enough." If you endure this long enough, you may no longer trust your own assessment of how you feel or your preferences. Over the years, many clients have said to me, "I don't even know what kind of TV show I like or what my favorite food is anymore." Checking in daily with yourself can help you start to trust your reality and experience, and it can be part of a mindfulness routine. Ask yourself questions out loud: *How do I feel? How was my day? How is my energy level right now?* Try to do this three times a day. When possible, talk through your routines: getting ready in the morning, preparing a meal, driving to work, or doing something for your job. Speaking out loud helps you be more in tune with your reality and get off autopilot. Gaslighting is only possible when you are not firmly in touch with what you know about yourself.

Time and time again, the research shows that healthy close relationships are one of the prime happiness-promoting elements of a well-lived life. When you are navigating narcissistic relationships, healthy feels far away. You need gaslight-free zones where you can share, be validated, live in a shared experience of reality, and feel accepted, seen, and heard. These spaces can include friends, colleagues, a therapist, safe family members, or support groups—people who hear you, hold space for you, and *do not* gaslight you. Simply one conversation with a respectful, reality-reflecting person can be more restorative than you can imagine.

The corollary to this is to be willing to disengage from people and systems that do gaslight you. You can't walk away from all the toxic or invalidating spaces in your life, but you can engage less. Think of a situation in which you are talking with someone, maybe sharing an experience or a feeling, and the other person retorts with something along the lines of "You have no right to feel that way. I think you twist everything and make it bigger than it should be." This is a wonderful opportunity to disengage and hold your ground, even if you are feeling a little doubtful.

Try saying something like "It's how I feel." And then slowly start physically distancing. No yelling, no door slamming, no engagement. Just put a bow on it, confirm that it is how you feel, and slowly get up. The other person will likely still verbally come at you—gaslighters don't just stop—but just a few episodes of disengaging will help you hone this skill. It's normal to feel sick as this happens and completely depleted when you walk away. Get yourself to a place you can be alone to sit, breathe, and recalibrate.

While disengaging means distancing and cutting out of dead-end and harmful conversations, you can also slowly start to quit a habit that plagues everyone in narcissistic relationships: stopping the "sorrys." Think of how often you have apologized in these relationships—*I'm sorry for always nagging*; *I'm sorry I didn't say that the right way*. Over time, it becomes reflexive, but start paying attention whenever it happens. Over-apologizing is usually a response to gaslighting, and it causes you to gaslight yourself. Find another way to communicate without the apology. Apologies are for when you do something wrong. Having a feeling, an experience, or not agreeing with someone's distortion of your reality is not "wrong." Imagine your partner is supposed to drive you to an appointment at eleven a.m. They insist it is at twelve p.m. and tell you that you are disorganized and always remember stuff wrong. You call the medical office and put the receptionist on speaker who confirms, yes, it is at eleven. They may then say, "Oh great, now I have to move my morning around to make this work," and you might say, "I am sorry." Instead, your response could be, "Thank you for getting me to the appointment." No apology, no further engagement. You also need to prepare for them to be no longer willing to drive you. Being narcissist resistant means forever maintaining realistic expectations and girding for the inconveniences that will follow.

You can also help other people catch their "sorrys." When you witness someone apologizing for something that needs no apology, remind them that there is no need. (All of my clients experiencing narcissistic abuse will apologize when they cry, and that's when we often begin dismantling the cycle of unwarranted apologies.) This awareness about other people's over-apologizing makes you more aware of these patterns in yourself.

It can be useful to keep a gaslighting journal. Writing down instances of gaslighting, big or small, helps you realize how often it occurs and with whom, and it can help you feel less "crazy." For example: *doubted the date of my sister's wedding and told me I always tell her the wrong dates*; *keeps telling me I am paranoid and denies it when I question why he is staying so late at work and his colleagues are not*; *raised his voice and told me I had the passport in my bag when he had put it in his*; *said that his management team's inaccurate report was well done.* Also consider making a note of the kinds of conversations or topics that are more likely to result in gaslighting in the narcissistic relationships in your life.

## Your Inner Critic Is Trying to Tell You Something

Your inner critic may be playing an endless loop of thoughts—you are lazy, nobody likes you, you are worthless, stop trying to be more than you are, just give up—but it'd be a mistake to just write it off as a bug in your brain.[1] Think of your inner critic as a part of you that may be trying to protect you from failing or getting hurt (not in a nice way, of course). For instance, you may listen to your inner critic and not apply for the new job and, voilà, you won't get hurt if you don't get it.

As you strive to heal, your inner critic may feel more like your inner tormentor, but when you can recognize its overzealous and misplaced protector role, you may stop experiencing it as an identity (*I am a lazy person*) and receive it as an internalized attempt to avoid more pain (*Ah, this inner voice may be trying to motivate me and I am afraid of failing*). In a sad sort of way, your inner critic is trying to get ahead of the narcissistic voices in your life and attack you before they can, though it also blocks you from actually seeing yourself clearly and may foster self-blame. Talk to your inner critic. If you have some privacy, do it out loud: "Hey, inner critic, I get it, you are trying to protect me, and thank you, but I am an adult, I got this." It may sound silly, but once you start reframing this voice as the way your psyche is trying to keep you safe in the narcissistic relationship, you may start being kinder to yourself.

## Understanding Your Sympathetic Nervous System

Christina felt almost light-headed in her relationship, like she was eternally on a carnival ride. She would find her heart beating a little faster when she got a text from her wife saying that she was on her way home. When Christina's wife came home after having a good day and was loving and warm, Christina would relax, almost forgetting how bad things could get. However, she could anticipate the tightening in her wife's shoulders when she would reach into the refrigerator and realize her favorite wine was not there. Christina would feel a lump in her throat and start sweating. Two weeks into a new job, as she met with a rather abrupt and entitled new colleague, Christina again felt that lump in her throat, her heart beat faster, and there was a tightness in her chest. It was a familiar feeling. The next few weeks showed that this colleague was brutally unkind and competitive, and Christina marveled at how her body was almost like an early detection system.

The fallout of narcissistic abuse, like other forms of relational trauma, is most potently held in your body. Close your eyes and envision your most painful narcissistic relationship. As you breathe and reflect on this relationship, pay attention to where these feelings are experienced in your body and what they are. Those bodily sensations will often be experienced when you encounter people with toxic behaviors that may be reminiscent of the narcissistic relationships you have already experienced. These physical responses in the face of fear and threat are governed by your sympathetic nervous system (SNS).

Your sympathetic nervous system is your fight, flight, freeze, and fawn/submit system—the part of you that is mobilized during times of fear to make you safe. Most of you are familiar with the fight-or-flight response: the urge to either yell, fight back, or run away when threatened. When you experience something that your brain and body have recorded as a threat, your sympathetic nervous system kicks in and responds to this threat, and you may experience a racing heart, dry mouth, hyperventilation, or other physiological symptoms. It's a great system when the threat you are perceiving is a clear and present danger, like a snarling dog, a fire, or an attacker. The challenge is that stimuli that may not be an actual threat to life, like someone yelling or giving you the silent treatment, are also associated with fear, threat, and dread, and so your SNS kicks in. And while there may not be a life-or-death threat from interpersonal stimuli such as the narcissistic person pulling away after an argument, the perceived loss of love and attachment and the fears about how others will react are also primal stressors that are experienced as threats, so you have a physiological response. SNS responses are reflexive: you don't "choose" to have these responses; they are your quicksilver reactions to moments of danger and risk.

Early in your relationship you may have fought because you didn't understand what you were dealing with, but the fight response typically doesn't work well in a narcissistic relationship. You would have better luck punching a snarling tiger in the face than trying to win an argument with a narcissistic person. SNS responses are involuntary and aren't about what tactically works in a relationship. If your response to a threat is to fight, then your narcissistic relationship may feel and appear very volatile, and people around you may even view you as complicit because you are embroiled in chronic conflict with the narcissist.

The flight response looks like running away to escape the harm. Now, while you may not literally run away from a narcissistic person, some people may psychologically flee from a narcissistic person by ending the relationship or ghosting them. More commonly, you may also flee by distancing or dissociating from your emotions or from yourself while in the relationship (feeling a more narrow range of emotion, no longer expressing needs, feeling like you are watching this relationship happen to you without really being connected to it, numbing yourself through work, food, or alcohol). You may also mentally check out when the narcissistic person starts in on you. Ultimately over time, you not only start detaching from your sense of "being" in the world but also become disengaged from other healthier relationships, get easily distracted, and become emotionally constricted. Flight is a common safety response in survivors, and in many ways it's not just about fleeing the narcissist but also your feelings.

The other *F*, freeze, occurs when something threatening is coming at you and you can't find the right words to say, scream, or move your body.[2] In the face of someone who is dominating, bombastic, grandiose, arrogant, or critical, you may find yourself completely tongue-tied and awkward, and after the interaction think, *I wish I had said this* or *I wish I had done that.* The freeze response may have been something that happened to you during childhood if you had a particularly rageful narcissistic parent and flight or fight weren't possible (which they often are not). The freeze response can foster shame and self-blame, because you may feel as if you are partially responsible, have let yourself or others down, or are foolish or weak for not responding. Remember, you aren't *choosing* to freeze. Their behavior, not your natural response, is what is unacceptable.

The fourth *F* is the fawn response.[3] The fawn/submit response is a surrender of your needs in favor of winning over and staying connected to the threatening person, and it is especially conditioned in people who grew up in abusive childhood environments. It may look like nodding with wide eyes, smiling, or complimenting the narcissist when faced with their invalidating, contemptuous, dismissive, or rageful behavior. You may continue to try to win them over throughout the course of your relationship with them. This is an attempt to maintain an attachment in a psychologically unsafe situation. People who fawn will often experience a sense of shame as though they are somehow complicit or weak, which is a harmful characterization of what is an expectable response to threat and adversity. Some people may intentionally "fluff up" a narcissist to get something done or for some other need; fawning isn't that. Fawning is your reflexive response to the invalidation and discomfort raised by a narcissistic person and driven by a fundamental need for safety, attachment, and connection.

## Learning to Manage Your SNS

Enduring narcissistic abuse, especially during childhood, means feeling on edge most of the time. You may live in a state of chronic tension, waiting for the narcissistic person's explosive rage, manipulation, or threats of abandonment. This tension may persist even if you are out of the relationship. Unfortunately, remaining in a constant state of physiological arousal is terrible for your health and can culminate in "survivor" patterns that are designed to keep you safe but can cause harm over the long run: walking on eggshells, not expressing your needs, being distracted, feeling dysregulated, or even experiencing symptoms of panic.

So how do we manage these sympathetic nervous system reactions? By tapping into our *parasympathetic nervous system* (PNS). While the SNS controls our response to threat, the PNS oversees our state of relaxation, rest, and digestion. Making sure that our bodies receive the repair and rejuvenation they need is essential to counterweighing the effects of remaining in a sympathetically activated state, even when the narcissistic people are not around. Start with all the stress management stuff you have been reading about for years—deep breathing, nature, exercise, meditation, and anything that downregulates and relaxes you. I often push my clients to get enough sleep. Sleep is not always easy for most of us dealing with the fallout of narcissistic abuse, but even an intentional bedtime routine—brushing your teeth, washing up, doing some breathing, maybe reading something that feels good, turning off those devices—can not only feel like reparenting, which most of us need, but also become a daily practice of bringing yourself down and giving your system a chance to rest enough to face another day. Healing is a slow evolution of being in harmony with your body, understanding that your body has been trying to keep you safe all this time, and intentionally bringing some relaxation into your life.

Over the years, many survivors have said to me that when they heard the jingle of the narcissistic person's keys as they came to the door, they would have a series of physical reactions. Listen to your SNS. It's not always easy to do because this system is designed to mobilize us out of danger and not just hang out and cogitate, but when you feel it activate, stop and ask yourself *What is the threat?* You may gaslight or pathologize yourself (*I am just a nervous wreck*) but, in fact, your body is on and feeling the truth of the situation. Ask yourself *What is happening?* especially when meeting a new person. At a minimum, take these reactions as a sign to move slowly and pay attention. After being through a narcissistic relationship, you may find that experiences like criticism and rejection can bring up these reactions. Over time, you will recognize that critiques at work are not the same as the cruel rejection of a narcissistic parent or partner, but since the SNS doesn't know the difference, figuring out the actual threat can help you be more discerning.

The SNS communicates using your body, so connect with your body. When your pulse starts skyrocketing, find that pulse at your wrist, with a hand on your chest, or with a few fingers to your neck, and count the beats. Simply connecting to your body in a focused way can start bringing down your heart rate. You can even go a step further and give yourself a hug. That kind of physical comfort can be soothing. The fear response can also mean that you may start breathing in a shallow manner, which can escalate your sense of panic. In your calmer moments, practice some form of deep breathing. Pick a number: 5, 6, 7, or 8. Breathe in on that count, hold for that count, and slowly exhale for that count. Do it at red lights, at the top of the hour, or before you begin a meeting. Being a better breather can ground you. Placing a hand on your chest or your belly as you breathe and humming on the exhale can allow you to feel the vibration, connect your breath to your body, and ground you as well.

You can also ground yourself by intentionally placing your feet under you and feeling that sensation of connecting to the ground with your body or by visualizing different sensations, such as a breeze or water flowing through your hands.

Difficult conversations and the anticipation of having them can also set off a cascade of SNS reactions, so it can be helpful to role-play these conversations with a friend or therapist—just make sure that the friend or therapist can fully play the toxic dynamics so you can feel best prepared. And if it is possible, use notes to help guide you in the conversation. If your mind freezes, at least you will have your thoughts organized. I initially wasn't a believer in rehearsal and role-play until I started doing it with my own clients. We would prepare for divorce mediations, conversations with invalidating friends, and holiday dinners. Most found that our rehearsals (and I was able to faux-gaslight them well!) helped them not feel as shocked and surprised during the event. In fact, one woman said, "I had to stifle a chuckle when my husband did exactly what you said he would. When I wasn't surprised by his behavior, I was able to have the conversation from a less emotionally raw place."

Remember, our SNS responses reflect our histories. You may find your heart racing when a conflict arises in a group, when you witness someone being scapegoated in a meeting, or even when you see someone behaving badly in public (e.g., yelling at a server). Reflect on your narrative about any activating situations you are in and ask yourself the following questions: *What do I think will happen if I speak up? Is the person dangerous? Have they been invalidating in the past?* At those times, take a minute, breathe, and connect your narrative to your SNS and the perception of threat.

# How Can I Support Someone Experiencing Narcissistic Abuse?

Some of us know people who are also experiencing or are currently healing from narcissistic abuse, and we may be wondering what we can do to support them. The good news is that being there for others can actually facilitate your healing, though there are a few things to keep in mind.

It is not useful to approach someone experiencing narcissistic abuse and tell them that the person who is the source of their pain is narcissistic. It's not that simple and can often result in someone who doesn't understand what narcissism is becoming defensive and justifying their relationship even more. Instead, let them know you are there for them, encourage therapy as a useful tool for everyone (and if you are in therapy, perhaps disclose that it has been helpful for you), and check in with them if you witness one of their difficult encounters. ("I just wanted to check in. How are you? I'm just worried after hearing that conversation the two of you had.") When you do this, be careful that there is no accusation as to the toxicity of the abusive person's behavior. Instead, you may plant a seed of doubt that could open someone's eyes a bit wider. Supporters should never force a survivor over to their point of view about a narcissistic situation, but rather should be there to validate their experience.

Cult expert Dr. Janja Lalich offers a technique to family members of those who have been pulled into cults, and it may also be helpful when supporting someone who is in the throes of a narcissistic relationship. She suggests sharing memories of a happier time with them: "Remember how much you loved our fishing trips?" "Do you recall those amazing paintings you used to make?" This is a slow process but bringing a person into happier times or reminding them of joys and skills they may have forgotten can also be quite useful for getting them to open up.

Finally, an article by Jancee Dunn in *The New York Times* gave the simple but elegant guidance of asking someone what they need most: to be "helped, heard, or hugged."⁴ Sometimes there is no help to offer, but listening, validation, and a gentle smile go further than you think.

## Building Resistance

So far, we've learned how to recognize when we're experiencing gaslighting or are having a sympathetic nervous system response to a narcissistic person. We've learned what our inner critic is trying to tell us about our insecurities and deepest desires, to breathe and connect with ourselves, and to recognize that these strong reactions relate to a perception of threat that we can revisit and reframe. Your narcissistic radar is on high alert. How do you avoid being further sucked into a narcissistic person's web or letting a new narcissistic person into your life?

## *Go No Contact*

The more contact you have with a narcissistic person, the worse you feel. Going no contact is exactly what it sounds like: no longer reaching out to them, but even more important, no longer responding to them. You don't take their calls, you don't reply to their text messages, you don't talk to them. You disappear from their lives. At the more extreme end, you may also block their number, email, or social media accounts, or you may even have a protective element like a restraining order. No contact is a heavy-handed but effective tool to end toxic cycles.

When you go no contact, be prepared for a toxic dance. The narcissistic person will alternate between angry and aggressive communication and hoovering manipulation, especially if you slip up and respond or if they realize that their anger isn't working. If you don't respond to hoovering, the rage communication will begin again. The amount of communication may also increase if you haven't blocked them—be prepared for dozens if not hundreds of texts, emails, and phone calls that grow angrier. They may threaten to blackmail you, or hire an attorney, or tell other people terrible things about you. They will double down over time, and the threats may become more unsettling until you contact them. They may even stalk you. If the stalking escalates—they drive by your home, the number of messages is overwhelming, they reach out to your workplace—consider consulting with an attorney or local domestic violence agency to learn whether legal remedies may be available to you (and sadly, there are fewer than you think—our current systems favor stalker-y behavior over survivor protection).

Unfortunately, going no contact is not viable in most situations and can sometimes create more distress. For instance, no contact doesn't work if you are co-parenting minor children, or in most workplaces, and it doesn't always work in family systems if you want access to some family members or have children who are invested in cousins or grandparents. For some of us, the overwhelming sense of disloyalty and grief at ceasing communication can be too uncomfortable or may cause pain for others in your life who matter to you. Ultimately, lots of stars need to align for you to be able to consider going no contact and then being able to stick to it.

## When You Have to Break No Contact

This is a sort of warning on no contact: You may approach it so zealously that it can result in distress. This can become an issue most pointedly in families. There may be a sense of pride in going multiple years with no contact and then life happens—someone gets sick or there is a death or some other major event that requires you to re-engage with the narcissistic person or system. If you have gone no contact, you may agonize about how to proceed and find yourself in a catch-22 of feeling uncomfortable maintaining no contact under the new circumstances but also afraid that breaking no contact means that you are giving in or the narcissist "wins." Keep in mind that all those years of no contact helped you heal; however, there also must be room for being circumspect, flexible, and accounting for the context. You may need to frame breaking no contact around bigger issues, including potential regrets for yourself if you remain no contact (e.g., a dying family member) and wanting to support people you do care about.

## Firewalling

I was once talking with a person who worked in the tech industry about narcissistic relationships, and they brilliantly suggested that maybe we need firewalls against narcissistic people. *Firewalling* is a term used in computing to refer to the safeguards that are placed on a network or computer to protect it from malware coming in, as well as requiring passwords to secure what information you give out. In narcissistic relationships, firewalling means having strong boundaries and walls around you so abusive "malware" doesn't come in and using your discernment when sharing vulnerable information that could come back and harm you.

First, let's talk about data coming in, because frankly that is where the most harm lies. Narcissistic people get in, gaslight you, mess with your head, and leave you with self-doubt. You can protect yourself with your knowledge about narcissism and narcissistic abuse. Here is where recognition and radical acceptance can come together with setting boundaries and moving slowly so you don't let someone with these patterns into your life too quickly. This is important because, many times, charming narcissistic people—like the innocuous-looking files you may download— look just like anyone else and may even be more enticing. In order to firewall and protect yourself, move slowly and learn the unhealthy behaviors that should make you doubt whether you need to "download" this person.

Now what about your data going out? This is also part of fire-wall protection—when you don't want to give away important information. You want to be able to share information about yourself, be vulnerable, and open up to other people, but this can be dangerous with people who may weaponize this information or are likely to shame or mock you. I wish we had a pop-up window that warned us right before we were about to share vulnerable information with the wrong person ("Are you sure you want to share your greatest fear?") so we could check ourselves before we move forward.

## Gatekeeping

Someone I once spoke with told me that one of the biggest leaps in her healing was that whenever possible, she stopped attending social and work events that she knew would put her in proximity to toxic people and situations. It was a game changer for her. She said it felt like self-care and that not only had she safeguarded herself from a variety of unhealthy situations, but she was also no longer doing things that she felt she "had" to do to earn the regard of narcissistic people, and she felt more free and whole as a result. For all the effort people make to be careful about what they eat, wear, and drink, being discerning about who you allow into your life seems like the most important decision of all. Being discerning means being comfortable with sometimes saying no to invitations that will place you in proximity to toxic people, refusing to work in places where narcissistic people run roughshod, leaving family events or conversations where you are being baited, saying no to a second date, and perfecting your Mona Lisa smile so you can be polite and gently exit.

## *Understanding the Enablers*

To become more narcissist resistant, you need to understand the chorus of voices that supports and emboldens them—the enablers. These are the people in your midst who keep cutting the narcissistic person slack: families or religious communities who may shame you for not forgiving the narcissist, a society at large that tells you that you can't "quit" your relationship or even call out bad behavior, people who minimize what you are experiencing or fall into tired explanations like "You aren't perfect, either," "They don't mean any harm," "I never had any problems with them," or, the ultimate enabler statement, "They did their best." Some of these folks may be what are sometimes called "flying monkeys"—enablers who will continue to overwhelm you with the narcissistic person's rhetoric, in essence "doing their bidding." Once other voices start excusing or signing off on the narcissistic person's behavior, it may undercut your instincts because you believe that everyone can't be wrong, so it must be you. You may believe that consensus is more meaningful than your subjective experience.

Imagine a narcissistic person who is gaslighting and baiting her sister. To push back and avoid the pain of these interactions, the narcissistically abused sibling sets a boundary and opts out of some family events. The narcissistic sibling then tells the family how sorry she is that her sister isn't coming around and that she is hurt by her, and behaves very nicely on group texts while being quite cruel one-on-one with her sister. What ends up happening is that the family rallies around the narcissistic sister because they just want the gatherings to happen, and when the sister who is being abused speaks out, the family characterizes her as the "problem" and says, "All your sister wants is for you to be a part of the family." Enablers are not necessarily narcissistic, and they may be people you retain in your life. However, to remain resistant to narcissistic relationships, you also have to develop an awareness of how others in your sphere may be giving the narcissistic person a free pass to maintain the status quo. Being discerning about the enablers is just as important as being discerning and aware of narcissistic patterns.

## The Twelve-Month Cleanse

I strongly recommend a one-year cleanse to anyone coming out of a narcissistically abusive relationship, during which you remain single. You may be thinking, "*What?* I have been so lonely for so long. I want to date, fall in love, have sex." I get it, but a narcissistic relationship hijacks you. A period of time alone—officially alone—is a time when you can get acquainted with yourself. After years of having your interests and preferences invalidated, walking on eggshells, and calibrating to the needs of someone else, you need time to reorient, to come home to yourself. As tempting as a rebound relationship, attention, touch, and feeling cherished can be, the risk of quickly subjugating your needs to a new partner—and succumbing to trauma-bonded patterns once again—is just too great during this time (and remember, transitions are a period of high risk for getting into a narcissistic relationship).

During this cleanse period, you become familiarized with your own rhythms, preferences, and needs and you begin to unearth your authentic self. You learn to be alone and in the unfamiliar space of not having to give in to the reality of another person. One of the only ways to dismantle the trauma bonds is to tolerate the discomfort of the unfamiliar. During these twelve months, you can do things that scare you, feed you, and enthrall you. This is one year of walking through birthdays, holidays, and anniversary dates alone, of rewriting your narratives actively instead of substituting them with another person's, and of recognizing your capabilities. And when you feel you are slipping and can't do the twelve months, stop, and catch yourself. Think of the worst days in the narcissistic relationship and remember how much you wished you could have a break. Well, here it is. Lean into it and feel the joy of not being destabilized by the relationship. It can also help to keep turning to those "Biscuits in Bed" or "It's My Turn" lists as a reminder of what you gave up, big and small, and to start taking those experiences back.

The cleanse principles can be applied to narcissistic situations in a family or workplace as well. The year after you end or significantly distance yourself from any abusive narcissistic relationship, ensure you give yourself time and space to heal. This can be a period in your life when you nurture your preferences and start establishing new rituals and routines. Remember that 2:00 p.m. toxic staff meeting every Monday, or the humiliating Sunday dinners? Do something soothing or rewarding at those times so you can experience the contrast between what was and what can now be.

When you come out of the twelve months, you may be more willing to exert your preferences and standards, so if a new partner rolls up and invalidates what matters to you or contemptuously pushes back on your cat or your enjoyment of reality television or a job you love, you may be in a better position to calmly step back and this time say, "No thanks."

### *The Power of Solitude*

Finding solace in your solitude is a big part of healing from narcissistic abuse and becoming narcissist resistant. Before all of you extraverts out there push back, let's break this down a little. Many times, the reason narcissistic people have the power they do is that many of us are afraid of being alone. Histories of trauma bonding and the self-blame and confusion created by narcissistic abuse can make being alone very difficult. But solitude is a critical healing space. This isn't about isolation; it's about holding space for yourself and scaling back the excessive caregiving, one-sided compromise, and personal censorship for a minute. Solitude is where we find our voice.

I remember working with a woman who was white-knuckling it through the periods of solitude after a forty-year marriage to a narcissistic man until we framed them differently. She learned to reflect on how she wasn't feeling on edge anymore or let down because once again he didn't come home and the dinner she painstakingly made went to waste, and instead she reflected on the healing that came from being able to laugh out loud at a TV show she wanted to watch without feeling judged. The solitude was where she finally, at the age of sixty-five, learned who she was and what she liked because she wasn't putting another person's needs first. She recognized that her negative scripts around loneliness had been driven by friends and family who were raising alarm bells about her "growing old alone." But when she contrasted it with the alternative, she stopped framing being alone as loneliness.

To become narcissist resistant, it is important that you realize that you don't need the narcissistic person and are now reclaiming the parts of yourself lost to this relationship. Some of that entails becoming so comfortable with your solitude that you are more discerning about whom you spend your time with. After years of your identity being shaped by the narcissistic person, it can be terrifying to think of yourself without that reference point. But when solitude becomes a meaningful alternative, toxic people lose ground in your life.

## Be Okay with Good Enough

It has long been said that perfect is the enemy of good, and nowhere is that more true than in a narcissistic relationship. Perfectionism is a defense and coping strategy for most survivors of narcissistic abuse who hold the eternal hope that if you could get yourself or the relationship "just right" then everything would be better. It can also be a form of self-sabotage that can result in procrastination or delays (*I can't submit this unless it is perfect*).

When you try to be perfect, you are still playing to the narcissistic person's projections and grandiose expectations of perfection. Try for "good enough" instead, a place where you acknowledge that what you did is fine. The laundry may be done but not ironed, the office may be a mess but the bills got paid, the cupcakes can be store bought. Striving for good enough is a key to healing. Once you radically accept and realize that you are no longer trying to do the impossible—getting it "just right" for them—you can pull back on this unhealthy standard.

## Practice Mindfulness

When you are meeting new people, breathing and being present with yourself and in the moment allows you to be more discerning, because your mind isn't racing. Instead, you are experiencing what is unfolding in front of you. The more present you can make yourself, the better you are at discerning unhealthy patterns and protecting yourself.

Practicing mindfulness doesn't need to be fancy. Try a simple exercise where you identify the following (and keep a little snack around for the last step):

- 5 things you can see.

- 4 things you can hear.

- 3 things you can tactilely feel.

- 2 things you can smell (keep some aromatherapy oils or a scented candle with you if you want).

- 1 thing you can taste.

As you practice this exercise, breathe deeply. Doing this once a day slows your mind down and can be especially useful if you are having a difficult interaction or are coming out of one. You can draw upon this any time you need to recalibrate your focus.

Another mindfulness exercise that can ground you is describing a space you are in with tremendous detail. Pay attention to the light, the sounds, the smells, the objects—where they are, what they look like. This can be useful to do in real time as well if you are feeling uncomfortable in an interaction with a difficult person (and if you are stuck in a car with a raging narcissistic person, it can help to mindfully note the landscape outside the window).

### *Embrace Joy*

And then there is that thing called joy. Remember that? If you have been in a narcissistic relationship for long enough, you may not. Narcissistic relationships are joy stealers: while you are in them, happiness, safety, and comfort are lacking, and you expend most of your psychological energy on trying to avoid threats instead of noticing passing moments of beauty. Joy has to be on the narcissistic person's terms, and if they are having a bad day, so is everyone else. Allowing yourself to experience joy is a highly effective form of narcissist resistance. This isn't about artificial positivity or listing out what you are grateful for. It's about giving yourself permission to savor the bits of joy when they waft by.

For all the time you spent monitoring the narcissistic person's every mood and need, becoming narcissist resistant means training yourself to mine the periods of joy that come your way. Finding joy in a small moment—a bright-red sunset, a delicious ice-cream cone, your child singing a song, hummingbirds outside your window—and not having it stolen reminds you that there is life outside of this relationship, and more beauty and hope than you thought. Narcissist resistance means relishing those private moments of joy that you do not diminish by sharing them with the narcissistic person who may minimize or devalue them.

At first, you may experience "joy guilt" at the idea of doing something so forbidden as experiencing delight outside of the narcissistic relationship or after a lifetime of being shamed for laughter or happiness. Then there is "joy regret," where you realize how much you missed after so many years of trying to eke out safety and survival. Find those moments of wonderment, joy, and goodness, be in them, and allow them to envelop you. In time those stolen moments of joy can become a richly colored life again. Consider keeping a joy journal so you can jot down these daily experiences. The more you notice them, the more you have them.

Experiencing joy is an act of defiance if you are experiencing narcissistic abuse. It was taken away for so long that I can only liken it to letting in the light after you have been sleeping in the dark. You sort of squint for a minute, but as time goes on you become more practiced at seeking it out and reveling in it when you find it. It's like your soul waking up after a long sleep, and you find you are still capable of feeling the good and not just the heaviness of constant rumination.

## 10 WAYS TO BECOME MORE
## NARCISSIST RESISTANT

These tools may help you shut the gate on a future narcissist—and perhaps keep yourself sane with the ones who are already in your life.

1. Own your truth and reality. This is, in essence, gaslight repellent.

2. Stop falling for charisma and charm.

3. Don't get lost in superficial qualities such as intelligence or education—or appearance, wealth, and success.

4. Watch how they treat other people (and don't justify it).

5. Learn their tells—watch how they behave under conditions of stress, frustration, or disappointment.

6. Breathe and take things slowly.

7. Disengage from the enablers.

8. Stop giving multiple second chances.

9. Cultivate a healthier social network. If you have enough healthy people in your life, then you have one of the ultimate narcissist antidotes.

10. Start getting comfortable with taking the less popular path. Know that by being narcissist resistant, you may get called out for being judgmental, demanding, or even difficult.

---

NARCISSIST RESISTANCE IS about past, present, and future: to start chipping away at those trauma bonds, to be present so you can identify unhealthy behavior, and to make sure you don't keep going down the rabbit hole. It is about knowing who you are, standing firm when it comes to your reality, setting boundaries that feel authentic to you, entering new relationships slowly, and proceeding with caution. When your mind starts making excuses but your body feels funky, pay attention and erect those firewalls. You've been taught to devalue yourself for so long, you may not even realize how wonderful your own company is.

Disengaging from toxic relationships is essential, but what about the ones you are already in and don't intend to leave? How can we heal if we stay?

# 8.

# Heal and Grow When You Stay

*Things do not change; we change.*

HENRY DAVID THOREAU

auline has come a long way in radical acceptance. She is managing a narcissistic adult child, toughing out a job with a narcissistic manager because she needs the benefits, and assisting in the care of her narcissistic father and her kind but enabling mother who never left and is medically fragile. She is exhausted, recognizes she can't change any of it, and encounters a daily sense of grief. But she loves her new job, finds solace in being alone with her beloved dog, and enjoys working in her garden.

Pauline also feels that after what she has endured with past and current narcissistic relationships, it is too painful to go too deep with others too often. She dislikes that she envies other people's lives, their happy families, their loving relationships with their adult children, and their family vacations, and she has found that as much as she loves her friends, she doesn't socialize as much as she once did to protect herself. She got off social media a long time ago for the same reason. She knows she cannot step away from the narcissistic relationships she is stuck in, so she doesn't entertain that as an option and gets depleted when people give her superficial advice about how to manage these situations ("Honor yourself and leave!" "Just go no contact"). Her superpower is finding joy in small moments: a hike with her dog, a pretty sunset, a new plant flowering, a show to binge watch. She has found purpose and meaning in the things she can control, and finds that healing, acceptance, and grief are a daily calibration.

The reality is, many of us cannot easily exit narcissistic relationships, and almost all of us have at least one relationship we cannot leave. It's too simple to tell yourself, *This is toxic so I'm getting out.* Maybe you stay because of children, because you need the job, or because you can't imagine walking away from your parents or family, no matter how toxic they are. You may feel you need your sidekick, even though the friendship with the narcissistic person is taking a toll on you. No matter why you choose to stay, the rules of engagement will need to change if you hope to heal. It is untenable for you to stay on the premise that the relationship will change or that you just need to get over yourself and adjust to it. To stay means maintaining the relationship in a way that doesn't hurt you as much and still allows healing to happen.

There are different levels of staying. At the more intense level, you may opt to stay in long-term toxic marriages or committed relationships, remain in regular contact with narcissistic parents, or continue to work closely with antagonistic business partners or long-term colleagues. The long history of these relationships and their entangled nature means that not only is the narcissistic abuse more impactful but leaving is also more difficult. At the milder end of staying, you may end the relationship but opt to continue having contact. Ongoing contact may happen with difficult friends you don't see that often, invalidating colleagues you do not work closely with, or toxic extended family members you rarely visit. You may not cut ties with these people because they are embedded in larger social groups that matter to you, you don't have enough contact with them for it to make a difference (but when you do it is unpleasant), or you see no point in deliberately ending contact because it is not worth the conflict.

This chapter will break down how to balance on the razor's edge of staying or having some contact in any narcissistic relationship without enabling the narcissistic patterns or blaming yourself. It will provide some key techniques and hacks for survival. Healing and growing while you are still in the relationship require mindful awareness of what is happening, preparing for and recovering from your conversations with the narcissistic person, being intentional, and always maintaining realistic expectations to manage the carousel of disappointment and grief. The exercises in this chapter will help you remain true to yourself and your goals, sidestep conflict, and construct workarounds while not allowing the invalidation of the relationship to clip your wings.

The primary challenge of healing while staying in the toxic situation is that narcissistic people don't really want you to heal. It's not that they care about your healing per se, but rather that your healing means they get less supply. Your healing means that you are experiencing yourself separate from them, which defies their expectation for domination and control. Narcissistic relationships are like sandbags on your hot-air balloon: as you try to fly, they attempt to keep you stuck on the ground. This chapter will teach you how to cut the ropes on those sandbags. It may look like you are still in the relationship with the narcissistic person, but at least your spirit can rise.

## Stop Shaming Yourself for Staying

It's easy to feel that by staying in the narcissistic relationship, or even just remaining in contact with the narcissistic person or people, you are doing something "wrong." But your reasons are yours, and these relationships entail enough shaming that continuing to invalidate yourself because you stay can impair the process of healing.

You may have stayed because you hope that your relationship will change or that a string of good days is a sign that the tide has shifted.

You may stay because you are fearful about being alone or growing old alone or you feel pity and guilt for leaving the narcissistic person to care for themselves, a dynamic that may be quite pronounced in relationships with vulnerable narcissistic people.

All of us are naturally drawn to the familiar, and even if it is toxic, there are routines and a sense of familiarity in your narcissistic relationship that can feel comforting.

You may stay for practical factors, including children, money, and housing.

You may stay because of cultural pressures, a sense of duty and obligation, and biases against divorce, familial estrangement, or relationship dissolution.

You may stay in a narcissistic relationship because limitations of systems that are in place—family courts, human-resource systems, or existing civil and criminal justice structures—mean that you have little recourse, and leaving can put you at even greater risk. This risk is magnified if you have less societal power because of factors including ethnicity, gender, sexuality, or social class.

Staying is a choice and seeing it that way is powerful. There is a reason for your choice. Dig into it and be mindful about the way you choose to stay. If it's for children, then be fully present with them, infusing their lives with empathy and emotional awareness, which are necessary for a child who has a narcissistic parent. If it's a toxic workplace, remain aware of what can be derived from the job, such as connections, technical skills, benefits, or retirement plans. Being shrewd can leave you feeling less passive and more strategic, maximizing what you can get from the situation. You may even try to use evenings and weekends to develop further training or a side gig that may be more enjoyable. If you are going to stay in a narcissistic situation, you already have to manage the ongoing narcissistic abuse. Don't add your own self-judgment to that.

# Barriers to Healing

Healing isn't about leaving—leaving is just a brick in the healing wall. But trying to heal while staying in a narcissistic relationship can feel like swimming against the current. You may think that if you do stay in the relationship or maintain contact with the narcissistic person, one day you may get so healthy that you will have to leave. You may also fear that healing could provide fuel to your family's gaslighted assertion that "Hey, your childhood wasn't that bad, look how well you are doing." If you keep getting better, you may start to find that you no longer fit into a narcissistic system, and staying can feel very disconnected. Your healing could be blocked by cognitive dissonance, with you justifying uncomfortable truths to avoid the tension of inconsistency (instead of "I am staying with an angry partner in an angry marriage," it is easier to say, "He is angry because he is having a tough time at work"). The version of you who justifies the relationship fits better into the dysfunctional relationship than the you that clearly sees it. All of this may create a sort of subconscious resistance to healing.

The truth is, *healing is more important than leaving.* You can still heal and not make the massive leap of leaving the relationship, disrupting contact, or upending your life. Healing is about taking back your power, even if you do stay. As you change, become more gaslight resistant, find your voice, and stop subscribing to their version of reality, the narcissistic folks may become less focused on you. You are only interesting as a source of supply, a prop, or a punching bag. Once you are no longer serving those roles, they may pack it in, disengage, or no longer want you around. Be prepared for that. This can be frightening as well, and your own fears of abandonment can put you at risk of wanting to put the brakes on your healing and individuation so the relationship can sustain.

## *I Hate to Admit This, but I Still Love Them*

We do not talk about this enough, with the general sense being this narcissistic relationship is unhealthy—you have to get out! But love and attachment are powerful forces and may still be very present for you. No matter how treacherous, hurtful, and painful your narcissistic relationship has been, you may still love the narcissistic person in your life and not feel ready to step away. I have had many a survivor say to me, "I wish I hated him, this would be so much easier . . ." You may sort through the trauma bonds and do the work but still recognize that you have loving feelings for the narcissistic person, and you may feel ashamed, heartbroken, or foolish. Healing means not judging your feelings. There are no mistakes in this process, just lessons. Do not shame yourself for it, it's normal, and no, it's not just the trauma bond—it may be very real for you. Healing from these relationships is about pushing back from the black-and-white thinking and embracing the complicated gray.

You may believe that the healing path forward is to see the narcissistic person as all bad, but that may require lying to yourself, which won't work. It's okay to love them. In fact, it may help you feel more authentic to recognize the simultaneous complexity of your emotions and the relationship history while loving a narcissistic person. Remember those multiple truths? Love is where that shows up most strongly—*They gaslight me, they manipulate me, we have a history, I love them, I wish it was different.* This intricate balancing act requires you to catch your breath on the good days but not let down your guard or burn your umbrellas, and to be honest with yourself about your feelings. It is not easy but it is possible, and nobody—not me, not anyone—can tell you to stop loving someone. You have your reasons for staying or remaining in contact, and the good days may reinforce that. Just don't let those days trick you into seeing this relationship or behavior in an unrealistic manner, which starts the cycle of hurt and disappointment again.

## What Will Staying Do to Me— and What Do I Do about It?

Healing is possible regardless of whether you leave the narcissistic relationship or not. However, and I cannot sugarcoat this, living with or regularly interacting with a narcissistic person is like living with a person who smokes cigarettes. Even if you have air filters, open the windows, and keep the house clean, you will still get a little sick over time.

If you stay, in most cases, there is no way to fully "work it out" with a narcissistic person. There will always be workarounds, minefields, and tension. It will never be easy. The person will not change, and your body and mind will not adjust to their impact on you. It's important for you to know these limits because if you don't, you can once again fall into the patterns of self-blame and think, "Oh, great, I can't even heal right." You are doing just fine. It's a new status quo: the narcissistic relationship remains the same; you are the one who is changing.

Remaining in a narcissistic relationship requires awareness, clear expectations, and self-compassion. Let's explore what this looks like.

## Depleted Bandwidth

Once you see and accept the narcissistic person for who they are, you may find yourself having to manage the situations created by their behavior: hurt children, angry family members, frustrated colleagues, upended plans. All of this depletes your bandwidth. Simultaneously, you may have to engage in behaviors like appeasing and avoiding: *I can't mention this*; *I won't tell them I had this good thing happen*; *I can't let them know we have to fix this mistake.*

Your bandwidth also gets depleted by scarcity,[1] and for years you have been living without compassion, respect, empathy, or balance in at least one primary relationship. Under conditions of scarcity, you are trying to survive and focus on short-term needs. If food is scarce and you are hungry, your entire focus goes to food; you aren't thinking about your process of individuation or life goals. A very similar process happens when you are in a narcissistic relationship: healthy emotional behavior and mutual regard are scarce and every day becomes about trying to get through, which makes it difficult to focus on higher-order growth or other relationships and may also culminate in burnout and illness.

To replenish your bandwidth, you need to engage in what I term *realistic self-care*. This isn't spas and massages and positive affirmations; this is recognizing when you are feeling depleted—when you have fatigue, brain fog, physical exhaustion, self-doubt, difficulty making decisions—and then giving yourself a minute. It may mean that you put down your email for a while, order in for dinner, take a walk, go to bed early, let the dishes sit in the sink, or call a friend. It also means addressing that scarcity—turning to spaces in your life where there is empathy, rationality, and kindness. Receiving those things can give you enough bandwidth to keep going. The temptation while staying in these relationships is to keep pushing through it because that is what you have always done. Take a moment, breathe, recalibrate, and recognize your experience.

### Not Feeling Like the Same Person

You may not like who you become with the narcissistic person or what staying does to you. Your daily thoughts can be uncomfortable. You may find yourself envying others whose lives aren't riddled with narcissistic people—people who are in happy marriages, or who have nice parents, or who work in collaborative workplaces. You may experience empathy fatigue or become numb. You may think mean or vindictive thoughts that are not your norm, such as wishing the narcissistic person were dead or that their business deal falls apart. These feelings are at odds with your self-concept as a decent human being.

First, it is crucial to recognize that these relationships require you to reshape your identity to survive, or even that your identity was shaped by these relationships in the first place. Then, to work on pulling back on the self-judgment, return to the idea of multiple truths. You can be happy for a friend and also envy them, and in your safest relationships or in a space like therapy, you may even consider exploring these feelings. The word *should* is dangerous (I *should* be happy for my sister's nice marriage; I *should* be happy my friend has such a close-knit family; I *should* not wish ill on someone else). These *should*s may be aspirational but none of us are perfect, and these are normal feelings. Catch your *should-ing*, recognize that it comes from a place of craving your own sense of normal and healthy, and practice self-kindness.

## Being Mean to Yourself

If you choose to stay, reflect on how you talk to yourself and the ways you view yourself. When you stay, you are staying in something in which you are devalued, so valuing yourself and healing are not consistent with staying and may even be mocked by the narcissistic person and others in your system. You may find that you are meaner to yourself than the narcissistic person is. Sadly, being mean to yourself is a way to make the pieces fit—you sustain the idea that you are "bad," reinforced by their treatment of you, and your self-talk mirrors that.

This exercise is a cold splash of water in your face, with the goal of learning to talk to yourself differently and treat yourself with kindness and nurturance. Find a picture of yourself as a small child and, just one time, imagine telling that little you that you are foolish, or too sensitive, or damaged. This will not be easy to say to an image of a small child. That little you is the same spirit as current you—when you speak badly to yourself now, it's as though you are speaking to that child (and may also be the way that child was spoken to all those years ago). When you look at a picture of you as a child, it may be more natural to muster up compassion for yourself, so when those self-deprecating words come up in you, please look at that picture. The way you talk to yourself shapes your reality, and when you tell yourself you are damaged or stupid, you live into that identity. Catch yourself when you do this and keep that picture of little you on your phone and at easy access. The narcissistic people will still invalidate you, but it's time for you to learn a new vocabulary and stop doing their dirty work for them.

## How Do You Stay?

If you cannot leave a narcissistic relationship or don't want to distance fully, how do you maintain it in a way that protects you from the impact of narcissistic abuse and still heal? There are several techniques and rituals that can help you navigate this complicated, toxic relationship so that you can heal and grow despite the ongoing narcissistic relationship in your life.

## Set Boundaries

Setting boundaries sounds like a good idea in principle—"Just set boundaries!"—but what does it really mean? It's about figuring out what you are comfortable with and setting limits in a relationship accordingly—and after years of enduring narcissistic abuse, you may not even be sure what is okay anymore. In a healthy relationship you can set boundaries, and when someone violates your boundaries, you can communicate and, gradually, they will acknowledge and shift the behavior. Boundaries in narcissistic relationships are an exercise in hypocrisy. While narcissistic people will expect you to honor their boundaries, they will not respect yours. But if you are going to remain in one of these relationships, boundaries are necessary, and you cannot set them overnight. Boundaries are meant to bring safety, something that is lacking in narcissistic relationships. Setting boundaries is paradoxical, a new and healthier safety behavior that in the short term can leave us feeling uneasy.

The key is to remember that boundaries are an inside job. It becomes less about you waiting for the narcissistic person to honor a boundary and more about you setting one for yourself that you can honor. This is about knowing what qualifies as acceptable to you. It is a slow process, gradually disengaging from sharing important things about yourself and avoiding sharing feelings, emotions, aspirations, or negative moods with the narcissistic person. You also need to be clear on your nonnegotiable boundaries. For some people it's cheating; for others it's physical violence. If the narcissistic person crosses the nonnegotiable line, you may feel empowered to set more clear boundaries or even get out. However, in many moderate narcissistic relationships, that clear boundary may not get crossed. There may not be the "big" breach (an affair, an arrest), but rather thousands of cumulative indignities. Setting boundaries under these more subtle circumstances is much more difficult.

In Mariana's marriage to a narcissistic husband, she had two "rules"—no cheating and no physical abuse—and she promised herself that if those rules were violated, she would walk. Ten years into the marriage, she learned he was unfaithful and left. Shortly thereafter, her mother died, she got sick, and he came back and promised it would never happen again (it did). The next time, she left for good.

After she moved out on her own and focused on friends and family, Mariana noticed patterns that had never registered before: friends who were disrespectful of her time, others who would expect her to watch their children at the last minute. It was a big first step to say "No" to her sister who called her with one hour's notice and asked her to run to the school to get her children—and then to have to tolerate her sister's accusations that Mariana never helped her, despite Mariana stepping in hundreds of times over the years. In another instance, she planned a weekend with an old friend, one who was prone to last-minute changes. When the old friend said she wanted to have her husband and a few of his friends join, Mariana said, "No, I had planned on this being a girls' weekend." She was genuinely shocked but heartened when her friend said, "Okay, thanks for letting me know. That's what we planned, and I am sorry I tried to change it." She'd first felt sick when she set a boundary with her friend, believing she would be angry or cancel the weekend, but Mariana had worked on recognizing her needs and valuing her time and pushed through and set the boundary. Protecting herself was a slow process, but she also recognized that a boundary slippage didn't automatically mean someone was narcissistic. While it was uncomfortable to set the boundary, she was realizing that it could happen without losing a relationship or facing unending rage.

Learning boundary setting as part of healing from narcissistic abuse means being clear on your fears. Ask yourself, *What am I afraid of if I were to set a boundary?* Anger, the relationship ending, guilt, the silent treatment? I have had numerous clients be completely clear on what their boundaries were, but the fear of being shamed or raged at for setting the boundaries was too overwhelming; for others it was the internal discomfort of guilt about setting a boundary and the fear that they hurt the other person's feelings or disappointed them. Understanding your fears may help you recognize the barriers instead of just assuming that you are bad at boundaries.

Boundary setting also involves your tolerances for the narcissistic person's reactivity. If the narcissistic person is very rageful, and that takes too much of a psychological toll on you, setting boundaries in those circumstances may feel impossible—and that is okay. If you want to work on healing, and you are going to stay, it can be helpful to evolve toward the stance of not caring what they think, though that sense of indifference may not be possible for all survivors. In narcissistic relationships, the best way to manage boundaries is to not engage, banter, spar, or take the bait.

Setting boundaries in your narcissistic situation may also be eye-opening for how you hold boundaries in your non-narcissistic relationships. Boundaries are often a lifelong struggle for survivors, and many of you may struggle with the fear of *If I set a boundary, I am afraid they will reject me or that they may get angry.* The truth is, they might. Setting boundaries becomes a revelation on what your relationships are made of—if you do "lose" someone or must contend with them becoming passive-aggressive or angry in the face of your boundary, this exposes some uncomfortable truths about these relationships. You may avoid setting boundaries if you are concerned about losing social support as you navigate this process of healing. However, pay attention to those uncomfortable truths that you do learn about others; this ties back to discernment, and perhaps a relationship you believed was "healthy" only worked because you had not set boundaries before.

Finally, work toward becoming resolute on your responses in the face of boundary violations and find your "No." With narcissistic people, boundary setting is not collaborative. You must be your own gatekeeper. Some folks assert that you must repeatedly set boundaries until the other person gets it. But when it comes to narcissistic relationships, that is not going to work. Waiting for a narcissistic person to finally get it and honor your boundary is like waiting for a submarine to show up at a bus stop. You will exhaust yourself if you keep setting boundaries expecting the narcissistic person to honor them and instead have them con- temptuously derided or simply not honored. Finding your "No" and recognizing that this is a process internal to you can trans- form boundary setting from a hopeless endeavor into a process of empowerment. Practice this in your healthier relationships as well, where you hopefully have successful experiences that allow you to see that your respectful relationships can grow and flour- ish while you express what you need.

## Low Contact

When Jessica figured out that her sister continued to spread un- founded gossip and rumors about her, even after Jessica repeat- edly asked her to stop, she had to find a different approach to the relationship. She never initiated any additional contact with her sister beyond family gatherings. Jessica got better at being able to ask her sister a few perfunctory questions about her children, the weather, and her home renovation, and then to step away and avoid further conversation. Radical acceptance meant that her sister's ongoing gossip still stung but no longer shocked, and low contact meant that she could maintain other important relation- ships within the family but avoid her sister's manipulative vortex.

Low contact means you show up for a few family dinners a year or only see the ex at children's soccer games. When you must converse, you stick to neutral topics like the weather or the new coffee shop in town. Low contact means you get out before the emotions start to flare. It is not as easy as it sounds because there can be baiting (the narcissistic person pokes at emotional issues that will get a rise out of you) and enabler pressures ("Oh come on, your brother isn't that bad," or "Stop being so cold, lighten up"). Low contact means holding your ground even when those sensitive topics or pressures surface. It is often a form of diplomacy, allowing family systems to keep running with you present, workplaces to continue operating, children to feel a little more comfortable, and friend groups to remain inclusive.

You have to pace your low contact—it doesn't mean the same amount of contact for everyone. For some people it means once a week, for others once a year. But low contact is also intentional: you have contact with the narcissistic people and enablers in settings and contexts that are comfortable or important to you (e.g., a child's performance); in order to be a supporter to people who matter to you; where escape is readily available, even if it is just a walk around the block; and at times when you feel you have the bandwidth to manage it or when you feel supported. You can have the superficial conversations and maintain a boundary, and you can extricate yourself when you start feeling uncomfortable. I have watched people use low contact to get through an adult child's wedding where the narcissistic ex was present, through funerals with multiple toxic family members, or at professional conventions where people would have to face up to former manipulative and narcissistic colleagues. (Here is a good low-contact hack: whenever possible, avoid being alone in a car with a narcissistic person, because then you are stuck listening to them and can't easily disengage.)

## Gray Rock and Yellow Rock

If you've read about narcissistic abuse before, you may have encountered the term *gray rock*. Gray rocking entails being as un-
interesting as a gray rock, with minimal response, flat emotion,
and simple answers. It's as close to no contact with a narcissist as
you can be while still having some contact. In essence, you are no
longer a source of good narcissistic supply. Gray rocking can be
used in real-time conversation, texting, and emailing—no long
shares, just the facts, yes and no, and a sort of "copy that" acknowledgment that a message was received. Gray rocking is a
specifically disengaged form of communication—unemotional,
perfunctory, brief, unembellished, and not vulnerable.

Initially if you start gray rocking, the narcissistic person may
get angry, because you are no longer feeding their need for argu-
ments, drama, validation, and admiration. The challenge becomes whether you can hold on during their initial escalation.
They may push harder, bait you more, and multiply their insults.
You will likely hear things like "What are you doing? You think
you're too good to talk to me now? What, are you in therapy
now? Did your therapist tell you to be like that?" Be prepared for
it—you may need to white-knuckle through this experience. But
the beautiful day may arrive when they finally get bored and
check out. Of course, this may trigger your own fears of abandonment or being alone, but don't succumb—that's just the
trauma bonds talking.

However, gray rocking isn't always a viable option if you are,
for example, co-parenting with someone or are in a job where

some collegiality may be necessitated or are close to some family members but not others. In those cases, you can use yellow rocking. Yellow rocking takes gray rocking and infuses it with more emotion and manners. The term was devised by coach and advocate Tina Swithin,[2] who recognized that cold, clipped communication is not appropriate when people are co-parenting and doesn't present well in settings such as courts or mediation. Children need to see some degree of civility between their parents, and a child may perceive the rather curt nature of gray rocking to be unsettling. Yellow rocking is a way to be yourself while understanding the traps of narcissistic communication. Yellow rocking includes warmth, forces you to stay in the here and now (you don't bring up old topics and hurts), and is still concise. I find yellow rocking to be a far better compromise in nearly all situations, because to people looking in from the outside, it feels more "normal" and undercuts the narcissistic person's argument that you are being standoffish. However, you still aren't giving up boundaries or territory, you remain polite and civil, you can show up with warmth and emotion that reflect who you really are, and you maintain realistic expectations, which is always a win.

What does this look like? When Gloria's mother, knowing Gloria was struggling financially, asked her at the family dinner if she had remembered to congratulate her sister on her new home, Gloria flatly responded, "Yes" (gray rocking). If Gloria had responded with some warmth in her voice with, "Yes, I responded yesterday when I saw the picture of her house," that is yellow rocking.

## *Don't Go DEEP!*

Callie's demanding and demeaning brother recently cornered her and asked, "Callie, tell me why didn't you come to our anniversary party? It meant so much to my wife, and you didn't come until late when everything was done." Callie explained she had to pick up an extra hospital shift to pay some bills. "Everything is a play for sympathy for you, isn't it?" he responded.

Callie tried to explain. "It's my furnace breaking, then my car dying; it was one of those tough months."

"It's always about you; you knew about this for months. She asked you to come specially," her brother replied.

"I know. I am so happy for you guys. Twenty-five years is a big deal! How can I make this better? Is there anything I can do, maybe take you out for dinner?" said Callie. Her brother said, "No thanks, you'll probably cancel that, too," then stormed off. Callie cried and told her friend, "I am a terrible person. I said I would come, and I came late."

How often have you had a conversation go off the rails with a narcissistic person because you interacted with them and actually thought they were listening? Survival in a narcissistic relationship means throwing away your usual playbook for communication and not getting into a toxic dance with the narcissistic person. The *DEEP technique* gives you a quick way to remember what *not* to do if you want to protect yourself and avoid falling into the typical mess of being gaslighted, baited, and invalidated. It is a tool to avoid getting into frustrating conversations and blaming yourself, and also results in you cutting off their supply

and retaining your bandwidth. When you practice not going
DEEP you do *not*:

- Defend
- Engage
- Explain
- Personalize

*Don't defend.* Defending ourselves is the most common mistake
we make in the face of narcissistic behavior. When someone is
accusing you of something you did not do or saying something
about you that you do not agree with, it's natural to want to defend yourself. But remember the cardinal rule of narcissism: they
aren't listening. So avoid putting in a lot of effort, giving them
lots of narcissistic supply, and ending up in unnecessary argu-
ments where you keep defending yourself. Where this gets tricky
is when you hear that the narcissistic person is speaking badly
about you to others. At those times, it's better to talk with the
people hearing these things—and if anyone is willing to believe
the narcissistic person, that is more of a reflection on that person
than on you. If their behavior is defamatory and resulting in professional and financial damages, retain an attorney. Not defending
is not about being a doormat; it is about not wasting your energy
on a pointless endeavor.

*Don't explain.* Because narcissistic people are so manipulative,
you may feel compelled to explain yourself whenever they gaslight
you. The difficulty is that they will distort your explanation, and
before you know it, you will be defending yourself. You may

believe that if the narcissistic person could just hear your point of view, things would be better—but they won't. With clients, I have them explain themselves to me in writing or in session, however they want, just to get it out and put their energy on not explaining all of it to the narcissistic person. Through radical acceptance they recognized explaining themselves to the narcissist was like explaining why it was raining to the rain: the rain doesn't care and will keep falling.

*Don't engage.* Here is where the gray rocking, yellow rocking, and firewalling come into play. Avoid getting into a back-and-forth with the narcissistic person. If they are going on about something, you can briefly acknowledge it, then move on. Don't voluntarily get into conversations because more often than not, they will end badly. Do not offer feedback or guidance or a critique—let them fail on their own. It is so difficult to live with or have regular contact with someone and not meaningfully interact or engage with them, but one exercise that can be useful is to play out the entire conversation in your head before you ever open your mouth. If you know the narcissistic person well, then you will see that even your "imaginary" conversation will play out to an endgame of gaslighting, rage, or invalidation. This exercise may help you stop yourself before you engage.

*Don't personalize.* This can feel tough to abide by because the narcissistic person's behavior *feels* personal—and it is personal, because you are hurt and having real emotions. Many people think, *Maybe it is something about me, that is why they are treating me like this.* But remember: it's not you! You aren't the only one the narcissistic person is treating this way, though you may be getting the worst of it. They aren't noticing you enough to actually devalue you; they are devaluing your narcissistic supply because that is all you or anyone else is to them. This can be difficult for survivors to accept because you have spent years mired in self-blame and thinking of course it's you! It's not, and the more you can disconnect from that belief, the easier it becomes to disengage.

While not going DEEP is a useful technique, it isn't always a smooth path forward. A person shared with me that once she used this technique and disengaged, her narcissistic spouse pushed back saying that he had no interest in being in a "polite" relationship and behaved even more badly. The DEEP technique will often show you the uncomfortable truth of your narcissistic relationship, which can fuel radical acceptance, but it still stings, especially if you are going to stay.

## Stop Making It about Them

The biggest challenge when you remain in these relationships is that the narcissistic people are still in your life, and they remain a big part of your context. Before you understood narcissism, you lived in their service (*I hope they are okay with this, I would be doing so much better if they were just happy*). As you begin to radically accept that they won't change, you may still hitch your psychological cart to them (*I am going to heal just to show them they don't have power over me; I hope I get this promotion just to piss them off; I hope they find out I am dating someone new*).

Here's the problem: When you do this, the narcissistic person is still a frame of reference—you're healing to prove something to *them*, succeeding to get one over on *them*. Healing means getting them out of the scene completely. It means focusing on your growth, success, and happiness separate from them. As you heal, they become less central to your story. Healing while staying requires caring less about what happens to them. This is not easy; it takes lots of work to get here (yes, I am talking to you, fixers and rescuers). You may even feel that you are being cold as you become a little more detached. It may not be possible to ever become fully indifferent to a person who caused so much harm in your life, but you can strive to make your story independent of theirs.

### Address the Self-Blame

Addressing self-blame requires self-monitoring: being mindful and catching yourself in the words, thoughts, and behaviors that foster self-blame. Start by talking about what is happening in the relationship either in therapy or with trusted friends or family members. Sunlight is the great disinfectant—it can lift the shame and blame and help you escape these harmful cycles. Try to track how often you say, "I'm sorry," because the frequent apologies may represent self-talk that underlies self-blame.

Journaling is also a useful tool. I recommend using a sort of flowchart approach, like in the example below where the asterisks highlight the self-blame patterns and the arrows reflect the flow from a behavior, event, or words to the next response or re-action:

> My partner yelled at me because he forgot the files he was supposed to bring to work—he said that if I had kept the house more organized, he would have remembered them. → I apologized* and frantically began cleaning the house. I created a little area by the front door for things that need to be taken to work.* → He yelled at me for putting a table by the door. → I apologized* for doing that but didn't feel safe asking him what would work better. The next day, I wanted to get it right, so I reminded him to double-check and make sure he has everything.* He got mad at me for treating him like he is a fool.

Documenting these kinds of sequences can show you where, when, and how you fall into these cycles. You may still think, *What else could I have done?* The fact is, anything you did would have been met with narcissistic anger and blame deflection, so you can simply acknowledge that forgetting the files must have been a nuisance and let them keep raging. Next time you may be more clear and avoid the reinforcing loop of apologizing and trying to fix it. If you make a mistake, you can acknowledge it— *Whoops, I cooked that for too long* or *I took the wrong route*—without framing it as your failure as a human being.

## *Find Your True North*

Aldo had stopped taking the bait from his narcissistic mom about so many things; he was proud that he was able to disengage and the conversations were pretty sparse. One day, she started in on him again and he didn't engage, then she started making barbs about his children. "I see Mariela is putting on some weight, and at lunch today I told her that she should focus on the vegetables and maybe skip the pasta." Aldo couldn't bear it and said she was out of line and that Mariela had been struggling. He grabbed his coat, stormed out, and was called out by other family members for "overreacting." He was so angry at himself for taking her bait, but he refused to not protect his daughter, even if it reinforced his mother's narrative about him that he was an inattentive son and not as successful as his brother.

Unfortunately, the reality is you can't disengage all the time. What do you do if the narcissistic person starts saying terrible things about someone or something that matters to you? Your child? Your family? Your religious beliefs? Or if they share racist or intolerant beliefs? Or that you must engage about a very important issue like a financial or legal matter within your family that affects people you care about? It may not be realistic to not go DEEP at those times. The things in your life you are willing to take the fight for, to go into the tiger's cage for, are your *True North*. Your True North can be your child or a family member, your work, or an ideology or a belief. For example, as you remain in a relationship with a narcissistic co-parent who may mock or scapegoat your child, all of the disengagement may go out the window and you may take the fight and defend your child.

Engaging with the narcissist only when it is about your True North can have a greater impact, because now you aren't arguing with them over everything and you have conserved your bandwidth for the meaningful battles. But it also means that the narcissistic people will learn your True Norths and use them to bait you or to draw you out. If that happens, go back to not going DEEP, or once again take a hard look at the relationship.

### *Prepare and Release*

Dove found that just sitting in their car, breathing about five times, and reminding themselves to not engage or personalize before going in to see a particularly toxic colleague made a difference. After one more invalidating meeting (which Dove intentionally put at the end of the day), they met up with an old and comforting friend on the way home and made a plan to go to bed early that night.

If you exercise, odds are you stretch before workouts to prevent injury so your muscles are prepared for the exertion, then you cool down to allow your body to prevent cramping. This can be a framework for how to approach interactions with narcissistic people. Preparing and coming down from these interactions can stretch out your radical acceptance muscle and allow you to recover after. You never want to go into one of these interactions cold. Even if it is just for a moment, close your eyes, take a deep breath, and remind yourself to not go DEEP. Then you have your interaction.

On the back end is what I call the release. Build in time after your interactions with narcissistic people. It may simply be another breath in, perhaps leaning into the mantra of "It's not me." If it was a particularly difficult interaction, when possible, don't just roll into the next thing in your day. Take a break, take a walk, have a cup of tea, listen to some music, take a shower, talk to a friend, exercise, watch TV—something to recalibrate yourself, to come down from the difficult interaction, and to simply give your psyche a minute to reset.

## Never Call Them Out as a Narcissist

This should make sense in the wake of not going DEEP, but many of us who finally have a name for the patterns in the relationship want the narcissistic person to know that we know who they are. But *do not call them out.* You may be thinking, *Why do they get to get away with it? It's not fair!* None of this is fair. If you do engage with them about their narcissism, you will be served a large bowl of word salad with gaslighting dressing on the side. It will not change the situation, it may end with you being called out as narcissistic, there will inevitably be rage, and it won't change their behavior. Even if you leave a relationship, there is little point to doing this, but it is absolutely a nonstarter if you are going to stay. The framework of this personality style and how it works is meant to be a navigational tool for you; sharing it will not facilitate your healing whether you stay or go.

## *Get Therapy and Support*

If you stay or have ongoing contact with a narcissistic person in your life, therapy is crucial. If you are in therapy, it's important to understand that there are no miracles in this process. Ongoing narcissistic abuse takes a toll on your mental health and having a sounding board can be extremely helpful. Group therapy can also be useful, especially if it is focused on survivors of toxic relationships, and it is often more affordable. Support groups can be another useful adjunct but may not be a substitute for therapy because they are often peer-led, and may not have the presence of a trained mental health professional.

In most of the world, therapy is not readily or affordably accessible. This magnifies the effects of narcissistic abuse in people who have fewer social and economic resources. The lack of resources means often being more stuck in these relationships—moving out, hiring attorneys, paying for the costs of a divorce, or quitting a job are not an option. For people who lack sufficient financial resources, life is already quite stressful, and narcissistic abuse on top of that can feel insurmountable. The marginalization of those who are less resourced means that folks with less money are more likely to be gaslighted and invalidated by all kinds of systems, including health care, justice, and law enforcement. Even as I issue the recommendation for therapy throughout this book, I remain painfully aware that it is not an option available to many, if not most, people.

Many therapists are still learning about narcissistic abuse, so while it is optimal to find a therapist who specializes in it, finding one who is well versed in narcissism and antagonistic personality styles, trauma, or domestic abuse can also be helpful. But above all else, choose a therapist with whom you feel heard and safe. You want a therapist who does not blame or shame you, doesn't ask you what your contribution is to the narcissistic person's behavior, doesn't scold you for wondering if a person in your life is narcissistic or toxic or gaslighting you, doesn't ask you to keep giving second chances or to repeatedly set boundaries that are never honored, and, above all, who never asks you, "Why don't you leave?" Therapy that is nonjudgmental, trauma-informed, genuine, and well-versed in how narcissism works is essential for survivors, especially when you are having ongoing contact with narcissistic people.

And then there is couple's therapy. Therapy is a great option for yourself, but couple's therapy with a narcissistic person can be tricky. It's important to go in with eyes wide open and with a very strong therapist. If you have a couple's therapist who doesn't understand narcissism, the therapist may fall hook, line, and sinker for the narcissist's charm, charisma, and confidence. If you do have a therapist who is willing to hold the narcissist's feet to the fire and ask for accountability, just know that the narcissistic person will most likely drop out of therapy. Narcissistic partners are notorious for manipulating the therapy and acting composed while you are emotionally shredded and sharing frustrations and strong feelings. If you have a great referral, are also in your own individual therapy, and can give yourself permission to end the couple's therapy if it doesn't feel safe, then it could be worth a tentative attempt. If the therapy feels like a place where the blame is being perpetuated or your narcissistic partner is weaponizing the process, you would be wise to reconsider. In the same vein, be careful when a workplace suggests mediation to work through a conflict with a toxic colleague or boss. If the mediator doesn't understand narcissism, this process may feel like gaslighting and more invalidation. Seeking therapy outside of the workplace can be essential to navigate these situations. Finally, as echoed throughout the book, social support beyond therapy—friends, family, people you may meet in a class—is crucial if you are going to stay. Validating, respectful, empathic and compassionate people, relationships, and experiences are essential to the process of healing.

## Soul Distancing

It may not feel good or authentic, but you can ostensibly be in a relationship and try to keep your soul out of it. I worked with a woman who would tell her narcissistic husband about a new idea or good news, and invariably he would half listen, ask her how much her "crazy idea would cost" him, or tell her that any successes she did have were due to dumb luck. She did not want to leave the marriage for a range of reasons, but we worked toward making it less of a soul-crushing place by teaching her to stop allowing him to be her first stop when she wanted to share something good. Over time, she recognized that this sharing of good news felt like a fawn response, and an attempt to win him over, much like she tried with her parents when she was a child.

Soul distancing may entail protecting your vulnerabilities, your dreams, and your hopes. It means being aware and attuned to the narcissistic behavior and the impact it is having on you and then changing your approach—engaging and sharing less, not taking the bait. It means saving your depth for the people who reciprocate. When you are attempting to soul distance, envision yourself sitting in a cloud of light, a sort of gauzy boundary between you and the invalidating behavior of others. Just envisioning yourself serene within that space can foster this experience of soul distancing.

LEAVING A NARCISSISTIC relationship or significantly disengaging from a narcissistic person isn't always an option but remaining in one of these relationships doesn't mean you cannot heal, adopt a new perspective, strive toward greater autonomy, and recover from narcissistic abuse. There are small and big things you can do to protect yourself, including using your knowledge about narcissistic behavior to disengage and giving yourself permission to grow despite being in a limiting and toxic situation. These small calibrations and shifts can help you cope, protect others you care about, and allow you to explore and occupy your authentic sense of self. Over time, you may find that healing while you remain in the relationship may lead you out of the relationship, but on a time frame that feels comfortable.

# 9

# Rewrite Your Story

We tell ourselves stories in order to live.

JOAN DIDION

When Luna looks back at her life, she sees herself as a "hopeful robot." She grew up in an immigrant family from a traditional and patriarchal culture, with a narcissistic father and an emotionally abused mother who lived her entire life appeasing her invalidating husband. In Luna's family she was the golden child, the fixer, and the truth teller. While she was an excellent student, her brother was the scapegoat, and she was saddled with survivor guilt over the preferential treatment she would sometimes receive from their malignant and vulnerable narcissistic father. Unless Luna yielded to what her father valued—doing well in school and pursuing tennis—he would never notice her. All of them were neglected, fearful, and walked on eternal eggshells for most of their lives. The extended family looked at her father as a titan and often enabled his bad behavior.

Luna was ambitious and smart, but her mother's trauma-bonded confusion and her father's criticism, disinterest in her as a person, and harsh comments about how she came up short when she didn't get into an Ivy League university resulted in her receiving little life guidance, and she just didn't trust herself enough to seek out mentorship and advocate for herself. Her raw intellect propelled her through an above-average college, and ultimately she went to medical school and became a physician. She had a solid career as a community physician and had the skills and ambition to be a leader in her area of medicine and research, but she talked herself out of that path. She had so deeply internalized the rhetoric of her childhood, the belief firmly implanted in her emotional DNA that she wasn't enough, that her dual fears of hubris and failure—and subsequent contempt and mockery—were a barrier. She truly believed she could not measure up to public appraisals and felt she couldn't cope with failing in such a big way. Her narrative was never open to the possibility of succeeding, only to the disaster that failure would bring. Luna found herself stuck between a fantasy of wanting to prove her father wrong and shut down his minimization and mockery, while simultaneously believing that she was a mediocrity who was ridiculous for wanting to strive for more.

Luna's relationships generally consisted of her choosing men who were accomplished but treated her in a dismissive manner. Eventually, she met and married a senior physician in the field who was ten years older than her. They had children together. Over time, her gifts and ambitions were further squelched with the focus on his career, and she was often belittled by him. Luna's career languished. She worked in a poorly run mid-tier community clinic overseen by invalidating management and was not achieving the recognition she deserved. Her husband was manipulative, rageful, controlling, and after an argument, he always convinced her that there was something wrong with her. Luna felt stuck, and in her therapy admitted that she even had fantasies of what it would be like if her husband died and she was finally free. Her therapist asked her, "Instead of fantasizing about someone's death as a way of getting free, have you ever considered getting out of this relationship?" Luna said, "I don't know if I have the strength for that."

Luna stayed in therapy, talked with a few trusted friends, and eventually realized that leaving this marriage would mean losing her family of origin, as her father believed divorce would bring shame on the family, and put her in a perilous financial position with her two children. But ultimately, she decided that leaving was the best choice and she moved into a small apartment. She and her ex-husband shared joint custody of their children.

The divorce was difficult, and for a variety of complex reasons, Luna ended up with fewer resources than expected. But she didn't fret. She thought, *I'm free. I can finally pursue my dreams and do what I want!* But things didn't always come together as she'd hoped. Luna would turn away some good opportunities because she thought that she was "getting ahead of herself" and wasn't good enough. In her marriage she'd conceded financial control to her ex-husband because he often berated her when it came to money matters, and as a result she was now having to play catch-up on a lifetime of financial education. Her father didn't think women needed to know about money and so she didn't receive that guidance from him, either. Luna was sliding deeper into debt, but she felt that at least her mistakes were her own, and it still felt better than the desolation of life in her marriage or with her family of origin.

Luna eventually began dating again and, wouldn't you know it, she met more narcissistic men. She got into new kinds of invalidating relationships with emotionally abusive men, and while her ex-husband had been faithful, she was now experiencing the sting of narcissistic infidelity. Although she managed to slowly crawl out of this new set of narcissistic relationships, she was psychologically exhausted. But she kept maintaining strong boundaries with her family. Every day, even when things were tough, Luna reminded herself that living on her own and being single still felt better than most days in any of those relationships.

Eventually, a business she started finally began to bear fruit. She had been invalidated at every turn as she developed it—and while the numerous barriers to launching it were stressful, they did not slow her down. The resilience and flexibility she cultivated after years of narcissistic relationships served her well. Her new business expanded enough to become a full-time gig, and while it is steadily growing and receiving great feedback, those inner invalidating voices remain loud, and every day she wonders if it is all going to fail. But she keeps at it.

Over time, Luna recognized that even though she had distanced from and set boundaries with her narcissistic family and ex-partner, their voices were still stuck in her head. She found herself in the loop of wanting to make her business work to prove them wrong or make them proud. Her ongoing work in therapy was about connecting with her feelings, who she was, and what she wanted, and detaching from how the narcissistic people in her life viewed her. She became better at not even talking to them about what she did, and gradually she came to care less about what they would think about her or her work.

By her description Luna is happy. She says that life has felt quite difficult, and has been painful, but now she sees her life and her relationships clearly. She does grieve how inefficient her life has been, and that it took her until almost age sixty to be where she finally wants to be. But she lives in radical acceptance. Her social circle has shrunk to a small group of people who are empathic and compassionate, and she doesn't give her time away to people who drain her.

On her darkest days, Luna admits to wondering what it would have been like to have parents who loved each other—a loving father, a thriving mother—to have had her own love story, to have been encouraged and supported. On other days, she recognizes that Luna wouldn't be Luna without the struggle. She is proud of her flexibility. When others around her are whining about something not going the way they wanted, she is grateful for the freedom that realistic expectations have given her, and that years of having to work around toxic people have left her well versed at thinking on her feet and making quick shifts as needed. She is well prepared for life's disappointments and is personalizing them less. What has saved her is her joy and gratitude when things do work out. She is deeply present with the good days—and is pleasantly surprised by them. She spots narcissistic people early, no longer engages, and has impressed herself by no longer caring about the opinion of enablers. She still carries grief about aspects of her life—like when she sees or hears about people with happy long-standing marriages, who are financially secure going into old age—but those moments now pass like a quick psychological pain spasm. At the same time, she revels in her freedom, a good day with her children, taking her mother on a day trip, and her career. Despite the pain, she stepped up to care for her father when he was ill. She expected nothing in return, and when she reflected on her "why" she recognized that it wasn't for him, it was for her. It is who she is.

This isn't the path Luna wanted. It's the path she got. She finally understands herself, and she can clearly see what the hurts and abuse from her family and prior relationships have done to her. She recognizes that there is no eraser that removes those scars. She is aware of who she is and lives in congruence with that self-awareness and with her values. Luna finally feels she can occupy her authentic self without fear and is rewriting her narrative. She is mindful and aware of the difference between a life with gaslighters and a life without. She no longer suffers fools. And a year ago, she met someone new. He is compassionate, respectful of her work, and not controlling. She keeps looking for red flags and insists the relationship move slowly. He had no problem with any of that, and in fact it is he who is bringing kindness, seeing her gifts, and not love bombing. Luna is falling in love, but she acknowledges that trust will always be a battle for her.

She slowly smiles and says, "Finally, after it just being a dish of salt and lemons, my life is a salted caramel—at this point the saltiness and the bitterness really do bring out the sweetness."

SO MUCH EFFORT goes into understanding narcissistic people and learning how to survive these relationships that you forget that the rest of your life will unfold as you heal, evolve, and mentally or literally move on. A narcissistic relationship can be a master class in your own potential, a reminder that you are worth fighting for, you are lovable, you have an identity outside of this relationship, and you can dump the worn fairy tales and rewrite your narratives. Narcissistic relationships render you unable to answer the simple question "How are you?" because you were not really allowed to have a feeling or experience outside of the narcissistic person—and that is a sobering recognition. These relationships are an eternal catch-22: speak your truth and be invalidated or give in to them and feel ashamed you don't have your own personhood. As healing evolves, the long game is about slowly claiming your personal sovereignty and not feeling guilty about it.

Of course it's not easy. Disengaging, letting go, less contact, proclaiming that you are "over it"—all of that is window dressing unless you are really willing to dig deep into yourself. The final steps to healing from a narcissistic relationship require recognizing that so much of your perception of yourself has been warped by the perspective of the narcissistic person, as if they made you wear a pair of distorted eyeglasses, and you now need to learn to see yourself without them. Lifelong healing is a journey of grief giving way to individuation and a more hopeful future. It's about finding a way to get through the pain and to seek joy despite all that has happened. As long as the narcissist is living in your mind, you probably won't like yourself. Evicting them and adjusting to the vacancy that follows from coaxing the narcissist from your mind, heart, and soul are necessary.

Many of the healing strategies up until now have been about how to "manage" the impact of the narcissistic people in your life. Those tools prepared you to begin the deeper work of shedding the narcissistic person as the central figure in your story. Instead of remaining stuck in the old narrative, it's time to begin revising your narrative from an honest and self-aware place and to reflect on the lessons learned from this difficult relationship.

Do we—*can* we—grow after trauma or the deep wounds of an emotionally abusive relationship? The answer is that it's complicated. The short answer is yes, and many people do. There can be an evolution from setback and fear to growth, including more gratitude, clearer priorities, greater empathy and sense of belonging, new interests and adaptability, increased confidence, a more meaningful personal narrative and beliefs, and a clearer sense of purpose.[1] A discussion of the issues around posttraumatic growth is beyond the scope of this book, but while the researchers argue about terminology and what constitutes posttraumatic growth,[2] we do know that in the wake of trauma, something happens to us, and not all of it is bad.

This shift within you can be harnessed and cultivated. You can and should talk about it in safe spaces, get it out in the light, and lift the shame from your journey. Elevate yourself out of the narcissistic narrative and give yourself the space to be the primary player in your own story. Recraft your narrative and recognize that it's time for a part two to your story that reflects what you have learned. Healing is about managing the negative emotions and trusting and feeling your body, which not only holds the pain of this relationship but also houses the intuition that you've strayed away from. It's not just about being the author and editor of your revised story but leaning into that pain, pushing back against perfectionism and negative self-talk, and creating space for meaning, purpose, and mutually recognized empathy.

We are built to heal; that is life. Nature is full of examples of organisms healing and continuing to grow and thrive. A tree continuing to grow even after a branch has been cut, a starfish regenerating a leg, flowers and forests flourishing after wildfires. You are no different. Your psyche may have been torn apart by this relationship, but like all living things, remind yourself that on the hardest days, living means healing.

## The Tale of the Lion

At the beginning of this book, I suggested that it's time to stop telling the tale of the hunter and instead start focusing on the story of the lion. But where do we begin?

To start rewriting and revising your story means understanding the impact of narcissistic relationships on you. For many of us, the narcissistic relationship has been there since the beginning. Our entire identity and personhood were shaped by a lifetime spent appeasing, pleasing, and trying to win over the narcissistic person, or merely trying to be noticed or acknowledged as a person with our own wants, needs, and experiences. We were living in the projected shame of the narcissistic person, holding back on our goals or dreams because they would be devalued and dismissed, or shaping them so they were no longer our aspirations but rather another attempt to win over the narcissistic person or avoid their rage and invalidation. It's time to consider who you are if you are no longer merely playing a role in the narcissistic person's story.

If we did attempt to rebel, even our act of rebellion was a response to the narcissistic relationship. The divergent opinions we held, preferences we voiced, even our hair color could have been a way of having an identity separate from this relationship or of screaming out to be heard and seen by the narcissist. Thus, even our attempts at autonomy were often a counterweight to the narcissistic suffocation or negation. Narcissistic relationships teach us that our needs are irrelevant, and we grow to believe that the other person's needs and wants are our needs and wants.

Even feeling our own feelings becomes fraught. Evolving past narcissistic abuse means owning and stating needs clearly without entangling them into the confusion of the relationship. Instead of "I want to be a mother, and I will show my mother how it's done because she was so bad at it and messed me up," we connect with our wants, separate from how the narcissistic person saw us or what they did, and simply say, "I want to be a mother." To be in this relationship meant to silence anything that was separate from them. Being able to identify and speak our feelings is a massive shift.

As you shape the second volume of your narrative, it's time to lean into the big questions: Who are you? What do you want? What do you need? What do you stand for? This is not always easy, but this is the work. All the exercises, information, and suggestions in this book are only useful as part of this all-important journey of giving your authentic self permission to be revealed. It's time to fade the narcissistic person out of the story and learn who you are separate from these relationships. Sometimes you believe you removed people from your life but they are still occupying prime real estate in your mind because you still devote hours to ruminating about these relationships. In Luna's story, striving was about proving her father wrong rather than pursuing her interests. But making your life a counterweight to the narcissistic person means that you aren't fully disconnecting from them and still live in their service, a familiar albeit toxic place. The true act of rebellion is to live a life that is not a response to them but a life as an authentic person with wants, needs, aspirations, mistakes, strengths, vulnerabilities, hopes, and feelings that are completely yours.

## Revising Your Narrative

Your narrative has been shaped by people who didn't want you to be you. Now it's time to swap out your old narratives and replace them with new ones that can release and empower you. These are old stories, so at first it may feel difficult to revise them. It's a bit like rewriting a childhood fairy tale you've heard so many times that now an alternate telling seems impossible. Imagine the Little

Mermaid rolling up and telling the Prince, "Hey, I actually like my tail, and if you want to swing by the ocean and hang out and get to really know me, give me a shout, but otherwise, no thank you."

The first step is to identify the old, warped narratives that have been holding you back. Write these down. This can be an outline, a few pages, or hundreds—whatever works for you. After you craft your original narrative, let it breathe. Now that you have a better understanding of narcissistic abuse, read your narrative through that lens and identify the misassumptions ("It was my fault"). Pay attention to how much of the story is really yours and how much of it belongs to the narcissist. Living in narcissistic abuse means that you end up confusing their story with yours, so rewrite those parts first—the parts you thought were yours. You might find that "I really wanted to be a doctor ever since I was a kid" morphs into "I loved science, and my father really wanted me to be a doctor like him. It made my life so much easier to want that too, and my parents loved that I was going to medical school. Being a doctor is fine, but I recognize that my real love was writing, so now I am trying my hand at writing about the personal process of being a health-care provider." Look at your story with clearer eyes. Stories can have different endings, and this is about writing a new second act for yours.

Your fears of rejection and abandonment may have stopped the process of individuation and taking back your story. Instead of the narrative "I am terrible at relationships and foolishly stayed for too long in this relationship," try "Relationships are sometimes difficult for me, and I am learning new ways of being in relationships. I can slow down and be kinder to myself." Tackling your narrative one piece or theme at a time and infusing it with self-compassion can make the entire process more manageable. It may take time and reflection, so don't rush it.

It's also time to rewrite your narratives on resilience. Your feelings and emotions were either not allowed or were gaslighted in your narcissistic relationships. People who have less power in their families, relationships, and the world at large learned long ago that their emotions are often not tolerated or permissible. Many of you learned long ago to push your feelings down, and that strength and resilience were associated with being stoic. In many cultures, not expressing emotion and leaving feelings unexpressed are mistakenly framed as resilience. But silent endurance is not resilience, even though it may be more comfortable for the people around you. As you reshape your narrative, connect to any feeling and emotion you have and are experiencing as you go through life. Give yourself permission to express these feelings; it is the truth of your feeling that will enliven your narrative with the truth of who you are. Your narrative is not just a story; it is the feelings you have long silenced to remain safe in toxic relationships.

As you revisit your narrative, remain mindful that you do not conflate individuation with a "you versus the world" style of independence. Human relationships can seem terrifying after narcissistic abuse. Be clear on the difference between understanding your identity separate from the narcissistic narrative and becoming an island who isolates from everyone. Human relationships can be safe, and a major element of your new story is allowing for the potential of healthy relationships, no matter how long it may take for them to unfold.

Ultimately, revising your narrative isn't a wellness hack. It is about the nuance. It is not about going from "I am not enough" to "I am great," or some superficial self-love mantra, but rather unpacking the lie of "I am not enough" and finally recognizing where it comes from and that your life story is telling you otherwise.

I worked with a woman who had a narcissistic mother, husband, sibling, former boss, and former best friend (who had been her maid of honor at her wedding). At first, she was resistant to do the exercise, feeling it was impossible to rewrite anything—and this many years in, who cares? But she was a good sport and agreed to do it. As she examined her old narratives and opened herself up to new ones, she learned that she had become quite good at coping with unpredictability, was not "unreasonable" as she had once been led to believe, had the ability to coordinate a large project, and had tremendous empathy. She also actually did know how to set a boundary (her original conception of herself was as a "doormat") and was able to ask for what she needed. Her past narcissistic relationships convinced her there was evidence for things that simply were not true, but she had heard the lies enough times that she believed them. She didn't change because a cheerleader therapist or coach told her she was great; the proof was right there in what she was doing in her life. Upon revising her narrative, she started talking to herself differently, and she disengaged from her mother and was no longer referring to herself as a doormat. A year later, she moved out of her marital home and started flourishing in her career.

Your revised narrative is dynamic, shifting and changing as you learn more about yourself. The narrative derived from your narcissistic relationships was a fiction. Your story, told by you, is the truth. The story of the hunt, told by the lion.

## The Treachery of Forgiveness

It seems that every single self-help book, healing practice, and spiritual scripture talks about the value of forgiveness. From the Bible to Instagram influencers to Gandhi, we are sold on the idea that forgiveness is divine and the path of the righteous. So for me to sit here and tell you, "Maybe not," is unorthodox to say the least. Psychological research highlights the value of forgiveness, and in healthy relationships it has tremendous value. But narcissistic relationships are not healthy, so all the conventional wisdom about forgiveness goes out the window.

*Merriam-Webster* defines the word *forgive* as "to cease to feel resentment against (an offender)." If you no longer feel resentment toward the person who betrayed you, then you are in the clear—forgive away. To try to forgive while still resenting may be what the world or the narcissistic person wants to see, but it is not an authentic process within you. What has happened in the past when you forgave the narcissistic person in your life? In most cases, narcissistic people didn't recognize forgiveness as the gift that it is and changed their behavior. Instead, they likely saw it as permission to keep on doing what they were doing. Forgiveness is narcissistic supply, one more thing that emboldens the narcissistic person's entitlement, and you may even get angry at yourself for forgiving them, especially if you get betrayed again.

Forgiveness also rarely happens in real time in a narcissistic relationship. It is something that, if it happens, tends to unfold long after you have safely extricated from the relationship.

Multiple studies suggest that forgiveness is not good for a person if it is not followed by an attempt to make amends or foster safety. When people repeatedly forgave a partner who behaved badly in a relationship, it negatively affected the well-being of the person doing the forgiving. Other researchers also found that less-agreeable partners were more likely to re-offend after being forgiven and didn't feel pressure to change their behavior because they believed their partner wouldn't be mad at them if they did slip up again. There is even a name for all of this: *the doormat effect*, which states that forgiving a less-agreeable partner who has behaved badly negatively affects self-respect. Most of what is written about the virtues of forgiveness does not account for narcissism and antagonism. When we do account for repeat offenders and disagreeable personalities, research suggests that it would be better for your well-being if you didn't forgive.[3]

Personally, I have not forgiven all the narcissistic people who showed up on my path. I have let go, moved on, and wish them no ill will, but I also see clearly that they harmed me and, in some ways, changed me, yet they never took responsibility for the harm they caused. I still spend time with some of them. But I always feel worse afterward, and because of these relationships, I am more vigilant, fearful, and less trusting. Embracing my non-forgiveness has significantly helped my healing and brought the volume down on my anger. The disconnect between resentment and forgiveness meant that if I claimed to forgive them, then I was holding something that held me back. Forgiveness for them meant internal tension for me. Doesn't seem very healing, does it? Some have told me, "Ramani, you have moved on and left them behind, just forgive them." But I don't view lack of forgiveness as a weight I carry. I view it as a realistic assessment of the situation. For years I did keep forgiving, or at least believed that I was forgiving, and I turned to the multiple truths to make sense of it. *They hurt me, I loved them, I tried to forgive, they betrayed me again, I stopped trusting other people, I still am afraid of their criticism.* Moving on wasn't as simple as forgiving and letting go. It never is.

Part of the struggle is that some things we call *forgiveness* aren't. Letting go, moving on, pardoning the narcissistic people's behavior, or forgetting it altogether can help set you free but they're not the same as forgiveness, which is a more active process. Rumination about forgiving (or not forgiving) can keep you mentally interlinked with the narcissistic relationship, even when they are out of your life. The balancing act is working through the overwhelming negative emotions raised by the relationship and recognizing that getting past those emotions is not forgiveness—it's you distancing yourself from those ruminations.

The key is that the forgiveness, if it does happen, should be authentic and not performative. Some people might say, "In forgiving the narcissistic person, I acknowledge how sad their life is, and I am not wasting bandwidth on loathing them." I will never posit forgiveness as a path forward for any survivors of narcissistic abuse. I support survivors who choose to, and I support those who don't—neither path is better or worse, though the research does suggest that it isn't good for us to keep forgiving repeat offenders. Healing, shaping a new narrative, and taking your voice back are about choice, and in the same way, forgiveness is about choice. It is astonishing to me how much of the discourse on narcissistic abuse is about forgiving the narcissist. It's ridiculous. If you don't want to forgive, you may have been shamed as somehow lacking compassion when, in fact, you are sorting through the wreckage of the narcissistic relationship. Or you may have been told that you will not be able to heal if you do not forgive. That is simply not true.

Healing is about clearly seeing what happened. To allow yourself to feel the sadness and the pain. This is not a story you just tell once. You need to tell it enough times so you can see it, but you can't do that without feeling it. It is sad, and grief-filled, and painful. To heal means to allow yourself to feel your pain and your story of narcissistic abuse. To slowly do this without shame but with self-compassion. Many people put their heads down and obsessively work or engage in other frenetic activity to get past narcissistic abuse. That's not healing; that's distracting yourself. Being busy can feel safe in the short term. The long game means you can't skip the pain step and go from busy to better. In our rush to heal, to get past it, we often forget to stop and *feel* it, and it is essential we do. Otherwise, we remain disconnected from the experience and are doomed to ruminate and perhaps even repeat it.

It can take years—or even decades—to get out of these adult narcissistic relationships, and even after you get out, you blame yourself for staying too long. *How could I have been so stupid? Why didn't I see it sooner? Maybe I didn't try hard enough. How much of this was my fault? Maybe I created this monster.* Forgive yourself for not seeing it, for confusing empathy with enabling, and for making excuses. You didn't know. No one is taught this, so why would you have seen it?

Self-forgiveness is about release. Releasing yourself from the narcissistic person's narrative. You may feel you let yourself, your own children, or your colleagues and employees down. But you just wanted to be loved, cherished, and protected by your parents; to fall in love with someone and be treated with kindness, compassion, and respect; to be treated equitably and respectfully in the workplace; to receive basic empathy. In return for that, you were met with gaslighting, invalidation, rage, contempt, dismissiveness, and cruelty. You did nothing wrong. It's time to stop crafting the story that you did. Forgiving yourself becomes a key step to working through the grief.

As you navigate your story, it can be very tempting to believe that the story ends with forgiveness. But your story may have a very different coda.

## From Survivor to Thriver

Is thriving possible after narcissistic abuse? Yes! Thriving isn't about bringing back the "old you"—you have been changed by this experience. It's about bringing forth the wise, more self-aware, authentic you. Thriving is not the day-to-day survivalist slog of decoding, confusion, anxiety, and self-doubt. Nor is it simply the day-to-day coping of getting meals made and work done. When you start to thrive, you no longer do things and wonder what the narcissistic person would think; they simply do not factor into your decision or experience. I have talked with, worked with, and heard the stories of myriad survivors, and their stories of learning to thrive are not always the big tales of "I started a business, I got remarried, I got my teaching credential." Thriving is often simply "I went through the entire day and didn't hear their voice in my head once."

Take a moment to see your journey and story clearly. You may judge your growth, aspirations, and even the praise you receive from others for how far you have come as "grandiose": *Oh, I can't talk about building a business, it sounds grandiose*; *Ugh, talking about my growth and my journey feels grandiose*. You've spent years being shamed for just wanting to live in sync with who you are rather than off a script that has been foisted upon you. Catch yourself when you silence yourself or write off your aspirations as "grandiose." That's not humility; it's the internalized voice of the narcissist. Your dreams and aspirations are not grandiose. You've got humility wired, so now learn to thrive, flourish, and reflect on yourself without shaming yourself.

## How Does the Story End If There Is No Closure?

The reality is that there is rarely closure in narcissistic relationships. You could waste a lifetime waiting for the fantasized moment when the narcissistic person says they get it or takes responsibility or is held accountable. They may never see your pain or all you lost. They may never face their karmic payback or their rock bottom, at least not on your watch. But even if you don't get closure, you still need to close out your story with them. Not every story has a neat buttoned-up ending, and healing and persistence mean a willingness to keep going even if their story line within yours isn't the ending you hoped. The closure is you moving forward and no longer having your sense of self and purpose stolen by them.

## Activities to Foster Healing and Recovery

The following exercises will help you address distorted narratives, support you in your healing, foster autonomy and independence from the narcissistic person, and recast yourself and your growth in a more empowering light. As you explore these exercises, take your time to reflect on your experiences and how you have transformed and learned from your pain. Be sure to show yourself compassion and kindness during this process.

### *Rewrite a Fairy Tale*

Why do childhood stories matter? Because they become the tropes for how adult romantic stories are constructed (pursuit, rescue, happily ever after). Most of us were raised on fairy tales, which basically reinforce gender roles, punish individuation, and glorify everything about narcissistic relationships: love bombing, forced narcissistic relationships, forgiveness, obedience, grandiosity, and future faking. If you come from a narcissistic family system, or even if you don't and these stories are still under your skin, this is a useful exercise.

Take a fairy tale you heard in childhood and reflect on how it may have perpetuated the justification of abusive patterns within your family, or how it may have reinforced patterns in an adult intimate relationship or in the workplace (*If I just work hard and never expect to be seen, then a bunch of mice and a fairy godmother will help me out and I will find true love*). Then rewrite this old tale in a realistic or balanced way. For example, the story of the Red Shoes was told as a story about a bad girl who didn't listen to her parents and was punished for disobedience. Instead, frame it as a story of a girl who cared about beauty and joy and was punished for just wanting to be herself. When you can unbraid these childhood stories, you may also be able to undo some of the rigid thinking that has pervaded your narrative.

### Reflect on How You Felt Instead of What Happened

If you tell your story enough, over time it can be easy to get separated from the emotions. As a therapist, I believe the stories are the "B-side" of a therapy session—the most important part is how a client felt in the moment and feels now. As you heal from narcissistic abuse and recraft your narrative, pay attention to your emotions. It's so easy to get lost in the narrative episodes (*My parents did this*; *This happened at my wedding*; *My partner cheated*; *My business partner stole my money*) that you don't feel the feelings. Simply recalling the things that happened in the relationship misses the one part of the story that is all yours: how you felt when it happened. Connecting to these feelings can break cycles of rumination, foster discernment, and allow you to be more present and self-compassionate.

## Bring All the Pieces of Yourself Together

You may want to completely leave behind the you that was in a narcissistic relationship, as though you are ashamed of that part of your story. You may think, *I don't want to remember myself as that broken, pathetic fool who stayed with the cheater* or *I am no longer that child who lived to please her selfish and competitive mother.* Not so fast. Hold space for you, the person who was confused, hurt, gaslighted, devalued, and still managed to have the strength to get out, or got through school, or survived a painful breakup. Denying your history, story, and yourself can mean you remain self-judgmental and fractured. Have compassion for all of you. Invite those harmed parts of you in, recognize that what seemed like weakness was often patience, empathy, and strength. Reintegrating yourself after these relationships means including your entire story with gentleness, respect, and love.

## Write a Letter

To see how far you've come and all you've learned in your healing journey, it can help to put all you now know in a letter to someone. That someone can be yourself while you were still in the narcissistic relationship; tell that prior you what happens once you decide to leave. Or you can write to yourself ten years from now, sharing what you hope will happen. You can write to your child-self who endured a narcissistic family dynamic. You can write to someone about to marry a narcissist or someone who is holding themselves back because they have a narcissistic parent or someone who feels lost in school or a job because of invalidating teachers or bosses. Writing what you've learned from this point of view can be healing because it offers a way to harness your experience by framing it as helping someone else or as a little detached from yourself. After you write the letter, put it down for a few days or weeks and then go back and read it. You may notice that you were using the language of self-compassion, self-forgiveness, and eradication of self-blame because you were talking to someone else or not directly to yourself. Now bring that compassionate language back to yourself.

## Pay It Forward

Many of you may be thinking, *I want to help other people who are going through this. I want to stop someone else before they waste as much time as I did.* Paying it forward can shape your narrative not only by recognizing the gifts you bring to others but also allowing yourself to learn from their stories as well. Paying forward what you have learned through your process of healing can manifest in different ways for different people. Some of you may go back to school to become therapists or counselors and work with survivors, while others may become divorce coaches. You may get involved in domestic violence advocacy or family court reform. Or you may find that talking about narcissistic abuse is still too upsetting or you just want to put it behind you, but you bring your empathy and compassion to animal welfare, community service, or simply the people in your life who cherish and benefit from it.

A word of caution: *Make sure you do not use paying it forward as a substitute for your own ongoing healing.* It is part of a larger spectrum of healing, but your desire to help others may mean you exhaust and deplete yourself by trying to be helpful (again).

## Witness Your Own "Survivor's Journey"

Have you ever heard of the hero's journey? It provides an outline for many myths and biographies across time and cultures. The framework is pretty simple: A heroic person is called to an adventure, faces down a critical crisis, often considers giving up, and returns home, permanently transformed. Along the way, the heroic person wanders through the unknown and is met with helpers, mentors, fellow travelers, threats, and existential crises, and upon returning is not only changed but also does good for others.

You are the heroic person in this journey. You hit rock bottom and wanted to give up on yourself, but you came through the other side. You faced the invalidation and eradication of yourself in the narcissistic relationship, and those fellow travelers may have been friends, family, therapists, and even strangers. As you grow, one of the most poignant and at times painful realizations is that not everyone, least of all the narcissistic people, can go with you to where you are going. As you heal and individuate, you will relate to people differently. It doesn't mean you leave people behind or even end relationships, but it means you have created a space within yourself that you are willing to safeguard. Returning home is about returning to yourself, but it's not the same home you left, because now you are able to fully possess it. The key is to remember that after navigating a narcissistic relationship you are forever transformed—and while it was painful, some of these shifts in you are remarkable and profound.

Break down your story into these components:

- What was your call to start your healing process/journey?
- Who walked alongside you for part or all of it?
- What was happening when you almost gave up?
- What did returning "home" look like?

You may not see yourself as Ulysses or Arjuna or Frodo or Sita, but the threats these mythic figures faced from outside of them were no match for the demons you have had to subdue from within. Shaping your story along the hero's journey framework transforms your perception of your healing process from someone who is dragging themselves out of a mess to a person who bravely undertook one hell of a treacherous trip. You could have chosen to keep things the way they were, to have left but never focused on individuation and healing, to have never attempted to take back your story, and never changed a word. That would have been easier. But that's not what you are doing now.

HEALING IS ABOUT divesting yourself from the story of the narcissist. It is about freeing yourself from the scripts and shame that the narcissistic person projected onto you. It is about creating an identity separate from your narcissistic abuse. It is about understanding, feeling, and grieving what happened to you. And then it is about having compassion for all the harmed parts of yourself: the part of you that feels not enough, the part of you that feels damaged, the part of you that feels unworthy of love, the part of you that feels like an object of abuse. Those are parts of you—don't just cut them out; receive them and love them. When you integrate those devastated parts of yourself into your larger authentic self, you give yourself permission to be separate from not only the narcissistic people in your life but also from their attempt to make you a mere player on their chessboard.

Healing from narcissistic abuse is more of a process than a destination. It's a delicately balanced space, where you detach from the narcissistic person's narrative for you and settle into your own without framing it around them any longer. It's not forced forgiveness. It's a place of detachment and even indifference toward them. But it is not about being detached and indifferent about what happened to you. It's self-compassion and growth in spite of, or perhaps because of, your grief, loss, and pain. Ultimately, these feelings may evolve into a resigned awareness that they did not choose to do right by you, and while that hurt, it's not because of you, it's about them. After years of seeing yourself as the broken one, you will recognize with sadness and maybe even a weary compassion that they simply projected their brokenness, fragility, and insecurity onto you. Some of you may even feel some pity and sympathy for them; some of you may not. There is no right way to do this. Ultimately, this messy process of recovery is trial and error. This journey culminates in the private and public launch of your authentic self, and that will be a gift to yourself, to the people who love you, and to the world at large.

I sincerely hope this book has helped you start processing and then releasing the pain of narcissistic abuse and opened you up to a pathway to *you*—your strength, gifts, wisdom, and grace. That it let you know that there is an act two, a volume two, a sequel, a fresh page to write on, and a new and more joyous life in the wake of healing. That after years or a lifetime of being gaslighted, manipulated, invalidated, and minimized, of being told you are not enough, that there is something wrong with you, that you have no right to feel the way you feel, of wondering, *What is it? What am I doing wrong? What can I do better? How can I be better?* you finally and fully recognize . . .

*It's not you.*

# Conclusion

In my ten years of graduate school, practica, internships, and fellowships, despite an excellent education, the terms *narcissism* and *antagonistic* were not taught to me once. Over twenty-five years later, I remain befuddled at the resistance to this conversation about how narcissistic relationships harm people and how to help them. As the therapists and researchers debate about semantics and whether it is "right" to discuss the harms of narcissism, or even what it is, people are hurting and suffering. I have spoken at conferences where the speaker in the next room was criticizing the concept of calling emotionally harmful relationships "toxic." It chills me to reflect on how much human potential we have lost from people who were blamed and shamed and felt stymied and silenced after internalizing the invalidating voices that echoed for a lifetime. These are intergenerational cycles and narcissism is a societally incentivized pattern. As we develop measurement tools and interventions designed for people experiencing narcissistic abuse, we are still building this airplane in the sky. I hope we get there, though most days I feel like a heretic.

To understand narcissistic abuse is to decolonize psychology and push back on old theories and models that don't make allowances for the harms of hierarchies, disparity, privilege, and traditionalism. I have watched thousands of survivors walk this tightrope and have balanced on it myself—and together we have learned that healing is possible, albeit messy. Their stories and mine remind me not just of the tyranny of narcissistic abuse but also of the courage of believing that there is always the chance for one more act. Remember that the world needs you—your true, whole, authentic you—so please don't hold back. This time, put that purple dress on.

# *Acknowledgments*

This book was something I didn't believe would get into the world, but through a series of almost otherworldly synchronicities, here it is. I was supported in so many ways in the writing of this book, and it stands not just as a guide for survivorship, but also as a testament to the blessings of community that make healing possible.

First and foremost, thank you to the many clients with whom I have had the privilege to work, and who have shared their stories, explored and felt the pain, and allowed me to share in their discovery of themselves. And to the people who every day, week, and month bring themselves to our healing program for survivors of narcissistic abuse—your vulnerable willingness to ask questions, share stories, and support each other while making the big leaps and small steps toward healing and individuation reminds me that it does get better. Thank you for your strength and for fighting another day, even when it breaks your heart anew.

To Kelly Ebeling and Irene Hernandez—you are the lifeblood of so much of this work. None of this would be possible without you—your creativity, resolve, flexibility, and willingness to be at my side during the hardest days allowed this book to happen. Zaide, it is a pleasure to have you join our tiny gritty team. All of you made those twenty-two years worth it.

To Nina Rodriguez-Marty, Meg Leder, Brian Tart, and Margaux Weisman at Penguin, thank you for your belief in the book. Nina, thanks for patiently, gently, but firmly guiding me through an evolving series of changes that strengthened the book, my voice, and the message. Lara Asher, for your editorial guidance on the earlier drafts of this book—thank you. Rachel Sussman, thank you for representing me and shepherding this work with a heartfelt commitment to the message. To Maria Shriver, thank you for believing in and welcoming this book onto The Open Field imprint. And much gratitude to everyone at Penguin and Penguin Life who has and is working on sales, marketing, and copyediting.

To my friends, and yes, I am looking at you, Ellen Rakieten—I don't know how this book would have gone this deep without our near nightly conversations on this topic. Thank you for being my "coach" and fellow traveler on some of the most difficult days of writing and life. Jill Davenport, my cheerleader and cactus friend since I was thirteen. Mona Baird, I do not know how I would have traversed those months at the end of 2021 without you. To all of my friends—thank you for the texts, check-ins, and forgiveness when I canceled plans over the past few years.

To my colleagues and friends in this field—Catherine Barrett, Tina Swithin, Ingrid Clayton, Heather Harris, Lisa Bilyeu, David Kessler, Jay Shetty, Matthew Hussey, and Audrey LeStrat and my colleagues through APA, MedCircle, Psychotherapy Networker, and PESI—thank you for creating community and providing me so much support and encouragement even when I was having a crisis of faith. To Pamela Harmell, for giving me the scissors to cut the trauma bonds. To Mari, for your development of the firewalling construct, thank you. To Nelia, for your unique courage in this work and incisive insight on how to share it.

To all of the guests on *Navigating Narcissism* who were willing to share your story in a public forum, your wisdom allowed me to re-think many themes in this book; thank you for entrusting me with your experiences.

Richard, thank you for always giving me the time and space to work and for believing in it and loving and seeing me.

To my sister, Padma, thanks for just listening to me talk about a whole lot of nothing, filling in the holes on our histories, making me laugh, and giving me a template for strength. To my nephew Tanner, for teaching me about goodness.

To Dad, I got here, and that may be enough.

To my beloved cat, Luna, may your furry soul recognize that I bounced more ideas off you than you know.

To my daughters, Maya and Shanti—once again, you tolerated an absent mother who ate meals with you between chapters. You remain always my True North. Please do what you love and know that you always have a soft place to land.

To my mother, Sai Durvasula—I live in the miracle that you are still here with us and getting stronger every day. This book is an homage to all you are and have become.

And to my sweet dear friend Emily Shagley. The world lost

Emily in 2022. Emily believed in me before I did. Her love and encouragement gave me courage years ago to put my voice out there. I will remain grateful all my days for her luminous presence in my life and in the world at large.

The goodness and light stay, even when we lose the angels in our lives.

# Resources

## DOMESTIC VIOLENCE HOTLINES

### National Domestic Violence Hotline

https://www.thehotline.org

Hotline: (800) 799-7233

Available twenty-four hours a day, seven days a week via phone and online chat.

### Rape, Abuse, and Incest National Network (RAINN): National Sexual Assault Hotline

https://www.rainn.org

Hotline: (800) 656-4673

Available twenty-four hours a day, seven days a week via phone and online chat.

## SUICIDE HOTLINES

### National Suicide Prevention Lifeline

https://suicidepreventionlifeline.org

(800) 273-8255

Text: HELLO to 741741

TTY: (800) 799-4889

Available twenty-four hours a day, seven days a week. Free and confidential support.

### 988 Suicide & Crisis Lifeline

Phone: 988

Chat: https://988lifeline.org/chat

https://988lifeline.org

For TTY users: Use your preferred relay service, or dial 711 then 988.

## MENTAL HEALTH SERVICES

### SAMHSA's National Helpline

https://www.samhsa.gov/find-help/national-helpline

(800) 662-4357

24-7 treatment referral and information service (in English and Spanish) for individuals and families facing mental and/or substance use disorders.

If you are experiencing acute distress, please call 911 or seek out local emergency services.

# Notes

## CHAPTER ONE

1　Z. Krizan and A. D. Herlache, "The Narcissism Spectrum Model: A Synthetic View of Narcissistic Personality," *Personality and Social Psychology Review* 22, no. 1 (2018), 3-31, https://doi.org/10.1177/1088868316685018.

2　Jochen E. Gebauer et al., "Communal Narcissism," *Journal of Personality and Social Psychology* 103, no. 5 (August 2012), 854-78, https://doi.org/10.1037/a0029629.

3　Delroy L. Paulhus and Kevin M. Williams, "The Dark Triad of Personality: Narcissism, Machiavellianism and Psychopathy," *Journal of Research in Personality* 36, no. 6 (December 2002), 556-63, https://doi.org /10.1016/S0092-6566(02)00505-6; Janko Međedović and Boban Petrović, "The Dark Tetrad: Structural Properties and Location in the Personality Space," *Journal of Individual Differences* 36, no. 4 (November 2015), 228-36, https://doi.org /10.1027/1614-0001/a000179.

4　Emily Grijalva et al., "Gender Differences in Narcissism: A Meta-Analytic Review," *Psychological Bulletin* 141, no. 2 (March 2015), 261, https://doi.org /10.1037/a0038231.

5　Sanne M. A. Lamers et al., "Differential Relationships in the Association of the Big Five Personality Traits with Positive Mental Health and Psychopathology," *Journal of Research in Personality* 46, no. 5 (October 2012), 517-24, https://doi.org/10.1016/j.jrp.2012.05.012; Renée M. Tobin and William G. Graziano, "Agreeableness," in *The Wiley Encyclopedia of Personality and Individual Differences: Models and Theories*, ed. Bernardo J. Carducci and Christopher S. Nave (Hoboken, NJ: John Wiley & Sons, 2020), 105-10.

6　E. Jayawickreme et al., "Post-traumatic Growth as Positive Personality Change: Challenges, Opportunities, and Recommendations," *Journal of Personality* 89, no. 1 (2021), 145-65.

7   Christian Jacob et al., "Internalizing and Externalizing Behavior in Adult ADHD," *Attention Deficit and Hyperactivity Disorders* 6, no. 2 (June 2014), 101–10, https://doi.org /10.1007/s12402-014-0128-z.

8   Elsa Ronnongstam, "Pathological Narcissism and Narcissistic Personality Disorder in Axis I Disorders," *Harvard Review of Psychiatry* 3, no. 6 (September 1995), 326–40, https://doi.org /10.3109/10673229609017201.

9   David Kealy, Michelle Tsai, and John S. Ogrodniczuk, "Depressive Tendencies and Pathological Narcissism among Psychiatric Outpatients," *Psychiatry Research* 196, no. 1 (March 2012), 157–59, https://doi.org /10.1016 /j.psychres.2011.08.023.

10  Paolo Schiavone et al., "Comorbidity of DSM-IV Personality Disorders in Unipolar and Bipolar Affective Disorders: A Comparative Study," *Psychological Reports* 95, no. 1 (September 2004), 121–28, https://doi.org/10.2466 /pr0.95.1.121-128.

11  Emil F. Coccaro and Michael S. McCloskey, "Phenomenology of Impulsive Aggression and Intermittent Explosive Disorder," in *Intermittent Explosive Disorder: Etiology, Assessment, and Treatment* (London: Academic Press, 2019), 37–65, https://doi.org/10.1016/B978-0-12-813858-8.00003-6.

12  Paul Wink, "Two Faces of Narcissism," *Journal of Personality and Social Psychology* 61, no. 4 (Ocober 1991), 590–97, https://doi.org/10.1037//0022 -3514.61.4.590.

13  Schiavone et al., "Comorbidity of DSM-IV Personality Disorders in Unipolar and Bipolar Affective Disorders."

14  Kealy, Tsai, and Ogrodniczuk, "Depressive Tendencies and Pathological Narcissism among Psychiatric Outpatients."

15  Jacob et al., "Internalizing and Externalizing Behavior in Adult ADHD."

16  José Salazar-Fraile, Carmen Ripoll-Alanded, and Julio Bobes, "Narcisismo Manifiesto, Narcisismo Encubierto y Trastornos de Personalidad en una Unidad de Conductas Adictivas: Validez Predictiva de Respuesta a Tratamiento," *Adicciones* 22, no. 2 (2010), 107–12, https://doi.org/10.20882/adicciones.199.

17  Tracie O. Afifi et al., "Childhood Adversity and Personality Disorders: Results from a Nationally Representative Population-Based Study," *Journal of Psychiatric Research* 45, no. 6 (December 2010), 814–22, https://doi.org /10.1016/j.jpsychires.2010.11.008.

CHAPTER TWO

1   Evan Stark, "The Dangers of Dangerousness Assessment," *Family & Intimate Partner Violence Quarterly* 6, no. 2 (2013), 13–22.

2   Andrew D. Spear, "Epistemic Dimensions of Gaslighting: Peer-Disagreement, Self-Trust, and Epistemic Injustice," *Inquiry* 66, no. 1 (April 2019), 68–91, https://doi.org/10.1080/0020174X.2019.1610051; Kate Abramson, "Turning

Up the Lights on Gaslighting," *Philosophical Perspectives* 28 (2014), 1–30, https://doi.org/10.1111/phpe.12046.

3 Jennifer J. Freyd, "Violations of Power, Adaptive Blindness and Betrayal Trauma Theory," *Feminism & Psychology* 7, no. 1 (1997), 22–32, https://doi.org/10.1177/0959353597071004.

4 Heinz Kohut, "Thoughts on Narcissism and Narcissistic Rage," *Psychoanalytic Study of the Child* 27, no. 1 (1972), 360–400, https://doi.org/10.1080/00797308.1972.11822721; Zlatan Krizan and Omesh Johar, "Narcissistic Rage Revisited," *Journal of Personality and Social Psychology* 108, no. 5 (2015), 784, https://doi.org/10.1037/pspp0000013.

5 Chelsea E. Sleep, Donald R. Lynam, and Joshua D. Miller, "Understanding Individuals' Desire for Change, Perceptions of Impairment, Benefits, and Barriers of Change for Pathological Personality Traits," *Personality Disorders: Theory, Research, and Treatment* 13, no. 3 (2022), 245, https://doi.org/10.1037/per0000501.

6 Heidi Sivers, Jonathan Scooler, and Jennifer J. Freyd, *Recovered Memories* (New York: Academic Press, 2002), https://www.ojp.gov/ncjrs/virtual-library/abstracts/recovered-memories.

7 Matthew Hussey, *Get the Guy: Learn Secrets of the Male Mind to Find the Man You Want and the Love You Deserve* (New York: HarperWave, 2014).

8 Patrick Carnes, "Trauma Bonds," Healing Tree, 1997, https://healingtreenonprofit.org/wp-content/uploads/2016/01/Trauma-Bonds-by-Patrick-Carnes-1.pdf.

## CHAPTER THREE

1 Jennifer J. Freyd, *Betrayal Trauma: The Logic of Forgetting Childhood Abuse* (Cambridge, MA: Harvard University Press, 1996); Jennifer J. Freyd, "Blind to Betrayal: New Perspectives on Memory," *Harvard Mental Health Letter* 15, no. 12 (1999), 4–6.

2 Jennifer J. Freyd and Pamela Birrell, *Blind to Betrayal: Why We Fool Ourselves We Aren't Being Fooled* (Hoboken, NJ: John Wiley & Sons, 2013).

3 Janja Lalich and Madeline Tobias, *Take Back Your Life: Recovering from Cults and Abusive Relationships* (Richmond, CA: Bay Tree Publishing, 2006).

4 Daniel Shaw, "The Relational System of the Traumatizing Narcissist," *International Journal of Cultic Studies* 5 (2014), 4–11.

5 Shaw, "The Relational System of the Traumatizing Narcissist."

6 988 Suicide and Crisis Lifeline: 988lifeline.org; dial 988 or 1-800-273-8255.

7 Bessel van der Kolk, *The Body Keeps the Score: Brain, Mind, and Body in the Healing of Trauma* (New York: Viking, 2014).

## CHAPTER FOUR

1  Daniel Shaw, "The Relational System of the Traumatizing Narcissist," *International Journal of Cultic Studies* 5 (2014), 4–11.

2  Andreas Maercker et al., "Proposals for Mental Disorders Specifically Associated with Stress in the International Classification of Diseases-11," *Lancet* 381, no. 9878 (2013), 1683–85, https://doi.org/10.1016/S0140-6736 (12)62191-6.

3  Jennifer J. Freyd, *Betrayal Trauma: The Logic of Forgetting Childhood Abuse* (Cambridge, MA: Harvard University Press, 1996).

## CHAPTER FIVE

1  Judith Herman, *Trauma and Recovery* (New York: Basic Books, 1992), 290.

## CHAPTER SIX

1  Pauline Boss and Janet R. Yeats, "Ambiguous Loss: A Complicated Type of Grief When Loved Ones Disappear," *Bereavement Care* 33, no. 2 (2014), 63–69, https://doi.org/10.1080/02682621.2014.933573.

2  Kenneth J. Doka, *Disenfranchised Grief* (Lexington, MA: Lexington Books, 1989).

3  Michael Linden, "Embitterment in Cultural Contexts," in *Cultural Variations in Psychopathology: From Research to Practice*, ed. Sven Barnow and Nazli Balkir (Newburyport, MA: Hogrefe Publishing, 2013), 184–97.

## CHAPTER SEVEN

1  Jay Earley and Bonnie Weiss, *Self-Therapy for Your Inner Critic: Transforming Self-Criticism into Self-Confidence* (Larkspur, CA: Pattern Systems Books, 2010).

2  Kozlowska et al., "Fear and the Defense Cascade: Clinical Implications and Management," *Harvard Review of Psychiatry* 23, no. 4 (2015), 263-87, DOI: 10.1097/HRP.0000000000000065.

3  Pete Walker, "Codependency, Trauma and the Fawn Response," *The East Bay Therapist*, January–February 2003, http://www.pete-walker.com/code pendencyFawnResponse.htm.

4  Jancee Dunn, "When Someone You Love Is Upset, Ask This One Question," *New York Times*, April 7, 2023, https://www.nytimes.com/2023/04 /07/well/emotions-support-relationships.html.

## CHAPTER EIGHT

1 Sendhil Mullainathan and Eldar Shafir, *Scarcity: Why Having Too Little Means So Much* (New York: Times Books, 2013).

2 Tina Swithin, One Mom's Battle, www.onemomsbattle.com.

## CHAPTER NINE

1 Richard G. Tedeschi and Lawrence G. Calhoun, "The Posttraumatic Growth Inventory: Measuring the Positive Legacy of Trauma," *Journal of Traumatic Stress* 9, no. 3 (1996), 455–72, https://doi.org/10.1002/jts.2490090305.

2 Eranda Jayawickreme et al., "Post-Traumatic Growth as Positive Personality Change: Challenges, Opportunities, and Recommendations," *Journal of Personality* 89, no. 1 (February 2021), 145–65, https://doi:org/10.1111/jopy.12591.

3 James K. McNulty and V. Michelle Russell, "Forgive and Forget, or Forgive and Regret? Whether Forgiveness Leads to Less or More Offending Depends on Offender Agreeableness," *Personality and Social Psychology Bulletin* 42, no. 5 (2016), 616–31, https://doi.org/10.1177/0146167216637841; Frank D. Fincham and Steven R. H. Beach, "Forgiveness in Marriage: Implications for Psychological Aggression and Constructive Communication," *Personal Relationships* 9, no. 3 (2002), 239–51, https://doi.org/10.1111/1475-6811.00016; Laura B. Luchies et al., "The Doormat Effect: When Forgiving Erodes Self-Respect and Self-Concept Clarity," *Journal of Personality and Social Psychology* 98, no. 5 (2010), 734–49, https://doi.org/10.1037/a0017838; James K. McNulty, "Forgiveness in Marriage: Putting the Benefits into Context," *Journal of Family Psychology* 22, no. 1 (2008), 171–75, doi: 10.1037/0893-3200.22.1.171.

# Index